Money Mistakes You Can't Afford to Make

How to Solve Common Problems and Improve Your Personal Finances

Paul J. Lim

D0757013

McGraw-Hill

New York   Chicago   San Francisco   Lisbon   London
Madrid   Mexico City   Milan   New Delhi   San Juan
Seoul   Singapore   Sydney   Toronto

The *McGraw·Hill* Companies

1 2 3 4 5 6 7 8 9 0   AGM/AGM   0 9 8 7 6 5 4 3

ISBN 0-07-141289-1

McGraw-Hill books are available at special discounts to use as premiums and sales promotions, or for use in corporate training programs. For more information, please write to the Director of Special Sales, Professional Publishing, McGraw-Hill, Two Penn Plaza, New York, NY 10121-2298. Or contact your local bookstore.

This book is printed on recycled, acid-free paper containing a minimum of 50% recycled de-inked paper.

Library of Congress Cataloging-in-Publication Data

Lim, Paul.
    Money mistakes you can't afford to make : how to solve common problems and improve your personal finances / by Paul Lim.
       p. cm.
    ISBN 0-07-141289-1 (pbk. : alk. paper)
    1. Finance, Personal. I. Title.
HG179.L4973 2003
332.024'02—dc21   2003005767

For Shirley

Contents

Preface

There's an old saying about money: With it you're a dragon. Without it, you're a worm. Somewhere in between, you're human. Being human, we're filled with a swirl of sometimes contradictory emotions and impulses that often get in the way of personal financial success. Some of these incongruities can be quite amusing. For instance, we tend to overestimate our neighbors' wealth while underestimating our own odds of financial success. Some of us underestimate the importance of investing for retirement, yet overestimate the difficulties of retiring comfortably. Meanwhile, we fixate on the "big" things, like trying to beat the market (which is a lot harder to do than many of us think) while overlooking the "little" things, like saving money and lowering our expenses (which are easier to accomplish than we think).

The ten common mistakes we've made with our money in recent years—which is the focus of this book—are rooted in these jumbled emotions. Hopefully, there are some lessons we can all draw from our experiences in the recent bull and bear markets. Once you come to understand these human foibles and find ways to overcome them, managing money doesn't have to be nearly as difficult or stressful as we sometimes make it out to be. Jack Bogle, who founded the mutual fund company Vanguard (and to whom I refer often), likes to say that "simplicity is the master key to financial success." He's right. And that's what I hope to convey in this book. In fact, throughout these ten chapters, I stress the importance of keeping things simple, playing the averages, and automating various aspects of your financial life. I hope you pick up on that.

While the book isn't divided into formal sections, there are general themes. Each chapter, or "mistake" as we term it, focuses on one of the ten common types of money mistakes that people make. **Chapters 1** and **2** focus on a topic that we're far too gloomy about: saving money. It's a lot easier to save than we think, especially over long periods of time.

Chapters 3 and **4** address another human foible: our tendency to overlook key elements of finances altogether. In **Chapter 3**, I talk about the importance of knowing and improving your credit score, since this could save you tens of thousands of dollars in interest payments over your lifetime. And **Chapter 4** addresses the *risks* we largely ignore when it comes to our investments. The chapters that follow are about investing, in particular the common mistakes we have made and continue to make with our portfolios. You'll notice a common theme running through **Chapters 5** through **8**: the danger of overconfident investing. I apologize in advance for repeating this theme over and over in several chapters. I just think it's that important. Finally, in **Chapters 9** and **10**, I'll address a few issues specific to retirement investors.

I hope you'll come away from this book with a basic understanding: When it comes to money, it's a lot harder to do the things we think we're good at, but it's a lot easier to overcome the things we fear. Though parts of the book may depress you (I've included a bunch of statistics that show that we're not really doing that well when it comes to saving and investing), I hope that by the time you're done, you'll realize things aren't as bad as they may seem. The truth is, many of us did make a lot of mistakes with our money in the 1990s. But there's a whole new decade—and era—ahead of us.

*   *   *

Before I begin, I want to be clear about something. I'm not a financial planner. I'm not a money manager. Nor am I a stockbroker or certified public accountant. I'm a journalist who talks to financial planners, mutual fund managers, stockbrokers, and CPAs routinely in the course of my work. For the past decade, I've covered the markets, mutual funds, 401(k)s. and other personal financial issues for a variety of publications, including *Money*, the *Los Angeles Times*, and most recently *U.S. News & World Report*.

So take this book for what it is: a journalist's observations. We could all benefit by observing patterns in our own lives when it comes to handling money, though this is something many of us are loathe to do. It's bad enough that we have to make myriad financial decisions in our busy livesit's worse to have to analyze how good we are (or aren't) at managing our personal finances. And it's even more unpleasant to have to make this assessment after the greatest bear market since the Great Depression. But it's something we all must do.

While it is true that the so-called "do it yourself" era of investing— symbolized by day-traders and online brokers—is over, the fact of the matter isthat more of us are responsible for managing our own finances than ever before. And more of us are responsible for more aspects of our finances than ever before. No matter how much we pine for the days when employers took care of our retirement needs, traditional pensions aren't coming back. Self-directed plans like the 401(k)—whether they go by that name in the future or not—are likely to be the dominant retirement accounts for at least another generation. Plans like this may evolve over time (the government is already talking about simplifying the alphabet soup of 401(k)s and IRAs). But self-directed, tax-deferred savings and investing will be with us for a very long time. That means more of us will have to save for our own futures. More of us will have to invest for our own futures. And more of us will have to retire on our own terms. And that's what this book addresses: saving money, investing money, and retiring with money.

Paul J. Lim
February 2003

Acknowledgments

I'd like to thank Jack Bogle of the Vanguard Group for showing me the light. I want to thank my old boss, Tom Petruno of the *Los Angeles Times*, for showing me the way. And I want to thank Shirley Leung for joining me on this and other journeys. Finally, I want to thank Jodie Allen, Tim Smart and Margi Mannix, my editors at *U.S. News & World Report*, for giving me time and encouragement.

INTRODUCTION

It should be painfully clear by now that the go-go '90s are gone, gone, gone. And they won't be back for a very long time, perhaps not in our lifetimes, perhaps not in our children's lifetimes. Bull markets and bear markets come and go. But drunken orgies such as we witnessed in the late 1990s come around about as often as Halley's comet. For savers and investors, it can take years, if not decades, to recover from the hangover. And that's where many of us find ourselves today—in personal financial detox.

We no longer have the luxury of a skyrocketing stock market, fueled by overhyped promises, overstated earnings, and overly mischievous corporate executives, to mask our financial shortcomings. Nor do we have the safety net of a seemingly endless supply of high-paying, stock-option-laden jobs that the dot.com revolution afforded us, if only for a few glorious years. After drifting below 4 percent—which used to be considered "full employment"—during the Internet boom, the nation's unemployment rate jumped back above 6 percent in 2003.

Just as the rising tide of the bull market lifted most boats in the 1990s, the downpour that was the 2000 bear market created an undertow that sucked many of our personal financial fortunes underwater. In some cases, deeply underwater.

The mistakes we now make every day with our money, both big and small, matter more than ever before. This means it's more important than ever to stop ourselves from making those mistakes. The good news is, if we take care of the little things—the basic or "mini" mistakes we can fix largely on our own when it comes to saving, investing, and retiring with money—we won't have to worry as much about the big things.

Why do we make so many mistakes with our money to begin with?

Some of it has to do with the way our brains work. It's a natural human impulse to think that things will forever be the way they are today. We can't help it. We think linearly. In the world of behavioral finance, it's referred to as "anchoring." We often base our expectations of the future by extrapolating from a point in the present and past. It's why we chase yesterday's hot stock. It's why we assume that if stocks have been generating 20-percent-plus returns a year for the past several years, they will continue to deliver those gains forever more.

In the late 1990s, we saw the world through rose-colored glasses. So we just assumed that our future would always be that rosy. Many of us were making more money than we ever dreamed of earning. Jobs were being created at a record pace. Personal incomes rose, stock portfolios mushroomed, and housing prices boomed. Meanwhile, inflation fell, interest rates tumbled, and energy prices stabilized. Even the social ills that threatened economic growth in previous decades—crime, poverty, and drugs—seemed to be under control for the first time in a long while. Economists and journalists quickly proclaimed the death of the business cycle as we know it, which was a fancy way of saying: "The good times are here to stay."

As a result, we came to believe that we had tremendous room for error when it came to our finances. So we took more chances with our money than we ever did before. And we took more chances than we ever needed to, which was probably our single biggest mistake. In the 1990s, we sought financial results that weren't tied to our goals, but rather, to greed or sometimes pride. And whoever it was who said that pride is at the bottom of all great mistakes was right. When the bubble finally burst in 2000, we saw the results of our unnecessarily reckless behavior. More stock-market wealth was lost in the three years after the bull market's peak, roughly $8 trillion, than existed a generation ago. Thank goodness our home values kept rising during this period, alleviating some of the stresses on our finances. And thank goodness interest rates kept falling throughout the bear market, allowing us to refinance our appreciating homes—in some cases, multiple times—to reduce debt payments and save some money.

All of this took place just as the first wave of "Baby Boomers"—the first group of Americans to retire in the post-pension, do-it-yourself era of the 401(k)—was preparing to leave the workforce. If history is any guide, it could take years, if not decades, for our brokerage and retirement accounts to return to their previous levels. Remember, the math works against you on the way back up. For instance, if your $250,000 IRA loses 50 percent of its value, you'd be left with $125,000. But to get back to $250,000 from a $125,000 portfolio, it would require a 100 percent gain.

It took a decade and a half—and a world war—for this nation to fully recover from the hangover that was the Great Depression. Japan's economy has been reeling nearly as long, since its stock market burst in 1989.

Today some of us may feel compelled to take even *more* risks with our money to make back what was lost. Yet this is Vegas-think, just as gambling on speculative "new economy" IPOs was back in the 1990s. The irony is, if we were to make fewer mistakes with our money to begin with, we wouldn't need to take bigger risks in the future to make up for the losses caused by the unnecessary risks we took in the past.

The point of this game isn't to recover every last dime you lost in the bear market. It's not to be as rich as you possibly can, the risks of getting there be damned. It's to make sure that at the end of the day, your needs are taken care of—and that you can live the life you intended.

SHORTCHANGING YOURSELF

Building up Savings and Paying Down Debt

We Americans are an optimistic lot, except when it comes to one thing—our ability to save money. Consider this sad but telling fact: More Americans of modest means think they stand a better chance of accumulating $500,000 by winning the lottery than by patiently and methodically saving small amounts of money each year.[1] That's what a survey by the Consumer Federation of America discovered. Yet the odds against winning a lottery can be as much as 10 million to one. In other words, working-class Americans think they stand a better chance of being struck by lightning, with odds of about 700,000 to one, than ever amassing $500,000 in wealth. So much for the American Dream.

Similarly, middle- and upper-middle-class earners believe there's a better chance of becoming "wealthy" by inheriting money than by saving it and investing it in the market, according to a separate survey conducted by *Money* magazine.[2] Is it any wonder, then, that nearly half of all households, or 48 million families, have no more than $1000 saved in their banking accounts?[3] And that an additional 12 million households have virtually no savings at all to speak of?

To be sure, some families simply can't save because they don't earn enough. After they pay their mortgage and utilities, buy their food, and cover their basic expenses, there is literally nothing left to save. Others spend too much—or have too much debt to repay. Recently, aggregate household debt in the United States grew to more than 100 percent of personal disposable income, which explains why the national savings rate is so low: There's nothing to save (see Figure 1-1). Yet even among middle-class workers—two-thirds of whom admit they have have the financial wherewithal to save—the unspoken but real feeling is: "What's the point?"

Figure 1-1. Rising Debt

Aggregate household debt now exceeds disposable personal income for the first time in U.S. history.
Source: The Jerome Levy Economics Institute

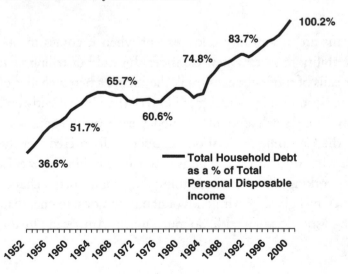

100.2%
83.7%
74.8%
65.7%
60.6%
51.7%
36.6%

Total Household Debt
as a % of Total
Personal Disposable
Income

1952 1956 1960 1964 1968 1972 1976 1980 1984 1988 1992 1996 2000

The point, of course, is to start taking care of tomorrow's obligations—sending your kids to college, covering unexpected medical bills, and taking care of your own retirement needs—today. By the time tomorrow rolls around, it might be too late.

While most of our money mistakes stem from being too optimistic—studies show that the vast majority of us think we are far better investors than we actually are (which we'll discuss in later chapters)—our inability to save is rooted in a deep-seeded pessimism. But this "glass half empty" outlook is just plain wrong, as I'll explain in a moment. Our situation isn't nearly as dire as we make it out to be.

Like an underachiever who sits in the back of the classroom and doesn't even try to learn because he fears he won't be good at school, tens of millions of us have given up on building savings because we just don't think we'll be successful at it. So we don't try at all, and then it becomes a self-fulfilling prophecy. It also becomes a vicious circle: We don't save because we don't think we'll be good at it. As a result, we find ourselves in a financial hole, at which point, even if we tried to do the right thing by saving money and paying down debt, it would be very difficult—and require tremendous sacrifice—to achieve our financial goals. That only adds to our sense of defeatism and gives us yet another reason not to try. And then we fall deeper into this sinkhole.

Add to this the fact that we get very little encouragement to save. Throughout the 1990s our friends and families put more stock in, well, stocks than in savings. When was the last time you and a coworker had a water-cooler conversation about how much money you saved over the weekend? More likely, you talked about how much money you *spent*. And before that, and our current economic situation, you probably chatted about what hot stock tip you had gotten from your neighbor.

Spending and investing are part of the modern consumer culture, reinforced by Wall Street, Madison Avenue, and, yes, even Uncle Sam. Truth be told, our government doesn't always encourage us to save, even though we're saving less in real terms than we did at the start of the

1990s (see Figure 1-2). During the bear market, the Federal Reserve cut short-term interest rates a dozen times in an effort to boost consumer and business spending to jumpstart the flagging economy. This cost savers billions of dollars in potential interest income as yields on government bonds, CDs, and even passbook savings accounts tumbled to multidecade lows.

For their part, the White House and Congress rebated tax checks to working families in hopes that we would spend it on cars, clothes, entertainment, and travel, thereby propping up the sluggish economy. We did. In fact, we purchased more new cars during the recent economic downturn—about 17 million new cars and trucks annually between 2000 and 2002—as unemployment rates rose and stock portfolios fell, than at the end of the 1990s, when we were flush with cash. Is it any wonder, then, that we are a nation of spenders, investors, and debtors, but not savers?

There's another factor at work. Put simply: We don't get the "rush" from saving money that we do from spending it—or doubling it, either in Vegas or the Nasdaq.

Spending money sends us through a euphoric roller-coaster ride of exhilarating, fast-paced emotions. Our heart rates literally jump when we hear the ka-ching of cash registers. Saving money, on the other hand, is about as much fun as running a marathon on a hot and muggy summer's day. Victory can't be spotted for miles ahead. Meanwhile, we feel pain all along the way.

Our Depression-era parents and grandparents gladly endured this pain to send their kids to school and give them a better life. But back then, instantaneous gratification wasn't in vogue as it is today. Now, many of us simply choose not to save because it's too hard, it's not fun, or it takes too long. As a result, too few households set aside too little money each week, each month, and with each paycheck to take care of basic financial needs, like establishing a rainy day fund, paying down debt, and funding longer-term goals such as college or retirement (see Figures 1-3 and 1-4).

Studies show that one of every four workers in America has saved less than $10,000 toward their retirement. This explains why less than

Figure 1-2. Personal Savings

Though there has been a recent pick-up in the savings rate, Americans are saving less today, in real terms, than they did at the start of the 1990s.

Source: Bureau of Economic Analysis

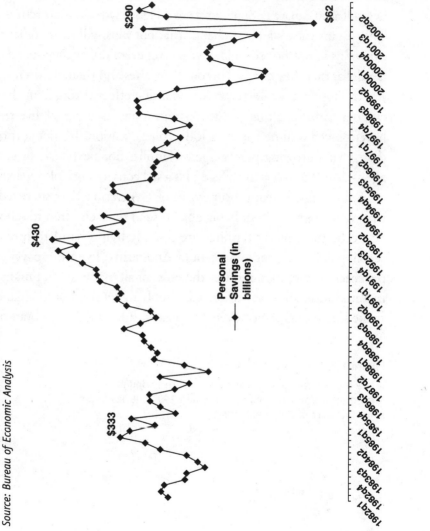

a quarter of Americans are "very confident" that they will be able to live comfortably after leaving the workforce.[4] The rest of us should be worried. At our current rate of savings, only 44 percent of working families will accumulate enough assets to adequately fund their retirement.[5] This means there's a good chance that our kids will have to help take care of us in our not-so-golden years. Yet every dollar they spend on us is a dollar that they can't spend on themselves and their children, which sets in motion a terrible economic domino effect throughout the generations. And speaking of future generations, two out of five parents haven't saved a dime for their kids' college tuition. It's not surprising, then, that a growing percentage of families don't expect—or encourage—their kids to go to college.[6] It's a sad consequence of our attitudes toward savings. Already, 90 percent of Generation Xers surveyed said they were worried about being able to send their children to school.

To be sure, many families are literally living hand to mouth. A recent poll found that 53 percent of Americans "live from paycheck to paycheck" sometimes, most of the time, or all the time.[7] For many low-income households, the priority is simply to get food on the table and make sure there's a roof over their heads. But while only about one in

Figure 1-3. Retirement Savings Trends

While the percentage of Americans who are saving money for retirement had been rising from the mid-1990s, it has fallen since the start of the bear market.
Source: Employee Benefit Research Institute

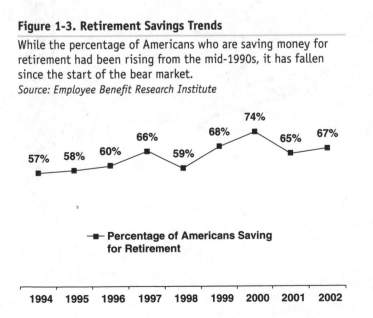

57%   58%   60%   66%   59%   68%   74%   65%   67%

—■— **Percentage of Americans Saving for Retirement**

1994   1995   1996   1997   1998   1999   2000   2001   2002

Figure 1-4. Retirement Savings

While more Americans are saving money for retirement today than in the past, a large percentage have less than $50,000 accumulated, a troubling sign for workers' ability to live comfortably in retirement.
Source: Employee Benefit Research Institute

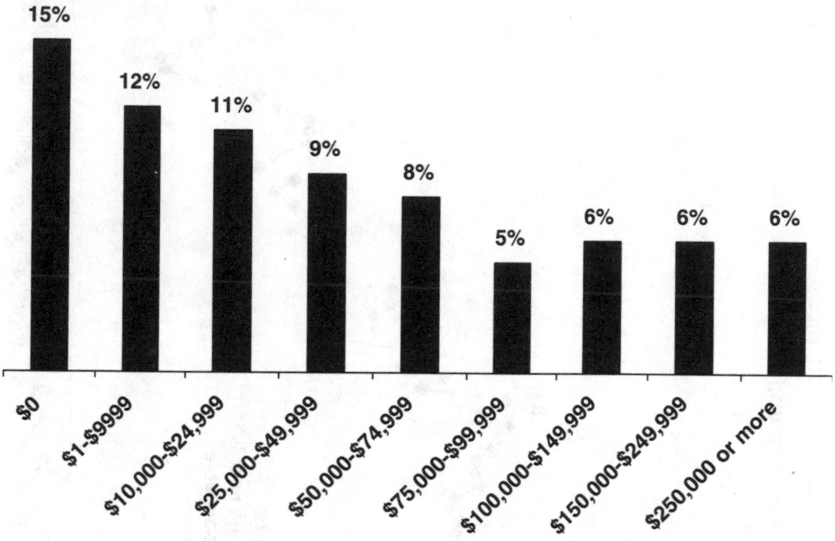

five such families save money routinely, the average middle-income household is woefully behind in saving anything for the future as well: Only 39 percent of all households set aside money on a regular basis.[8]

Worse still, those of us who are saving aren't saving that much. Between 1967 and 1982, the average family socked away almost 10 percent of its disposable income every year, like clockwork, into savings accounts. In October 2001 that figure had fallen to less than 1 percent. Our savings rate improved somewhat during the recent economic slowdown—the personal savings rate climbed back to around 4 percent of disposable income in 2003—as consumers tried to put their financial houses in order. Still, the national savings rate is but a fraction of what it was in the 1970s, '80s, and early '90s[9] (see Figure 1-5). Meanwhile, American workers are also putting less, on a percentage basis, into their employer-sponsored 401(k) retirement accounts, making this trend even more worrisome.

Figure 1-5. Personal Savings as a Percentage of Disposable Income

Americans are saving a far lower percentage of their disposable income today than they did a generation ago.

Source: Bureau of Economic Analysis

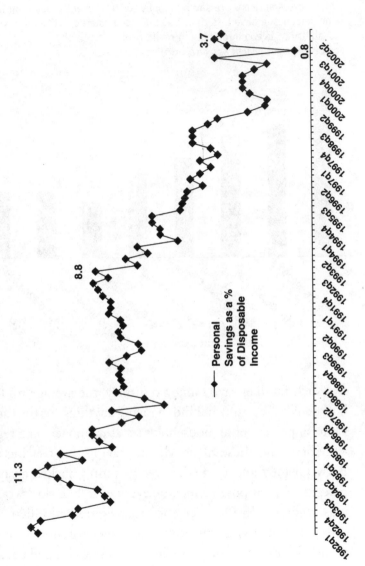

Not surprisingly, then, the typical American household has accumulated less than $10,000 in total financial assets.[10] And there's little indication even among families that have saved less that they plan to save in the future. In fact, 41 percent of these families say they don't save at all, and 78 percent say they don't save money on a routine basis (see Figure 1-6).

Even that $10,000 figure is somewhat misleading, because our consumer debt relative to our savings keeps growing. The typical household now owes more than a dollar in consumer debt, such as credit card balances, for every two dollars it has in savings. So while many of us may have $10,000 in gross savings, it may be really closer to $5000 on a net basis. Households in this situation are "only a layoff or emergency expenditure away from financial disaster," says Stephen Brobeck, executive director of the Consumer Federation of America.

Figure 1-6. Saving and Spending Patterns

According to surveys, savings isn't a priority for most American households.
Source: Consumer Federation of America

	Households with Less Than $10,000 In Net Assets	All Households
% Americans who don't save at all	41%	23%
% Americans who don't save regularly	78	61
% Americans who spend more than they earn	22	14
% Americans who spend less than they earn	36	56

Crunching the Numbers: It's Easier to Save Than You Think

If we had a better grasp of how effective a simple savings plan can be, if we understood the true power of compound interest and appreciated the true value of time, I'm sure more of us would try to save. For an optimistic people, Americans greatly underestimate and underappreciate their ability to accumulate wealth through an incremental and routine savings program (see Figure 1-7).

When asked in a recent survey how much they would accumulate if they set aside $25 a week for 40 years at a 7 percent annual rate of return, the average consumer guessed around $122,500. Wrong. The correct answer is more than double that: $287,000. For what is essentially a cappuccino a day at Starbucks, you could amass a retirement account of nearly $300,000 over the course of a working career. And $300,000 will go a lot further toward funding a comfortable retirement than most people think.

When asked how much they would accumulate if they saved $50 a week—which you could easily do by packing your own lunch and making your own coffee at home—for 40 years at a 9 percent rate of return, the average saver guessed just under $240,000. Wrong. The correct answer: more than $1 million.[11] There's your lottery.

"The good news is that . . . most unprepared households could get ready by taking advantage of the magic of interest compounding," says Brobeck. "Saving just $25 a week for 40 years, with a 5 percent yield, will result in an accumulation of more than $165,000."[12] Indeed, the silver lining in this dark cloud is that it's so much easier to save money than we think. So cheer up.

The irony—or is it tragedy?—is that the vast majority of Americans who don't save admit that they have the financial wherewithal to set aside small amounts of money in this fashion. In other words, they *can* save, but they just choose not to. According to a recent survey by the Employee Benefit Research Institute, 62 percent who classify themselves as "nonsavers" admit that they make enough in salary to set aside at least $20 a week toward their retirement. And an astound-

Figure 1-7.

The amount of wealth you can accumulate over time by saving $25 a week, based on various rates of return.				
Interest	10 Years	25 Years	30 Years	40 Years
5%	$16,850	$64,600	$90,300	$165,580
7%	$18,775	$87,725	$132,000	$283,700
10%	$22,280	$144,600	$246,510	$690,650

The amount of wealth you can accumulate over time by saving $50 a week:				
Interest	10 Years	25 Years	30 Years	40 Years
5%	$33,700	$129,230	$180,610	$331,170
7%	$37,550	$175,450	$264,060	$567,360
10%	$44,570	$289,190	$493,020	$1,381,315

The amount of wealth you can accumulate over time by saving $100 a week:				
Interest	10 Years	25 Years	30 Years	40 Years
5%	$67,400	$258,470	$361,200	$662,300
7%	$75,100	$350,900	$528,120	$1,134,720
10%	$89,130	$578,380	$986,040	$2,762,630

ing 70 percent who are already saving admit that they can afford to save more—an extra $20, over and above what they already set aside for retirement.[13] The hurdle we face isn't financial so much as it's psychological. Intellectually, we understand the problem, but we just don't have the discipline or the energy to overcome financial inertia.

Concentrate on the Short Term

Whatever you do, don't fixate on the hundreds of thousands of dollars it will take to retire comfortably. For the moment, forget the tens of thousands of dollars you'll need to send your kids to college. Or the thousands of dollars it will take to pay off all of your credit cards. Big, depressing numbers like this will only serve to remind you how long and grueling this marathon is. They will only serve to motivate you to give up, like that slacker in the back of the classroom.

Many financial planners and experts advise families to sit down at the start of the process and calculate their personal balance sheets and income statements. You can do this by summing up all of your assets (such as your house, stock portfolio, and retirement accounts) and liabilities (loan balances and other forms of debt) on one sheet of paper, and your income and monthly obligations on another. Some believe that this exercise will literally scare nonsavers straight.

In theory, this can be a useful exercise. But focusing on your financial balance sheet too early in the process can also scare some people out of saving and into giving up. For many households, the figures are just too depressing. How many of us stopped opening our 401(k) statements during the bear market because we got sick and tired of looking at losses? How many of us stopped logging onto financial websites to track our stocks once they started showing losses? The fact of the matter is, it's a natural human tendency to shy away from unpleasant things. Who wants tangible proof of their shortcomings? Yet the whole point of our personal financial detox program is to recognize human shortcomings that lead to mistakes, and to overcome them.

As with everything in life, finding the right motivation is key. In this case, it's vital that you find enough *positive* reinforcement to make sure you (1) start saving money and (2) continue to save money for the rest of your life. It's like counseling an alcoholic: You don't tell them how weak they are and how difficult it will be to stop drinking day in and day out, week in and week out, year in and year out for the rest of their lives. You make sure they get through day one and feel good enough about themselves to get to day two. Then you deal with the rest of the week. And then you take it from there.

Similarly, when it comes to saving money, you can't focus on the finish line. Concentrate instead on making it through to the one-mile marker. And then you can take it from there.

But what is the first mile in this marathon of savings? Is it saving for retirement? Should you use a greater part of your paycheck to start funding a 401(k)? Is it saving for a short-term goal, like paying for your daughter's wedding or putting a deck in the backyard? What about paying down debt? Should that be your first priority? If so, what kind of debt should you pay off first?

MINI MISTAKE

NOT ESTABLISHING AN EMERGENCY FUND

Before you try to climb out of your savings sinkhole, it's important to make sure you don't slip even further. Your first order of business, then, ought to be establishing a rainy day fund—a stash of cash intended to cover your basic expenses should an emergency arise.

Let's say you lose your job tomorrow. How will you pay the mortgage? How will you pay for food? What if you have to take an extended leave of absence, without pay, to take care of a sick child? Who's going to pay the bills then? Emergencies such as these are a major reason why many Americans find themselves in debt. In fact, medical emergencies explain why seniors are racking up debt at a faster rate than younger, and presumably healthier, Gen Xers, and Boomers.[14] Indeed, in the 1990s, household debt among senior citizens grew at nearly twice the rate as for the rest of the population.

Many of us are just one health scare away from being awash in debt. (Ironically, those of us who are in debt are more likely to run into a medical emergency. One study found that people in credit card debt are typically in worse health than people who aren't, in part because of the stress caused by financial concerns.[15])

But it doesn't have to be a major crisis. Emergency funds also come in handy when water heaters bust or cars break down. Most families have the financial means to cover such expenses. But if you have to sell a longer-term investment such as bonds or stocks to cover unexpected bills, it could end up costing you substantially more in the form of opportunity costs.

In establishing an emergency fund, there's a general rule of thumb: Set aside at least three months' worth of living expenses. Notice, I said three months' worth of *expenses*, not three months' worth of pay. Different people earning the exact same salary may have widely divergent monthly obligations.

If you have no children, for example, and no family to speak of, no credit card debts or car payments to make, and your mortgage is paid off or is manageable, you probably can afford to save less and invest more. On the other hand, if you're a single parent with three children to support, with big car payments, college tuition, and credit card bills to cover, your emergency fund should be much larger. So it's important to sit down and actually calculate your monthly expenses.

And when calculating the costs of an emergency fund, be sure to focus on your needs, not on your desires.

The whole point of saving is to meet your obligations, not your cravings. This means you should focus on the necessities: monthly mortgage and car payments, utilities, insurance, food, and health care. And don't forget to include other basics, such as monthly maintenance costs for your home and cars, and for taxes. And add in some extra cushion when it comes to insurance. Remember, if you lose your job, your health-care costs will likely rise, and substantially so. This is especially true if your spouse doesn't work and if your family has no other access to medical insurance. You may also experience greater out-of-pocket costs for life insurance, since you wouldn't have access to group life coverage either.

Because your bills aren't exactly the same from month to month—your utility usage can change, for example—you should write down everything you spend for three months. Then average your expenditures to come to a reasonable guesstimate of your monthly needs.

While this sounds basic, the fact is more than 4 out of 10 families—or some 71 million Americans—have yet to establish a three-month financial cushion, according to a survey by Fidelity Investments. Among families in debt, the situation is even more dire. One nationwide survey conducted by a credit-counseling firm in 2002 revealed that 9 out of 10 families in debt do not have an emergency fund. Yet those in debt have greater need for an emergency fund than those who aren't. After all, if you have no credit card bills, if you have no car loans, if you've paid off your mortgage, you have fewer monthly obligations to worry about. And with fewer bills, there's less need for an emergency fund, or at least a large one.

Having said this, there are a few caveats to the three-month rule. During economic downturns, such as the one at the start of this decade, you'd be wise to increase your emergency stash to at least six months of living expenses. Why? The chances of you losing your job — one of the reasons for having emergency savings—will rise during such times. Emerging from the Gulf War recession of the early 1990s, the nation's unemployment rate rose from 5.2 to 7.8 percent. Similarly, at the start of this decade—following the September 11 terrorist attacks in New York, Washington, D.C., and Pennsylvania—the economy shed more than 2.6 million jobs, pushing the unemployment rate up from 3.9 percent in 2000 to 6.1 percent by May 2003. Based on historic standards, 6.1 percent unemployment is still relatively low. But it won't feel low if you find yourself one of the unemployed.

Worse still, in 2003, it took the average out-of-work American 4.2 months to find a new job, a 17-year record high, according to the outplacement firm Challenger, Gray & Christmas. Under these circumstances, a three-month fund might not cut it.

Other Emergency Fund Considerations

- If you're self-employed or generate a sizable portion of your income from commissions and/or bonuses, think about permanently increasing your emergency fund to three to six months' worth of expenses. While a salaried employee might be able to take some time off—with pay—to take care of minor emergencies, commissioned workers and the self-employed don't have this luxury. Plus, the self-employed must shoulder more of the cost of their benefits, such as health insurance.

- If you work in an economically sensitive industry—the travel, retail, or manufacturing sectors, for instance, where layoffs come in cyclical waves—think about increasing your emergency fund permanently to six months. Workers in other industries, such as health care, are often cushioned from severe layoffs even in recessions, given the steady nature of those businesses. The nursing home industry, for one, will continue to get business whether times are good or bad. Private-sector educators find themselves in the same situation. But employees in cyclical industries like technology, telecommunications, financial services, transportation, leisure and travel, don't enjoy those same assurances.

- If you're the sole breadwinner in your household, think about permanently increasing your emergency fund to six months. An emergency in this situation could wipe out 100 percent of your family's income. Plus, your family may no longer have access to health or life insurance through your work. This means your monthly obligations could rise significantly at the same time your household income will be falling.

- If you're the sole breadwinner in your household and *have* children, think about increasing your emergency fund to at least six months. Not only do your monthly obligations rise with the presence of children, but the potential for family emergencies increases too. And those emergencies are hard to budget for in a rainy day fund.

- Think about increasing the size of your emergency fund as you age. You might wonder why. A 50-something, after all, tends to have more wealth than a 20-something. And by the time you hit your 50s, a number of your obligations go away. You're done paying off your own college loans. Your kids are probably out of the house. You may have already paid down most if not all of your mortgage. But the reason for a 40- or 50-something to maintain at least a six-month stash of cash is actually quite simple. Today's job market is crueler to 50-somethings than their younger counterparts. While it can take 14 to 18 weeks for an average laid-off worker to find a new job, it often takes older workers considerably longer, given the vagaries of the job market. Health is also a consideration as you age. If you're out of work and have to pay for your own health-care coverage—especially if you have a pre-existing medical condition—your out-of-pocket costs for health care could be considerably higher than you budgeted.

Of course, life isn't always precise. Some workers who are laid off can't find work for a year or more. As a result, it often makes sense to have a safety net for your safety net. That doesn't mean keeping more money in cash. Remember, a rainy day fund is for short-term emergencies only. Any money that's not needed for short-term reasons ought to be invested in longer-term securities, such as stocks and bonds.

Here, you can make good use of your home. A simple step that homeowners can take is to establish a home-equity line of credit now—before an emergency arises and before retiring. Note that I said a home-equity *line of credit*, not loan.

While a home-equity loan immediately taps a lump sum of equity from your house, a home-equity line of credit does not. Instead, it simply gives you access to borrow money against your home later if a need should arise. And unlike a loan, where you get a specific amount of money sent to you which you then need to start repaying, a home-equity line of credit allows you to tap only what you need, when you need it. In other words, if you never borrow money off this line of credit, you'll never have to pay anything back. At the same time, if a need does arise, you'll have a source of cash to meet that need without disrupting other aspects of your financial portfolio.

If you think you need such a safety net, it's important to take this step now, while you're still employed. It will be that much harder to get such a line of credit—and at favorable rates—after you lose your job.

MINI MISTAKE

BANKING IN THE MARKET

Now that you've established an emergency fund, the question arises: Where should you put the money? Keep in mind that this is your emergency *savings*, not your emergency investments. Not a single drop of this money belongs in the stock market, not even in the most well-diversified, dividend-paying blue chip stock fund you can find.

During the bull market, many of us were literally using our stock fund accounts as de facto banks. When stocks were consistently returning 20-percent-plus returns a year, cash accounts, with their single-digit yields, looked paltry by comparison. But anyone who "saved" money in Enron stock or even in a broadly diversified S&P 500 fund learned how risky it can be to bank *in* the market.

It's imperative to match your money with your needs. The less time you have to work with—that is, the less time there is to make up for losses, should they occur—the more conservative you need to be with your money.

Money that you'll need to tap in a year or two, or sooner, should be put into the most conservative and accessible asset: cash. Money that you won't need for, say, two to five years, should be allowed to grow. But it should be held in moderately safe securities such as short- and intermediate-term bonds, so there's little chance that its value will diminish during that period of time. Money that you won't need for five years or more should be invested more aggressively, in a combination of stocks, bonds, and perhaps other assets, in order to meet your long-term financial goals and outpace the long-term effects of inflation.

Because an emergency could arise tomorrow, an emergency fund, by definition, must be held in an ultrasafe and ultra-short-term account. Though fixed-income investments, or bonds, are inherently safer than stocks, they still aren't safe enough for emergencies. Even Treasury bonds, backed by the full faith and credit of the federal government, should be considered investments, not savings. Held in a mutual fund, for instance, government and corporate bonds can easily lose value in the short term. It typically happens when market interest rates spike, as they did in 1994 (see "Mistake 4: Overlooking Risks"). Over time, this risk subsides. But if you need to tap your emergency fund tomorrow, you'll require an account that offers total principal protection.

One option is a bank certificate of deposit, or CD. The problem is, most CDs, which are federally insured, hit you with penalty fees for withdrawing money before the term of the contract expires. And who knows if an emergency might arise before a one- or two-year CD comes due? (As an alternative, there are so-called penalty-free CDs that allow customers to withdraw money early, but, as you would expect, they return less than traditional CDs.) Early-withdrawal fees on traditional CDs vary, depending on the financial institution and the term of the CD. But an early withdrawal would typically cost you three months' worth of interest income on a one-year CD and up to six months' interest on a two-year CD.

A money market account at a bank, then, may be a better option, especially if you shop around for an account offering better-than-average rates. Like a CD, money market accounts are federally insured, but you can withdraw money more frequently. Typically, a bank will allow savers to pull money out of these accounts three to six times a month. That's certainly flexible enough for emergency purposes. Yet unlike a regular checking account, you don't have *unlimited* check-writing privileges either, which could work to your advantage. In most money market accounts, customers who exceed three to six withdrawals a month (in particular, three checks a month) are assessed a penalty fee of $10 to $15. Some banks even threaten to cancel accounts if customers write too many checks. Hopefully, this will deter you from casually tapping the account.

An added bonus is the fact that you can open up a money market account, often for as little as $500. And many accounts waive annual fees if your balance is greater than $1,000 or $2,500. (For more information on these accounts or to shop for money market yields and terms, go to *www.bankrate.com*.)

Why not go with a basic passbook savings account or an interest-paying checking account? "There's the opportunity cost to consider," says Greg McBride, an analyst with Bankrate.com, which tracks trends in banking services. Interest-paying checking accounts at traditional banks were yielding only about 0.5 percent in the spring of 2003. That means if you maintained a $7500 emergency fund, you'd be earning only $37.50 a year in interest—hardly enough to cover the incidental fees that many checking accounts charge (see "Mistake 2: Getting Fee'd Up"). At the same time, the average money market account was yielding around 1.4 percent, and some were paying more than 2 percent.

If you're looking to boost your yields slightly, you might want to consider a money market mutual fund. A money *fund*, as opposed to a money market *account*, is a portfolio that invests in a diversified collection of extremely short-term debt securities. Depending on the type of money fund, it might invest in short-term Treasury securities, high-quality commercial paper, and even negotiable bank CDs. By law, the average maturity of debt in a money fund can't exceed 90 days, which means these funds are significantly less risky and much more stable than bond funds. However, money funds aren't federally insured.

To compensate for the slightly higher risk, money funds sometimes pay out a slightly higher yield than a bank money market account. But that wasn't the case in 2003, when average money fund yields fell to less than 1 percent, thanks to record low short-term interest rates. Part of the problem was that the average money fund charged about 0.36 percent in annual expenses. At $36 a year per $10,000, those expenses ate away at many fund's already anemic yields.

In very rare cases some money funds might drop in value after expenses are deducted. But should that occur, fund companies would almost assuredly step in and make the investor whole. Financial institutions often waive fees, temporarily, to protect money fund returns in low interest-rate environments. Since it would be considered a scandal if an established financial institution did not protect money fund investors, it's in your best interest to stick with funds run by large, reliable companies (such as Fidelity, Vanguard, Schwab or T. Rowe Price) that charge lower-than-average fees.

MINI MISTAKE

NOT DIGGING OUT OF DEBT

After making sure you have proper footing through an emergency fund, your next priority has to be paying down debt. Just as you can't learn to run before you walk, you can't save money until you free up money. And a good chunk of our money every month is going to credit card companies.

In the aggregate, the situation seems dire. Today, the average American household carries more than 14 credit cards, split among bank cards, department store cards, and gas cards, according to *The Nilson Report*, a card industry newsletter (see Figure 1-8). And the typical family owes more on those cards than ever before.

In 2002, the average household had nearly $9000 in outstanding balances spread out among their cards, according to an analysis by *Cardweb.com*, which tracks the credit card industry. That's up 35 percent from 1998, when the average family's card balances were about $6600 (see Figure 1-9). Think about that for a moment. We carry far more credit debt today, after having lived through the greatest bull market in history, than we did before the best bull market years of 1997, 1998, and 1999.

Figure 1-8. Credit Cards Run Amok

Source: The Nilson Report

Year	Average Cards per Household
1997	13.76
1998	14.02
1999	13.68
2000	13.95
2001	14.27

Figure 1-9. Credit Card Balances Run Amok

Credit card balances have risen throughout the recent bull and bear markets. Numbers in table denote average annual household credit card balances in dollars, 1992–2002.

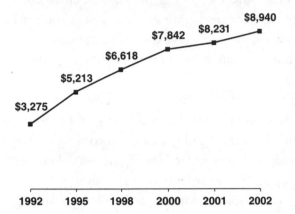

The good news is, paying down credit card balances ensures high returns on your money. If, for example, you pay off the remaining $5000 balance on a Visa card that charges an annual interest rate of 18 percent, it would be the equivalent of earning 18 percent on your money in the stock market. Put another way, paying off this $5000 credit card is like investing $5000 and immediately seeing it grow to $5900. If you're sitting on credit card debt that charges even higher interest rates, it makes even more sense to pay it off quickly.

Despite falling interest rates at the start of the decade, credit card rates didn't come down that much. In March 2003, the average credit card rate stood at 14.9 percent, according to CardWeb. That was down from the average rate of 16.2 percent two years earlier. Yet during this period, bank prime lending rates were cut in half (see Figure 1-10).

Many credit card issuers have actually *increased* rates on some customers during the recent economic downturn, especially for cardholders with less–than stellar credit scores (see *Mistake 3: Not Knowing the Score*).[16] A number have also begun imposing "penalty rates" on customers who are delinquent with one or more payments. A growing number of card companies are imposing this higher interest rate not just on customers who are late with payments, but on customers who are late with any bill to any other creditor. In other words, the interest rate on your Mastercard could jump from 12 to 24 percent because you were late paying your American Express bill. And in some cases all it takes is one or two delinquencies to trip this "penalty rate."

Of course, if you're charged 24 percent interest, you can make the best of a bad situation by paying that card off first. By doing so, you earn 24 percent returns on your money—guaranteed. What's the likelihood of earning 24 percent a year on your money in stocks? Most experts believe we're in store for an extended period of low- to mid-single-digit returns in equities for much of this decade.

There was a time, not too long ago, during the bull market of the late 1990s, when some of us—especially younger investors—were literally borrowing money off credit cards to buy stocks. Their thinking was simple, if not perverse: With the stock market returning nearly 30 percent a year, at a time when their credit cards were charging them around 18 percent, why not borrow at the lower rate to invest at the higher?

Figure 1-10. Credit Card Rates

While interest rates in general have fallen over the past couple of years, credit card interest rates have not fallen as much.
Source: CardWeb.com

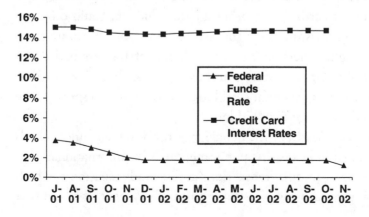

Obviously, those investors never factored the concept of risk into this equation (see *Mistake 4: Overlooking Risks*). There is absolutely no risk in paying off a high-interest credit card. In fact, you end up lowering the risk of potentially defaulting on your debt and harming your credit profile, which is vital to being able to borrow money cheaply in the future. There is tremendous risk, on the other hand, that you could suffer a short-term loss—and a steep one at that—in the stock market. So take your pick: the stock market, with high risk and no guarantees on what your money will earn, versus paying off credit card debt, with no risk and guaranteed double-digit gains.

Step 1: Freeze Your Spending

The first step toward paying down card balances is to stop adding to them. There are a couple of easy ways to start this process. First and foremost, stop using your cards to make basic purchases. Wherever possible, use cash for day-to-day transactions, such as paying for groceries or buying clothes.

There is a tendency among consumers to differentiate their money sources. The cash in our wallets is ours, but money pulled from a credit card feels like someone else's. All things being equal, we have an easier time spending other people's money than our own.

Two professors at MIT documented this fact in an experiment a few years ago. They set up two different auctions for a pair of Boston Celtics tickets. In the first auction, would-be bidders were allowed to pay by credit card. In the other auction, bidders could only use cash. You might assume that the average bid from both auctions would be roughly the same, since both sets of bidders had equal knowledge of what they were purchasing: basketball tickets. As it turned out, the average credit card bidder was willing to spend twice as much as the average cash bidder.[17]

A more recent study, of the behavior of fast-food customers, sheds some additional light on this phenomenon. Visa International analyzed more than 100,000 transactions at fast food restaurants, which are increasingly accepting plastic as a form of payment. It found that the average purchase made by a person paying with a card was 20 to 30 percent higher than purchases made by cash-paying customers.[18] This puts a modern-day spin on that famous phrase that Wimpy used to utter in those Popeye cartoons: "I'll gladly pay you Tuesday for a hamburger today." The implication is clear. When posed with the classic question, "Would you like fries with that?" consumers paying with cash are far more likely to say no than those paying with plastic. It's important to recognize this all-too human foible.

Obviously, some things are hard to purchase with cash. Hotel rooms, for instance, require a credit card for insurance and security. Some customers can pay with cash, but they would have to call the hotel weeks in advance and jump through several hoops. It's also hard to rent a car with cash. And you're actually better off renting with plastic due to the insurance coverage many cards provide. Nevertheless, given our propensity to spend more on credit, it's in our best interest to avoid plastic when possible.

Another way to freeze your spending is to freeze your plastic. Literally. This is an idea that a financial planner, Dee Lee, mentioned to me, and I think it's inspired. Put your credit cards in a sealable plastic bag, and immerse the bag in a tin of water. Then put the tin in your freezer, creating a block of ice. The purpose of this exercise is to force you to wait to make purchases. The next time you get an impulse to buy something with plastic, you'll have to wait for the cards to thaw out—which could take hours—before you can use them. Hopefully by then your urge to splurge will have subsided.

Of course, you may decide to use cash to make the purchase. But since, as the MIT experiment showed, consumers aren't willing to spend as much using cash as plastic, I'm guessing this will end up saving you some money in the long run. Or you could get your credit card number off of your latest statement. But that's only good for Internet and catalog purchases. To buy something in a store, you'd have to thaw out the card. If you really want to spend that badly, you'll find a way to break through the ice. For instance, you might try to microwave the card, but then, that would destroy the magnetic strip on the back.

Step 2: Win the Small Victories First

In general, it makes sense to pay off cards with the highest interest rates first. But remember that in addition to financial victories, there are psychological ones to consider too.

Let's say you have two credit cards, one with $10,000 in outstanding balances that charges 24 percent interest, and another with $1000 in outstanding balances that charges 18 percent. And let's say that after establishing an emergency fund, you have $1000 left over to start paying off some debt. You can't go wrong paying off the higher-rate card. A $1000 payment on a 24 percent card is the equivalent of earning $240 in the stock market instantly. However, in this case there could be a bigger benefit in paying off the $1000 card first.

Why? Our problems with savings and debt stem from pessimism. So to whatever extent you can demonstrate to yourself that you're making real progress, the less pessimistic you're likely to be, and the better off you'll feel. And the emotional impact may embolden you to keep on saving.

In this example, if you were to pay off the higher-rate card, you might not notice much progress. You'd still have two cards with outstanding balances. The only difference would be, one of those cards would now have a $9000 balance instead of $10,000. If, on the other hand, you used the $1000 to pay off the 18-percent-interest card first, you'd only have one card left to tackle. It just feels less daunting. Plus, you'd still be earning 18 percent on your money— and that's nothing to sneeze at.

Step 3: Prioritize Your Debts

All forms of debt are not equal, so it's important to prioritize your obligations before you pay them down.

It actually pays to have some forms of debt. Home mortgage interest, for example, on acquisition loans of up to $1 million are fully tax deductible. Mortgage interest on a second home can also be deducted in many cases. Meanwhile, $2500 of your student loan interest can be deducted if you're a single taxpayer with a modified

adjusted gross annual income of $50,000 or less, or a married cou-
ple filing jointly earning $100,000 or less.

In addition to serving good purposes, these loans also happen to
charge relatively favorable interest rates. Anyone who purchased a
new home recently or refinanced their existing mortgage is paying
only around 5 or 6 percent interest. In 2003, student loans were being
consolidated at 4 percent rates or lower. By comparison, the average
credit card was charging nearly 15 percent, and many were charging
21 percent or more.

It seems obvious, then, that you should pay off your cards first.
Not only do cards charge the highest rates, the interest isn't
deductible. And by paying off your cards first, you're also likely to
improve your credit profile faster. A person's credit score—used by
lenders to set interest rates on loans—factors in that person's mix of
debt (see *Mistake 3: Not Knowing the Score*). And unsecured revolv-
ing debt is looked upon less favorably than mortgage debt.

After you're done paying off your cards, attack other forms of
high-rate nondeductible debt, such as car loans. Then work your way
down the food chain. If you have a home-equity loan outstanding,
consider paying that off next.

Home equity loan interest is deductible provided the loan itself does
not exceed $100,000. Home-equity loan rates also tend to be relatively
low. And the money can be used for any reason, such as paying off
credit cards or going on vacation. Home equity loans aren't always
desirable, however. Despite rising home values, many Americans own
less of their houses today than 20 years ago. That's largely because of
the record amount of equity we pulled out of our homes through
"cash-out refinancings," where a homeowner refinances a mortgage for
more than is currently owed on the property, in order to pocket the
difference. To whatever extent you can restore that equity, great.

Despite the attention we pay to our stock portfolios, our homes
are by far our most valuable assets. Among middle- and upper-middle-class families, home values represent more than 40 percent of total
wealth (versus just 17 percent for retirement accounts). It's in our best
interest, then, to own a larger percentage of this appreciating asset.

Next, pay off the student loans, particularly if they charge higher rates.

Finally, that leaves you with the mortgage, which offers the most flexibility of all debt. And thanks to record–low-interest rates at the start of this decade, it's also probably your lowest-rate loan.

Step 4: Regiment Your Savings Plan

The amount you save each month and the amount you set aside to pay down debt ought to be based on what you make and what you need to live on. That's a simple budgeting exercise.

Sum up all of your income sources, including salary, commissions, bonuses, and dividends. Then subtract your obligations. Everything left over should be fair game for savings. If you have the ability to do it, try to save 10 percent of your income each month. That's how much the average American family used to save.

Unfortunately, many families today can't achieve this goal because of mounting debt. If you were to only save enough to meet the minimum monthly payments required by your lenders, it could easily take 25 years or more to pay off some of your debts. It could also cost you thousands of dollars in additional interest costs over time. So pay off as much as you can as soon as you can.

It's important to stick with this approach even as your debt shrinks. Let's say you have balances on four credit cards, and your minimum monthly payments run about $200. And let's assume that you're able to direct $400 a month toward paying down that debt. Once you start making progress, don't lower the amount of money you dedicate to paying down debt just because there's less debt to pay down. If after knocking off one or two of your cards your minimum monthly payments fall to $100, don't lower your monthly payment schedule. Keep paying $400 toward your card balances as long as you can.

By channeling a level amount of money toward an ever-smaller amount of debt, you'll speed up your pace of debt repayment. That should free up extra money sooner, which you can use to build up savings and investments for specific goals.

NOT AUTOMATING YOUR SAVINGS

Behavioral finance scholars Shlomo Benartzi of UCLA and Richard Thaler of the University of Chicago have done some fascinating research in the area of 401(k)s.

Several years ago they noticed that a growing number of companies, concerned that too few workers were taking advantage of company-sponsored retirement plans, were experimenting with "automatic enrollment" 401(k)s. In a regular 401(k), it's up to workers to decide whether they want to participate in the savings plan. Employees who want to join are required to fill out enrollment papers. They have to decide how much they want to contribute to their 401(k)s and how they want to invest the money. In other words, it's up to the worker to *opt in* to the system.

In automatic-enrollment 401(k)s it's just the opposite. A new employee is automatically swept into the plan upon joining the firm. The only people who have to do anything are those who want to opt *out* of participating. "These plans are remarkably successful in increasing enrollment," Benartzi and Thaler say. Indeed, when companies switch to automatic enrollment plans, the participation rate in those 401(k)s can jump from below 50 percent to more than 80 percent. In some cases, 9 out of 10 workers end up participating. [19]

The lesson: automate your savings regimen wherever you can. Save small amounts of money each week or month like you do in a 401(k). And make inertia work for you.

This is simple to do. Most brokerages and mutual fund companies allow customers to set up automatic investment programs. Money can be automatically deducted from your checking account into a money market, bond, or stock fund each month. At places like T. Rowe Price and Fidelity you can set up a savings program for as little as $50 or $100 a month. The appeal of these plans is that, once set in motion, they allow individuals to set aside a small amount each month without having to make a conscious decision to save. If you want to quit, you have to fill out the paperwork. This way, inertia is working for you.

Today, only a minority of savers and investors take advantage of such plans. Yet the majority recognizes that automatic plans are useful tools toward building up savings. In a recent survey, 68 percent of Americans said that saving automatically each month would be somewhat or very useful in building their own savings accounts (see Figure 1-11). And in general, 79 percent think that setting aside a fixed amount of money each month would be useful in overcoming the inertia that hinders so many savers.

Benartzi and Thaler cite one problem with automatic 401(k)s: "The very inertia that helps increase participation rates also can lower the savings rates of those who do participate."[20] They note that many investors in automatic 401(k)s never increase their payroll deductions into the plans. In such plans, companies often establish a default rate of contribution, typically 3 percent of a worker's salary. Benartzi and Thaler found that workers tend to stick with those default rates, even if they eventually can afford to contribute more.

Figure 1-11. What People Find Useful in Creating a Savings Plan

According to surveys, consumers think setting aside a small amount of money each month can be among the most effective ways to save over time.
Source: Consumer Federation of America

Savings Method	Somewhat or Very Useful
Participating in 401(k)	80%
Saving Fixed Amount Each Month	**79%**
Developing Long-Term Plan	69%
Paying Off Mortgage Before Retiring	68%
Saving Fixed Amount Each Month Through Automatic Plan	**68%**
Paying Off Credit Cards	67%

Their solution is to automate these plans even more. Whenever workers get raises, automatically raise 401(k) contributions too: "By timing the increase to coincide with the pay increase, workers are assured that their paycheck will not fall."

Savers should try something similar. Every time you get a raise, increase the amount of money you put into your automatic savings and investment plan. The idea is simple but smart: By moving money out of your basic checking account and into your savings plan immediately, you'll never get to enjoy the raise in the first place. And you can't miss—or spend—what you don't see in your checking account.

Bottom Line

For all of the talk in the late 1990s about the importance of maximizing one's stock investments, creating a basic emergency fund, paying down debt, and creating a savings strategy are the first steps in any financial recovery plan. Only after you pay down your debts can you start saving. And only after you start saving can you start investing for the future.

The good news is, having a plan is half the battle. Surveys indicate that less than 40 percent of American families have ever—not even once—mapped out a financial plan. But those households that create such a plan wind up saving twice as much money as those that don't, according to research. Perhaps it's because once they sit down and study the situation, they discover just how easy it can be to save for a long-term goal.

If you do the math correctly, you'll come to understand that building up a savings account isn't about big sacrifices as much as it's about making small, routine contributions, just as you do with your 401(k). The battle to save money is literally won in $5 and $10 increments. Once you understand this, hopefully, pessimism will turn to optimism and you'll be on your way.

Checklist: Things to Do

❑   Start an emergency fund.
❑   Freeze your credit card spending.
❑   Freeze your credit cards.
❑   Start setting aside $25 a week in basic savings. This can add up to more than a quarter of a million dollars over 40 years.
❑   A few months later, see if you can save another $25 a week on top of that.
❑   Establish an automated savings and investment plan through your brokerage or mutual fund company.

MONEY **2** MISTAKE

GETTING FEE'D UP

Saving More by
Losing Less to Fees

No matter how smart we are, there are certain things in life that none of us has direct control over. The stock market is one of them. Interest rates are another. And our salaries are a third. True, we might be able to manage our stock investments, our income instruments, and our careers over time. But we cannot, at the flip of a switch, dictate their terms. Try as we might, we cannot force U.S. Treasury bonds to pay out more than they are yielding at the moment. We cannot will stock prices to rise through prayer. And we cannot give ourselves an instantaneous raise, no matter how much we think we deserve it.

The irony is, when it comes to managing our finances, we spend most of our time worrying about these things rather than the things we do have control over, like the fees and expenses we routinely pay out to our banks, brokerages, and mutual fund companies. Year in and year out, many savers overlook the detrimental effects of fees and expenses on their overall savings and financial plans. That's a big mistake.

It's easy to understand why we overlook fees and expenses. In the grand scheme of things, they seem like little annoyances. Two dollars to your bank for using a competitor's automated teller machine. Twenty dollars for being one day late with a credit card payment. Fifty dollars for letting your account balance fall below a certain level. And a thousand dollars to pay your mutual fund manager, even though he or she routinely underperforms the market. Soon it adds up to real money.

Just counting basic banking fees, like those for credit cards and ATM charges, consumers shell out more than $150 billion a year to financial services firms.[1] Add in investment-related costs, such as brokerage commissions and money management expenses, including the annual fees investors routinely pay to mutual fund companies, and the figure rises to around $300 billion a year. Compared to the $8 trillion investors collectively lost in the recent bear market, $300 billion might sound like a drop in the bucket. But the $8 trillion lost was a onetime event. Or at least we hope it was. Historically, stock prices rise more often then they fall. Fees, on the other hand, continue to grow year in and year out, in good markets or bad, in good economies or bad.

In a decade's time, the $300-billion-plus we lose to fees every year turns into more than $3 trillion lost, not counting the opportunity cost of investing that money. And over 25 years it balloons to more than $7.5 trillion, which is about what we lost to the bear market. No wonder banks, credit card issuers, and even brokerage firms are looking to generate a greater percentage of their annual revenues from fee income. It's simply more dependable than investment income. In the bear market of 2000, for example, while interest income fell for banks and credit card issuers and commission income fell for brokerages, fee income actually rose for many financial-services firms. for many financial-services firms and guess who paid for all of that?

You may shrug off fees as a necessary expense of being a saver and investor, but that would be a mistake. Fees and expenses can be devastating to a savings regimen. If you don't get a handle on such routine costs, your savings plan may be no more effective at retaining money than a sieve is at holding water, further discouraging you from setting money aside. A good place to start, as we will discuss throughout the book, is with the little things.

`MINI MISTAKE`

IGNORING BANKING FEES

For the past quarter of a century, banks have been aggressively moving to generate a greater portion of their revenues through all sorts of fees, ranging from transaction fees—like ATM charges and loan-processing expenses—to penalty fees, such as those associated with late payments on a credit card. In other words, they're doing what we should be doing: focusing their efforts on matters that they can control. So far, they're succeeding. In 1976, fee income represented just 18 cents of every dollar of operating revenue that commercial banks generated. Today it's more like 43 cents. In all, the nation's banks pocketed $157 billion in fee income in 2001.[2]

Given this fact, it's clearly in our best interest to shop for financial services providers based on the fees they levy, in addition to intangible considerations such as brand loyalty, convenience, and familiarity. To be sure, there's nothing wrong with choosing a bank because it has a branch across the street from your office. But consider expenses too, just as you would weigh the cost of other goods and services—like groceries, clothes, and airplane tickets—before making major purchases.

Unfortunately, 36 percent of savers and investors don't give much weight to matters such as fees and expenses when shopping for banks, brokerages, or investment firms. The sad thing is, we don't know enough to complain. The majority of consumers don't know how much they're losing to financial services fees annually. Meanwhile, another 35 percent are indifferent to costs altogether, as surveys show.[3]

This attitude might be understandable when it comes to choosing a financial planner, which is more subjective. There, you're paying an expert not only to manage your money, but to hold your hand and to let you sleep well at night, knowing that your assets are properly cared for. Personal relationships matter in addition to investment success when it comes to selecting a financial adviser. You're paying for peace of mind and comfort as much as functionality. Hopefully, you're paying reasonable prices for both.

Banking services, however, are essentially a commodity. The routine goods and services—maintenance of a checking account, availability of cash through ATM machines, the printing of checks, and the servicing of loans—can be done in virtually the same fashion by any bank or financial services provider. Just as an ounce of copper is the same no matter who you purchase it from, banking services are banking services whether Bank of America or Bank One is your primary provider. Of course, one bank may offer better customer service than another, and some banks have better online services. But at the end of the day, your checks get processed the same way through Wachovia as they do through Washington Mutual. This means that fees, rates, and prices ought to be the biggest things you worry about when selecting a bank.

Basic Checking Fees

Though we're supposedly entering an age of electronic bill payment, we still need basic checking accounts. That's just a fact of life. But do you know how much you're paying each year for that basic service? By one account, a typical checking account customer with, say, $1500 in his or her account, who writes 12 checks a month and bounces one check a year, could easily expect to pay about $125 in annual fees.[4] Now, if you found a way to avoid such fees and invested that sum every year for 25 years, earning 8 percent annual interest, you could amass more than $9000.

Nowadays, there are more types of bank fees to be wary of than ever before (see Figure 2-1). In addition to monthly service fees, there are account-balance-minimum fees, for not having enough money in your account; "nonsufficient funds" fees, for bouncing checks; per-item charges for writing too many checks; teller fees, for utilizing the services of a bank teller; online-access fees, for not using a teller and instead relying on the bank's Web site; point-of-sale fees, for using a debit card to make purchases; and bill-pay fees for using the bank's computer to pay your bills electronically.

And don't forget the truly pesky fees, the little things that even the most cost-conscious saver often overlooks, like coin-counting fees, check-printing fees, temporary-check fees, lost-debit-card replacement fees, currency-exchange fees, money-order fees, telephone-banking-inquiry fees, fees for photocopying old checks, and wire-transfer fees.

Figure 2-1. Banking Fee Terms

ATM Foreign Fee: The amount of money your bank charges for using a competing bank's automated teller machine.

ATM Surcharge Fee: The amount of money banks charge noncustomers for using their automated teller machines.

Annual Fee to Use ATM: Some banks charge their customers an annual fee for the right to use an ATM or debit card.

Account Balance Minimum Fee: Many savings and checking accounts impose a minimum account balance. Should your account fall below that threshold, you will be assessed a fee—and will continue to get hit with the fee until you bring your balance above the threshold.

Bill Payment Fee: Many banks provide bill payment services through their Web sites. But in some cases the service comes with a monthly fee, often $6 to $8 a month.

Figure 2-1. Banking Fee Terms (*Continued*)

Foreign-Exchange Fee: A surcharge levied by credit card issuers on card purchases made overseas.

Late Fee: Penalty fee assessed by credit card issuers on customers who are late paying their monthly bills. It typically ranges from $29 to $35 per incident. In recent years, card issuers have shortened grace periods, causing an increasing number of customers to be hit with this fee.

Monthly Service Fee: A monthly fee imposed to cover the administrative costs of maintaining your account. This could run between $5 and $15 a month.

Nonsufficient Funds Fee: Fees assessed on customers who bounce checks.

Overlimit Fee: Credit cards often let customers exceed their credit limit—but assess them a penalty fee. A typical overlimit fee ranges from $29 to $35.

Point of Sale Fee: Amount of money banks charge account holders to use an ATM card at a point of sale, such as a retailer or gas station.

Banks levy fees for the same reasons that governments impose taxes: They serve as primary and predictable sources of revenue. Take the credit card business. While interest income on bank cards fell 1 percent in 2001, as market interest rates tumbled during the volatile year, merchant fees—which card issuers charge retailers every time consumers buy goods and services on plastic—rose a steady 7 percent. Annual bank-card fees rose 5 percent, penalty fees rose 11 percent, and cash-advance fees soared 12 percent. In total, bank-card fees rose 9 percent, despite the recession and bear market (see Figure 2-2).

Like taxes, some fees are also assessed to curb what is deemed to be negative or "undesirable" behavior. Just as a state might levy a cigarette tax to curb smoking or a liquor tax to curb drinking, banks want account holders to stop bouncing checks across town. Hence, NSFs, or non-sufficient-funds fees, aren't only levied, they're routinely raised. Indeed, the average bounced-check fee at a traditional

Figure 2-2. Rising Credit Card Fees

While interest income fell at the start of the decade, bank credit card fees rose.
Source: Credit Card Management

Revenue Source	2001	2000	% Change
Interest Income	$64.17 bil.	$64.63 bil.	−1%
Merchant Fees	14.12	13.18	+7%
Annual Fees	2.40	2.29	+5%
Penalty Fees	7.32	6.57	+11%
Cash-Advance Fees	3.83	3.42	+12%

bank is more than $25 per incident, according to a study conducted in 2002 by *Bankrate.com*.[5] At the nation's biggest banks the situation is even worse. The average bounced-check fee went up from around $23 in 1999 to an average of $26.18 in 2001, according to a separate study by the U.S. Public Interest Research Group. That's $5 more than what small banks were charging.[6]

Obviously, the simplest way to avoid this fee is to balance your checkbook and stop bouncing checks. But let's be real. Try as we might, some of us occasionally bounce a check or two. One option is to apply for overdraft protection from your bank. But that too comes with fees. Some banks charge $20 or $25 a year just for the right to have overdraft protection—and then might assess an additional fee of $10 or $15 or more every time overdraft protection kicks in. In other words, you would be paying an annual fee for a service that simply charges a lower fee for bouncing checks than it normally does.

> **TIP:** A better solution may be to go with an Internet bank (see Figure 2-3), where the average bounced-check fee is slightly less than at a traditional bank. Also, consider a smaller community bank, rather than a big financial services provider. While fees for bounced checks at big traditional banks were rising 13 percent at the start of the decade, they grew just 3 percent at small banks, to $21.74, according to the U.S. Public Interest Research Group.[7]
>
> *(Continued)*

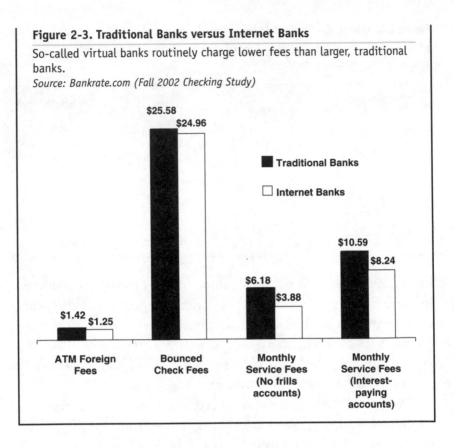

Figure 2-3. Traditional Banks versus Internet Banks

So-called virtual banks routinely charge lower fees than larger, traditional banks.

Source: Bankrate.com (Fall 2002 Checking Study)

Clearly, banks want customers to be with them for an extended period of time. They want a stable customer base from which they can draw a predictable and growing stream of revenues. This is why some banks impose yet another type of fee, acount-closure fees, for customers who shutter their accounts before a set period of time has passed. Typically, it might cost you $25 for closing your account less than 90 or 180 days after you opened it. Keep that in mind before you casually open up a new checking account.

Studies show that the typical U.S. household has relationships with more than three financial services providers. And one-fourth of all households have at least five banking relationships.[8] Obviously, it's in your bank's interest to accumulate more of your assets, off of which it can generate more investment and fee income. This explains why many banks impose "minimum account balance" fees—to get you to bring more of your money to them.

Nationwide, the average minimum balance required to open a traditional interest-paying checking account is more than $700. However, the more meaningful statistic for cost-conscious consumers is the minimum balance required to open a checking account while avoiding monthly service charges. These charges, which can range from $5 to $20 a month, depending on your bank and the nature of your account, are deducted from your checking account every month to cover the costs of basic account administration.

In the case of traditional banks, that minimum is now about $2600. Worse still, the number of banks requiring at least $5000 to avoid administrative fees is soaring.[9] Unfortunately, as we discussed, 48 million families maintain account balances of less than $1000. And "many simply can't avoid being zapped with extra fees by their bank because they don't meet the onerous minimum balance requirements," says consumer rights advocate Ralph Nader.[10]

If you don't have that much in savings, and you think your balance on occasion might fall below certain minimum thresholds, the best option may be to go with a "no frills" checking account that doesn't pay interest. As short-term interest rates have fallen to multidecade lows, so too have yields on bank checking accounts. The average yield tumbled to around 0.5 percent at the end of 2002. Fewer than one out of five checking accounts were paying 1 percent interest or more during that year.[13] Under such circumstances, the meager yield your account will earn would more than likely be overwhelmed by the fees you'll incur if your balance dips below a threshold. You may be better off, then, going with a no-frills checking account that doesn't pay interest but offers lower minimum balance requirements.

The average minimum balance required to open a *non*-interest-bearing checking account is only about $75. By comparison, the

Tip: A way to significantly cut service fees—which average nearly $11 a month, or $127 a year—is to consider an Internet bank. The average minimum balance required to avoid monthly service fees at virtual banks is roughly half the amount required by traditional institutions[11] (see Figure 2-4). You may not think it's worth the effort to save a few dollars in service fees, but according to surveys, consumers who are unable to maintain adequate minimum balances are paying upwards of $266 a year in annual fees at big, traditional banks. That's up from $235 a year in 1999. If you were to invest that sum for 25 years, you'd have close to $20,000.

Figure 2-4. The Internet Bank Advantage

While account balance requirements are typically higher on average at Internet banks, the minimum required to avoid fees is lower at virtual banks. *Source: Bankrate.com (Fall 2002 Checking Study)*

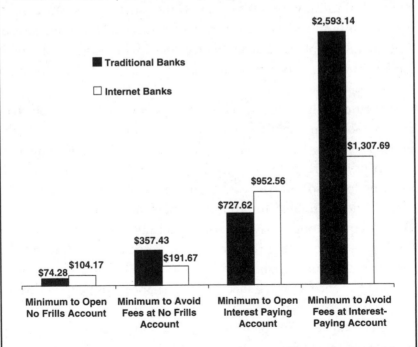

Alternatively, you might consider a small community bank, where average annual fees for a consumer with low account balances is about $191. Even better, consider opening a regular checking account through your credit union, if you're eligible to participate in one.

(Continued)

According to surveys, the average annual fees for a regular checking account at a credit union is only $101. That's actually lower than it was in 1999[12] (see Figure 2-5). In part, this is because average minimum balances to avoid monthly fees for checking accounts at credit unions is just $345.

Figure 2-5. Checking Account Costs

In general, small banks and credit unions offer lower overall fees than big retail banks. (Figures for 2001 were based on a survey of 521 banks in 32 states and the District of Columbia. Figures for 1999 were based on a survey of 526 banks in 33 states plus D.C.)
Source: U.S. Public Interest Research Group

	Interest-Bearing Accounts		
	2001	**1999**	**Change**
Big Banks	$266	$239	+11%
Small Banks	204	225	−9%
Credit Unions	131	124	+6%
	Regular Checking Accounts		
	2001	**1999**	**Change**
Big Banks	$266	$235	+13%
Small Banks	191	203	−6%
Credit Unions	101	112	−10%
	No-Frills Checking Accounts		
	2001	**1999**	**Change**
Big Banks	$169	$161	+5%
Small Banks	122	136	−10%
Credit Unions	88	82	+7%

average minimum balance to open an interest-bearing account is 10 times higher: $728. Meanwhile, the average minimum required to avoid fees in a no-frills checking account is only $357.

But even if you have more than enough money to meet minimum balance requirements to avoid fees, there's still a strong argument for going with a no-frills account. Instead of putting, say, $3000 into a checking account that pays 0.5 percent interest, or $15 a year, you could keep $1000 in a non-interest-paying checking account and move the remaining $2000 into a money market account yielding, say, 2 percent, or $40. The higher yield of a money market account will allow you to earn more interest than a checking account—even with smaller balances. Plus, by maintaining a no-frills checking account, you stand a better chance of avoiding unnecessary fees that interest-paying accounts often charge.

Other Ways to Avoid Fees

- *Think small.* In general, smaller banks offer savers a competitive product, with fees typically about 30 percent lower than at big banks. Credit unions, which are run as nonprofit organizations, are even cheaper. A typical credit union customer will pay 60 percent less in annual fees than big bank customers pay. Furthermore, while regular checking account fees at big banks are rising, credit union charges are actually falling; they're down 10 percent from 1999.

- *Direct deposit.* About 11 percent of all banks offer "free checking" to consumers if they agree to electronically direct deposit paychecks into their accounts. Still other financial institutions may discount fees for customers who direct deposit. From the bank's point of view, direct depositing not only reduces the need for teller assistance and the cost of processing checks, it assures a steady stream of assets coming into the bank week in and week out, or month in and month out, depending on your payroll schedule. It also has a huge benefit for customers: Your money will clear much faster than if you manually deposit each check. If your paycheck arrives every Friday, for instance, that money will be in your account first thing Friday morning. If you were to take a physical check and deposit it into your bank, it might not clear until the end of the day the following Monday—perhaps later if your company issues your paycheck from an out-of-state bank. If you're like the tens of millions of households who literally live paycheck to paycheck, as we mentioned in the first chapter, than having this money credited to your account sooner means there is less likelihood of bouncing a check. That, in turn, lessens the likelihood of incurring yet more bounced-check fees.

- *Consolidate accounts.* Some banks will exempt you from fees—or will discount them—if you maintain a large enough percentage of your overall assets with that institution. It's an enticement to get you to do more business with them. Less than 20 percent of American households do all their financial business with a single company. The majority have multiple financial relationships primarily because we think it's too risky to hand over all of our money to one firm.[14] If you don't agree with this assumption, see if it makes sense to consolidate more—though not all—of your money at a single financial institution. At the very least, consolidate enough of your basic banking assets to meet minimum thresholds to avoid penalty and service charges. That might mean opening a checking account at the bank where you purchased a certificate of deposit, or through which you invest in a money-market fund. According to a study by the Council on Financial Competition, Americans keep more money outside their "primary checking accounts" than inside them. Close to 60 percent of the $600 billion kept in checking accounts in the late 1990s was held in so-called nonprimary accounts.[15] That's a stunning statistic, and one that could lead some households to pay minimum-balance fees they don't need to incur.

- *Don't pay for services you don't want.* Many bank customers don't want to receive their canceled checks, yet some banks charge an additional monthly fee for this service. Worse still, many of us don't even realize we're paying for this. Make sure you aren't being assessed fees for services you don't absolutely want or need.

Credit Card Fees

Credit card issuers have been finding new and ever more creative ways to hit us with fees. "There's really been a fee frenzy" in the industry, says Robert McKinley, CEO of *CardWeb.com*. It's no wonder, then, that the vast majority of cardholders say they've been hit with at least one unnecessary fee—be it a transaction fee, a penalty fee, or an annual fee—over the past year. Card fees now represent the fastest growing source of revenue generation for credit card issuers[16] (see Figure 2-6). While credit card interest income rose 84 percent between 1994 and 2001, credit card fee income grew a stunning 279 percent during this same period.

The irony is, a growing number of us are doing a better job of managing our credit, despite what you read in the headlines. For

Figure 2-6. Rising Fee Income

In recent years, credit card issuers have started to generate a greater percentage of their revenues from fees, as interest income has plateaued.
Sources: Cardweb.com and Credit Card Management

	Credit Card Revenues	
Year	Fee Income	Interest Income
2001	$27.7 billion	$64.2 billion
2000	25.5 billion	64.6 billion
1998	18.9 billion	58.1 billion
1997	14.8 billion	53.1 billion
1996	10.0 billion	52.3 billion
1995	8.3 billion	42.2 billion
1994	7.3 billion	34.8 billion

instance, a greater percentage of households are rejecting the tidal wave of unsolicited credit card offers that perennially clog our mailboxes (see Figure 2-7). You know the ones I'm referring to: "Congratulations, Mr. or Ms. Fill-in-the-Blank! You have been preapproved for a brand-new, elite titanium credit card that sports a $30,000 credit limit." Of course, in the fine print the card issuer indicates that your limit may only be $1000, depending on your credit score.

In 1992, 3 percent of the 920 million credit card offers mailed out to consumers were accepted. But that acceptance rate fell steadily throughout the 1990s and now stands at just 0.6 percent. This is due to a combination of factors. For starters, Americans are getting smarter about unsolicited offers of all kinds. In this "shredder" nation, it's that much easier to throw away all sorts of unsolicited mail. Furthermore, it's so easy these days to get credit from one's own financial institution, unsolicited credit cards are redundant. Plus, most Americans have more than enough cards already in their

Figure 2-7. Saying No to Plastic

The percentage of Americans who accept unsolicited offers for credit cards is shrinking, studies show.
Source: BAI Global.

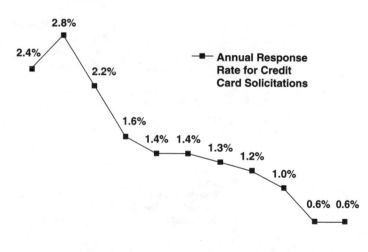

wallets. As we discussed earlier, the average household maintains a collection of more than 14 credit cards.

Of course, the banks aren't sitting still. With acceptance rates at recent lows, credit card issuers are simply pumping up the volume. Americans now receive more than 5 billion unsolicited credit card offers each year through the mail, which is double the rate from the mid-1990s and more than triple the volume of the early 1990s (see Figure 2-8).

Another sign that we're more careful with our credit is that though card delinquencies rose during the recent economic downturn, more than 95 percent of cardholders kept making their payments in recent years, despite the confluence of several negative factors—the recession, the threat of terrorism, a weak stock market, falling consumer confidence, and rising unemployment (see Figure 2-9). Furthermore, more Americans are paying off their card balances in full every month, something that rarely gets talked about

Figure 2-8. Credit Card Solicitations

Over the past decade, credit card issuers have flooded consumers with billions of unsolicited credit card offers.
Source: BAI Global.

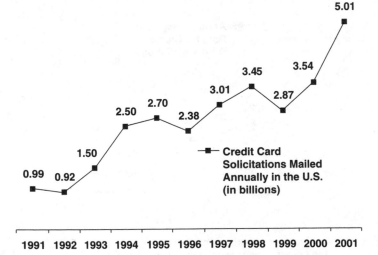

Credit Card Solicitations Mailed Annually in the U.S. (in billions)

1991 1992 1993 1994 1995 1996 1997 1998 1999 2000 2001

in the news these days (see Figure 2-10). We'll address this topic in greater detail in the next chapter.

Still, while a growing number of us are trying to do the right thing when it comes to managing our credit, card companies are making it more difficult. Over the past decade, grace periods for credit card bills—the time between the end of a billing cycle and when payment is due—have quietly fallen. According to *CardWeb*, the average grace period for a credit card bill is now just 21.2 days, down more than eight full days from 1990. This may explain why such a large percentage of cardholders are being slapped with late fees. According to one recent survey, three out of five cardholders reported being hit with a late fee at least once in the past year.[17] A separate survey found that one-fourth of all Americans pays one or more bill late each month.[18]

Figure 2-9. Credit Card Delinquencies

Though there's plenty of room for improvement, Americans have started to do a better job of paying their credit card bills on time. (Data are based on figures collected in the second quarter of each year.)
Source: CardWeb.com

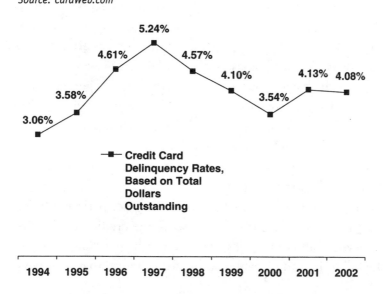

Figure 2-10. Paying Off Plastic

A growing percentage of cardholders are paying their credit card balances in full—and on time.
Source: CardWeb.com

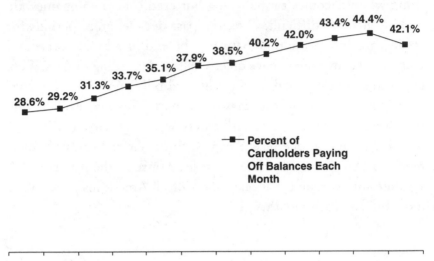

1990 1991 1992 1993 1994 1995 1996 1997 1998 1999 2000 2001

Worse still, late fees themselves are on the rise. The typical late fee on a credit card is now $29 (see Figure 2-11). That represents a 128 percent increase from 1995, when the average late fee was a little less than $13. Many card issuers charge much more—$35 or even $38 for each late payment, which helps explain why late fees are now the credit card industry's third biggest revenue source. The way it works, typically, is that the bigger your account balance, the larger your late fee. Many card issuers have gone to a tiered system in which consumers with no or low account balances get a lesser fee, while those with substantial balances pay the maximum. So, if you mismanage your credit cards, you get hit with a double whammy: higher interest payments and bigger penalty fees.

Clearly, it's in your best interest to know the grace period on your cards. Sometimes, you have to be precise. Some credit card issuers will say that your bill is late if it's not received by a certain time on the day the bill is due. You might assume, for instance, that your pay-

Figure 2-11. Late Fees Rising

Credit card issuers are slapping higher penalty fees on consumers who are late paying their monthly bills. (Figures represent averages measured in February of each year.)
Source: Cardweb.com

Year	Average Late Fee
2002	$28.79
2001	27.12
2000	25.99
1999	22.89
1998	19.30
1997	14.62
1996	13.25
1995	12.64

ment is on time as long as it's received by the end of the business day on the due date shown on the bill. But some card issuers say that payment is not technically "on time" unless the bill is received by noon or 2:00 P.M. on that date.[19] Given the unpredictable nature of mail delivery, the only way to ensure that your payment is on time is to make sure it's there the day *before* your due date.

One way to make sure that your bills are getting to where they need to go *when* they need to go is to pay them online. For one thing, more banks are doing away with other fees—such as online banking fees—for customers who agree to pay their bills electronically.[20] Moreover, the more you can automate your finances, the better off you'll be. We'll emphasize this theme throughout the book.

One option is to link your checking account to a specific credit card company, such as American Express. Under this scenario, when your Amex bill is due, you can simply go onto the American Express Web site, log in your information, and at the click of a mouse transfer money out of your checking account into your American Express account. Typically, this is free. Still, make sure your credit card company does not charge for this type of bill payment.

If you go with an online payment service to pay your bills, your checking account is linked to the service, which in turn pays your bills for you. In some cases the money is transferred electronically. In others, the online bill payment firm may cut a check to whomever you ask it to. According to Forrester Research, 17 million households paid bills online in 2002, up more than 40 percent from just the year before.[21] But a separate study found that less than 10 percent of Americans routinely pay their bills online.

Today, myriad financial services firms offer online bill payment services. They range from banks to brokers to credit card companies to the U.S. Postal Service and even financial Web sites like Quicken. Typically, they charge a monthly fee of about $6 to $8 to pay all of your bills. That's about as expensive as buying stamps to mail all your bills the old-fashioned way, if you pay more than 15 bills a month. And these days, it's common for a family to receive more than 15 bills a month: your mortgage, car loan, local phone bill, long-distance phone bill, cellular phone bill, heating bill, electric bill, water bill, at least three credit card bills, a gas station card bill, college tuition bill, and the list goes on and on.

Not that errors can't occur online. There have been reported incidents of missed, late, or incorrect payments on some online transactions. Recently, the *Wall Street Journal* speculated that these errors may explain why only a minority of households regularly use such services.[22] But to be fair, there are as many, if not more, incidents of old-fashion mailed checks being lost, delayed, or improperly credited. So don't let that deter you from considering online bill payment. Just be judicious. Keep an eye on your electronic bill payment service. Routinely check with lenders to see if they are receiving your payments in full and on time.

Another solution, if you're running late on a single bill—and fear that it won't get there on time if you mailed it—is to phone it in. Nearly all credit card issuers have an established 1-800 phone number to make payments by phone. The only catch is, some card issuers charge fees for accepting payments by phone, and for those companies, a typical fee for phone payment services is about $10 to $15 every time you use the service. But then, while that's steep, it's certainly less than the $29 or $35 late fee you'll incur if you throw your payment into the mailbox too late.[23]

For their part, banking industry officials note that penalty fees, especially late payment fees, are totally avoidable.[24] They're right. All it takes is discipline to ensure that you're not late with payments. If you plan ahead and plan properly, other fees can also be avoided. By comparison shopping, for instance, it's easy to find cards that don't charge annual membership fees. In addition, there's no reason why consumers should be making credit card cash advances. Yet cash-advance fees are the fastest-growing category of all charges. Consumers lose a staggering $13 billion a year to avoidable transaction and penalty fees.

Other Fees You Can Easily Avoid

- *Overlimit fees.* Fees for going over your credit limit have sky-rocketed 116 percent since 1994, according to *CardWeb.*[25] The average overlimit fee is now $29. But if you routinely carry out-standing balances on your card, you're likely to pay more. Cardholders with more than $1000 in balances might expect to pay as much as $35 every time their balances exceed their credit limits.
- *Foreign exchange fees.* Increasingly, banks have been adding additional surcharges to the fees Visa and MasterCard already charge consumers traveling abroad. Today, you can expect to be hit with combined surcharges of as much as 3 percent every time you use your card overseas. That means you could be paying $100 or

$200 in transaction fees for a week-long trip to Europe.[26] In the spring of 2003, a California court declared that Visa and MasterCard failed to adequately disclose its currency-conversion fees to consumers and ordered the card networks to pay state cardholders up to $800 million in restitution. But it's important to note that the California case was not the final ruling on this matter, and that the court itself determined that such fees were legal, if properly disclosed. So don't expect high foreign-exchange fees to go away.

- *Account closing fees.* Be sure to read the fine print of your credit card agreement before signing on the dotted line. That's because some cards will hit you with a fee when you close out your account. Some will charge a flat fee of, say, $35, while others charge a higher interest rate on the remaining balance on your card.

ATM Fees

Automated Teller Machine fees really get my goat, but not necessarily because of what banks charge—though, for the record, they charge way too much. Of all the fees we can avoid, it's this one. We can do so by picking banks more judiciously. We can read the fine print of our ATM card agreements. (According to one recent survey, many of us aren't even reading ATM *signs* correctly. Twenty percent of us think that we aren't subject to ATM fees as long as the automated teller machine we use bears the same financial network logos—such as "Star," "Cirrus," or "Plus"—shown on our bank cards.) Or we can just drive a few extra blocks to get to our own banks, where chances are we won't be hit with as many ATM fees. The funny thing is, many of us routinely drive several miles out of our way to buy cheaper gas, but won't do the same for cheaper money.

While some critics of bank fees harp on the very existence of ATM charges, I don't. Listen, if you withdraw money from an ATM that doesn't belong to your bank, you're getting a service. And you're getting that service from a bank that you don't do business with.

Why shouldn't you have to pay for it? My only complaint is how much they charge and whether they make it clear that they're charging that much.

Think about the number of times you withdraw money from an ATM. It could be as often as once a week, which translates into four times a month or 52 times a year. Now think about what banks routinely charge today. Nine out of 10 banks charge noncustomers who use their ATMs, and the typical "surcharge" is about $1.50 per transaction.[27] A growing number—13 percent in 2002—are charging $2.00 or more. That's $2.00 for the right to access your money through another bank's ATM.

But there's more. In addition to the surcharge that the other bank will hit you with, you'll likely be slapped with a second fee, this time by *your* bank for two-timing it. This is sometimes referred to as a "foreign ATM fee," which is simply a penalty for going outside your bank's network of automated tellers. These days, 9 out of 10 banks levy such foreign ATM fees on customers who use other banks' machines, and that fee typically amounts to another $1.50 to $2.00 per transaction.[28] So, assuming you're one of those folks who doesn't comparison shop, you're looking at $4.00 per transaction in a worst case scenario, which works out roughly to about $208 a year. If you were to invest that amount every year for 25 years, you could amass $16,500, assuming an 8 percent average annual rate of return.

Remember too that a minority of banks also charge their own customers a fee even if they use an in-network ATM. And still others—about 9 percent—charge customers an annual fee for the right to have an ATM card in the first place. It's no wonder, then, that banks collect more than $2 billion a year in ATM fees each year. That's up more than 40 percent from 1998.[29]

Of course, we sometimes find ourselves away from home and our banks when we need cash. We may be on vacation. We may be on a business trip. In that case, take out enough funds to tide you over until you're near your own bank. A $4.00 ATM fee, for instance, for withdrawing $20 means your transaction fee is actually 20 percent of your take, which is in the ballpark of what loan sharks charge.

> **TIP**: Because of the number of times you're likely to be hit with these ATM fees, this should be one of the key variables you consider when shopping for checking accounts. You can comparison shop for banks within individual cities at *www.bankrate.com*. If you click on the section that discusses ATM fees, and identify the city in which you reside, the Web site will indicate what each bank in that market assesses in surcharges and foreign fees, and which banks charge their own customers for using an in-network ATM. In addition, make sure that whatever bank you choose has a sufficiently large and convenient network of ATMs for you to routinely withdraw cash without being robbed.

Withdraw $400 instead, and that surcharge drops to just 1 percent of your withdrawal. And you avoid having to go back to that ATM again during the same trip, incurring yet more fees.

MINI MISTAKE

IGNORING INVESTMENT FEES

Some investors I've interviewed say they don't mind paying higher than average fees to mutual funds for higher than average returns. In other words, they're willing to pay for performance. But it's not quite that simple when it comes to mutual funds.

You have to appreciate how money management fees work. In a mutual fund, expenses are calculated as a percentage of your assets, not as a flat fee. The bigger your investment in a fund, the bigger your annual fee in dollar terms. For instance, if your fund charges annual expenses of 2 percent of assets, and if you have $10,000 invested in the portfolio, your fee will amount to $200 a year. If you invest $100,000 in the same fund, your fee would be $2000 a year.

Whatever your fee, it will be *automatically* deducted from your gross total returns. This is not an insignificant point.

One reason why many investors haven't a clue as to how much they're paying in mutual fund fees is because they never receive a bill. You don't pay a fund out of your checking account, like you do a gas bill. You pay it out of your returns. The mutual fund returns you see in your account statements reflect the performance of that investment *after* fees have already been deducted. All things being equal, then, the higher your fee, the worse your returns are likely to be.

If your fund gained 10 percent on its investments on a gross basis but charges fees of 2 percent of assets, your net return will be 8 percent. If your fund gains just 1 percent in the market on a gross basis but charges 2 percent fees, your net return will be negative 1 percent. This arrangement raises an interesting dynamic: While a fund charging higher than average fees won't necessarily deliver better than average returns, the fact that it charges high fees to begin with means that it will have to be better than average simply to be average on an after-fee basis. Got that?

Put simply: The higher the fees, the higher the bar the fund sets for itself to be successful. Conversely, the lower the fees, the lower your costs and the better the performance of your mutual fund, all things being equal.

Consider the following hypothetical situations:

- You have two funds that perform equally, and both returned 8 percent a year in gross terms. But Fund A charged lower than average fees of about 0.6 percent of assets. So its after-cost returns were 7.4 percent. Fund B, on the other hand, charged higher than average fees of 2 percent. That means its after-cost return was just 6 percent. On a $100,000 investment, that's the difference of about $1400 in fees each year. But over the course of 10 years, the cost doesn't just grow to $14,000, as one might assume by doing the simple math. Remember, in a fund, your returns compound annually. When you factor that into the equation, you wind up losing about $25,000 more over the course of a decade to fees by investing in Fund B—or one-quarter of your original investment (see Figure 2-12).

- Instead of gross returns of 8 percent, let's assume that your funds return 12 percent in the marketplace. Fund A, with annual fees of just 0.6 percent, would then return 11.4 percent on an after-fee basis. Fund B would return just 10 percent. The difference between those two figures over a decade would amount to nearly $35,000—or more than one-third the size of your original investment.

- Now, if you were to invest in a passively managed, low-cost index fund (which we will discuss in later chapters), you could easily find a fund that mirrors the S&P 500 for 0.2 percent of assets or less. The Vanguard 500 index fund, for instance, one of the biggest mutual funds in the world, charges shareholders just 0.18 percent of assets. Under this same scenario, assuming a 12 percent annual rate of gross returns, a fund charging 0.18 percent of assets would return 11.82 percent, on an after-fee basis. Over a decade, a $100,000 investment would grow to $305,629. That's $46,255 more than a similar fund charging fees of 2 percent would return.

Sadly, most investors don't appreciate or understand this dynamic. Studies show that more than 80 percent of fund investors can't even *estimate* the fees they pay out to even one of their mutual funds. It may be the result of the bull market we grew up in. When our funds were returning 30 percent a year in the 1990s, the thought of paying out 2 or even 3 percent of those returns in fees seemed trivial, so none of us complained. But in a stock market where funds are gaining just 5 or 6 percent a year, fees of 2 percent represent about 30 percent of your gross returns. And if your funds are losing money, as they did throughout the bear market, fees simply exacerbate an already frustrating situation.

Researchers at the investment advisory firm Kanon Bloch Carre recently studied the real cost of investing in a mutual fund. They

Figure 2-12. Mutual Fund Fees

Because expenses are deducted from total returns, fund investors don't often know how much they lose each year to fees. Yet the costs can be significant.

	Market Returns	Expense Ratio	Net Returns	Growth of $100,000 Year 1	Growth of $100,000 10 Years
Stock Funds					
Low-cost funds	8%	0.60%	7.40%	$107,400	$204,194
Average-cost funds	8%	1.30%	6.70%	106,700	191,269
High-cost funds	8%	2.00%	6.00%	106,000	179,085
Difference: High vs. Low				*$1,400*	*$25,109*
Stock Funds					
Low-cost funds	12%	0.60%	11.40%	$111,400	$294,342
Average-cost funds	12%	1.30%	10.70%	110,700	276,360
High-cost funds	12%	2.00%	10.00%	110,000	259,374
Difference: High vs. Low				*$1,400*	*$34,968*

(Continued)

Figure 2-12. Mutual Fund Fees (*Continued*)

Because expenses are deducted from total returns, fund investors don't often know how much they lose each year to fees. Yet the costs can be significant.

	Market Returns	Expense Ratio	Net Returns	Growth of $100,000 Year 1	Growth of $100,000 10 Years
Bond Funds					
Low-cost funds	5%	0.40%	4.60%	$104,600	$156,789
Average-cost funds	5%	0.90%	4.10%	104,100	149,454
High-cost funds	5%	1.50%	3.50%	103,500	141,060
Difference: High vs. Low				*$1,100*	*$15,729*
Bond Funds					
Low-cost funds	7%	0.40%	6.60%	$106,600	$189,484
Average-cost funds	7%	0.90%	6.10%	106,100	180,781
High-cost funds	7%	1.50%	5.50%	105,500	170,815
Difference: High vs. Low				*$1,100*	*$18,669*

studied fund expenses over a five-year period—March 31, 1997, to March 31, 2002—that encompassed a raging bull market and a grisly bear market. Instead of weighing a fund's expenses relative to assets, though, they analyzed costs relative to performance. After all, if some investors say they're willing to "pay for performance," why not see how much they're actually paying?

Some of the findings were staggering. Though portfolios in the major fund companies in the study charged fees of between 0.5 and 1.4 percent of assets, the fees represented upward of 10 to 12 percent of gross total returns (see Figure 2-13). For instance, American Express mutual funds were charging average annual fees of 0.99 percent of assets during this period, according to Kanon Bloch Carre. But on average, the funds returned just 7.76 percent. This means the company pocketed nearly 13 percent of its total performance in fees. Alliance Capital was even worse, with average fees of 1.37 percent of assets between 1997 and 2002. However, the average total return for those funds was just 8.64 percent a year, meaning fees represented nearly 16 percent of gross returns.

Unfortunately, this seems to have little bearing on where investors put money to work. A recent survey by Vanguard and *Money* magazine found that the majority of investors don't know how much they pay in fees. Three-quarters of all investors can't even define the term "expense ratio," a key concept in measuring mutual fund costs. And another 64 percent don't understand how expenses impact mutual fund returns.[30] Yet, as we have discussed, the impact can be enormous. Over even longer periods of time, it can make or break a person's retirement plan.

Jack Bogle, a founding father of the modern mutual fund industry and a champion of individual investors, offers this eye-opening example: Had you invested $1000 in the stock market in 1950, it would have turned into $514,000 by 1999, based on the performance of the S&P 500 index of blue chip stocks (see Figures 2-14 and 2-15). Yet that same $1000 invested in the average stock mutual fund grew to just $193,000 during that period of time, largely thanks to fees. "The investor lost 63 percent of the market's cumulative return to the intermediaries . . .," Bogle notes.[31]

Figure 2-13. Fund Fees Versus Performance

Between March 31, 1997, and March 31, 2002, mutual fund investors lost a significant portion of their stock market returns to investment fees.

Source: Kanon Bloch Carre

Fund Family	Average Exp. Ratio	5-Yr Mkt. Returns	5-Yr Returns After Fees	% of Returns Kept by Fund Companies
Vanguard	0.46%	11.05%	10.59%	4.2%
American Funds	0.65	13.71	13.06	4.7
Fidelity	0.67	11.97	11.30	5.6
Janus	0.83	13.29	12.46	6.2
Merrill Lynch	0.97	14.44	13.47	6.7
T. Rowe Price	0.88	11.82	10.94	7.4
Amvesco	1.18	14.24	13.06	8.3
MFS	1.10	12.97	11.87	8.5
Franklin Templeton	0.99	11.60	10.61	8.5
American Century	1.00	11.33	10.33	8.8

Salomon Smith Barney	0.98	10.87	9.89	*9.0*
Oppenheimer	1.23	12.87	11.64	*9.6*
Fleet/Liberty	1.05	10.74	9.69	*9.8*
Morgan Stanley DW	1.23	12.33	11.10	*10.0*
Fidelity Adviser	1.25	12.01	10.76	*10.4*
Dreyfus	1.08	9.13	8.05	*11.8*
Deutsche/Scudder	1.18	9.95	8.77	*11.9*
Putnam	1.02	8.25	7.23	*12.4*
American Express	0.99	7.76	6.77	*12.8*
Alliance Capital	1.37	8.64	7.27	*15.9*

Figure 2-14. The Impact of Fees

Over time, fees can erase a huge amount of
your potential stock market returns. The figures
reflect performance from 1950 to 1999.
*Source: Vanguard, The Bogle Financial Markets
Research Center*

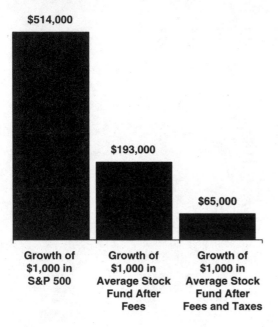

$514,000

$193,000

$65,000

Growth of	Growth of	Growth of
$1,000 in	$1,000 in	$1,000 in
S&P 500	Average Stock	Average Stock
	Fund After	Fund After
	Fees	Fees and Taxes

Sales Commissions

Of all the fees that funds charge, the most familiar are sales commissions, or so-called "loads." The majority of funds today are not
purchased directly by investors through fund companies but are sold
through brokers, financial advisers, or other intermediaries. That's
because more of us are seeking the services of financial planners and
stockbrokers to help us manage our money. Indeed, a majority of
Americans think that financial planning is more important today
than it was at the start of the bear market, and more of us are now
willing to pay for that advice, especially when it comes to picking
mutual funds. It's easy to see why, given that the stock market has
been so unforgiving in recent years and there are more than 10,000
funds to choose from.

Figure 2-15. Diminished Returns

Average annual returns for the stock
market and stock mutual funds between
1950 and 1999.
*Source: Vanguard, The Bogle Financial Markets
Research Center*

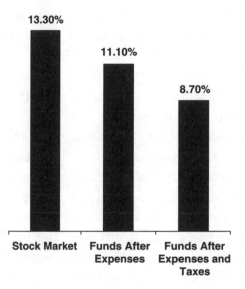

To compensate those so-called financial intermediaries, broker-sold funds come with a sales commission, or "load." There are basically three types of load funds: those that charge the commission up front, when you purchase the fund; those that charge the commission when you sell; and those that spread out the commission cost somewhat evenly over time. Funds that charge front-end loads are often known as A class shares. Those that charge back-end loads (also referred to as "contingent deferred sales charges") are B shares. And level-load funds are referred to as C shares. The underlying fund is the same, but the shares dictate how you pay for the financial advice.

According to Morningstar, 2568 of the 10,184 stock funds that existed in 2002— or roughly 25 percent—charged a front-end load. Typically, the front-end loads ranged from 1 to 5.75 percent of your investment, with an average commission of about 4.6 percent.

Do these commissions affect your returns? Absolutely. The load is automatically deducted from your investment before it gets put into the market. In other words, if you were to put $100,000 in a load fund that charges a 5.75 percent front-end commission, only $94,250 of your money would be invested. The rest would be pocketed by the broker. By comparison, if you were to invest that same $100,000 in a no-load mutual fund, all of the money would work its way into the market.

Over time, the effects of a front-end load should diminish somewhat, provided the fund produces better than average returns. But what if the fund produces returns that are no better than the overall market? Assume that you invest $100,000 in that 5.75 percent load fund while your friend invests $100,000 in a no-load fund. And assume that over the next 25 years both funds return exactly the same amount: 7 percent a year after annual expenses. While your account would grow to $511,500 over that time, your friend's investment would be worth $542,740—more than a $31,000 difference (see Figure 2-16). That's because you only started out with $94,250, not the full $100,000. The question you have to ask yourself is: How much are you willing to pay for advice?

The good news is, many investors are getting better at avoiding front-end loads where possible. According to a study by the Investment Company Institute, the mutual fund industry's trade group, the average actual cost of front-end loads, on a sales-weighted basis, has fallen to 1.1 percent, down from around 2 percent in 1997, 4 percent in 1989, and nearly 6 percent in 1970. This means that while more of us are paying sales commissions, we're putting money to work in *low*-load mutual funds.

The bad news is, we should be paying even less. In 2003, the Securities and Exchange Commission, the New York Stock Exchange, and the National Association of Securities Dealers found that a number of fund investors eligible for so-called breakpoint discounts—price breaks on front-end loads for investing large sums of money at one time, such as $50,000, $100,000, or even $1 million— aren't receiving them. In fact, the study, which was conducted

Figure 2-16. Heavy Loads

Sales charges can be harmful to a fund's real returns. Though the effects of a fund's "load" may diminish gradually over time, even after 25 years you can see a significant difference in total returns. The table shown here indicates the performance of mutual funds based on 7 percent annual growth.

Mutual Fund	Initial $100,000 Investment	Year 1	Year 3	Year 5	Year 10	Year 25
No Load	$100,000	$107,000	$122,504	$140,255	$196,715	$542,743
1% Load	99,000	105,930	121,279	138,853	194,748	537,316
3.25% Load	96,750	103,523	118,523	135,697	190,322	525,104
5.75% Load	94,250	100,848	115,460	132,191	185,404	511,536
No Load vs. 5.75% Load	$5,750	$6,152	$7,044	$8,064	$11,311	$31,207

between November 2002 and January 2003, found that nearly one in three fund transactions that should have received commission discounts did not get them. The cost to investors: approximately $364 per transaction.

Meanwhile, more stock funds are imposing back-end loads. Nearly 3400 equity funds imposed such a commission in 2002, according to Morningstar, and the typical back-end load ranges from about 1 to 6 percent of the investment, with the average being more than 3 percent.

Often, a back-loaded fund will start off with a higher deferred commission, say 5 percent, and will gradually lower that over time. However, keep in mind that to recoup the commissions it loses by forgoing a front-end load, the fund will want to keep you around for at least five to seven years. That means your back-end load may not disappear altogether until you hold the fund for more than half a decade. Moreover, the annual fees charged by a fund with a back-end load is typically going to be higher than those charged by front-end load funds. According to Morningstar, the average A share fund charged annual fees of 1.55 percent at the end of 2002, whereas B shares, which charge back-end loads, sported average annual fees of 2.07 percent.

Expense Ratio

While investors have done a decent job in avoiding sales commissions, the same cannot be said for high annual expenses. Annual expenses are something all fund investors face, whether they invest in a no-load or load fund. But, for a variety of reasons, investors don't seem as willing to shop for funds on this basis as they do loads.

In a recent paper, finance professors Brad Barber, University of California at Davis, Terrance Odean, U.C. Berkeley, and Lu Zheng, University of Michigan, concluded that "investors are more sensitive to salient in-your-face fees, like loads and commissions, than operating expenses."[32] Yet commissions are onetime charges, whereas annual expenses continue to be assessed, year in and year out, whether your fund makes money or loses it.

Of course, there are real costs associated with running funds. They include investment management fees, to cover the expense of hiring a fund manager and paying for stock research. Often, funds hire teams of equity analysts, sometimes numbering in the dozens, to support fund managers. Their job is to pore over company filings and to run earnings, revenue, and cash-flow projections to help the manager determine whether a particular stock is (a) worth investing in and (b) worth investing in now. Typically, management fees can run anywhere from 0.25 to 1 percent of assets, depending on the fund. In some instances, funds will lower this fee if it fails to meet certain performance guidelines, such as underperforming its assigned benchmark. (To learn how your funds stack up in terms of management fees, total expenses, and loads, you can research that information at *www.morningstar.com.*)

There are also administrative fees to consider, which cover the costs associated with record keeping and account maintenance. Remember, someone has to pay for the monthly statements that get mailed out and the customer service representatives you call. What's more, from time to time mutual funds incur other operating expenses, including taxes and legal expenditures.

Finally, there are so-called marketing and distribution fees to consider. Of the 14,609 funds in existence as of this writing, 9236 portfolios charged something called a 12b-1 fee, supposedly to help defray marketing costs. Typically, this fee ranges from 0.25 to 1 percent of assets.

These fees, sometimes referred to as "hidden loads," are controversial for a couple of reasons. For starters, while other fees have fallen in recent years, 12b-1 fees really haven't. These fees, which bring in about $10 billion a year to mutual fund companies, have stayed fairly level on average for the past several years, according to the Investment Company Institute. However, on a sales-weighted basis, 12b-1 fees on load funds have grown from 0.23 percent in 1990 to 0.43 percent.

What's more, 12b-1 fees aren't absolutely necessary to operating a fund. Fund companies make the argument that 12b-1 fees are helpful in marketing funds, which in turn keeps them viable and brings in more shareholder assets. That, in turn, they say, should help funds lower their overall fees in the future. But there is no research that I'm aware of that shows funds with 12b-1 fees grow significantly faster than funds without them. And there is absolutely no evidence whatsoever that funds that impose 12b-1 fees lower their overall costs down the road more—or more quickly—than other funds do. And there's a dirty little secret in the fund business: Some funds that are closed to new investors—and therefore don't need to be marketed—still charge 12b-1 fees, which says something about the need for these fees.

Regardless of what you think about any specific fee, it's important to weigh expenses in the aggregate. Combined, all three of these costs—management fees, administrative fees, and 12b-1 fees—are known as your *expense ratio*. This represents the total annual fees you will pay your fund, based on your assets.

Today, the average stock fund's expense ratio is about 1.28 percent of assets, according to the ICI. That's down from 1.54 percent in 1995. Still, they could be lower. Fund assets more than doubled from $2.8 trillion in 1995 to nearly $7 trillion today. Meanwhile, fund returns, thanks to the recent bear market, have sunk like a rock. Over the past decade, through the end of 2002, the average domestic stock fund returned on average slightly more than 7 percent a year, after fees.

TIP: Obviously, it's in your best interest to seek out funds with lower than average expense ratios. If you feel it necessary to seek out the assistance of a financial professional—which is fine—make sure they direct you to low-load funds (or even no-load funds) with lower than average expenses and, if possible, no 12b-1 fees. After all, if you're paying a load to begin with, you're already doing your part to help distribute and market the portfolio. You are paying a commission to an adviser or broker who distributes and markets that fund. This is especially important in a low-return stock market such as the one we're likely to be stuck in for a while.

It's even more important to be stingy with fees when it comes to bond funds, and especially money market mutual funds because they return less over time than stock funds do.

The average bond fund returned 6.18 percent a year over the past 10 years through the end of 2002. Meanwhile, bond fund fees have fallen from 1.25 percent in 1995 to 0.90 percent today, according to the ICI. Still, even at 0.90 percent, the average bond fund pocketed about 13 percent of its gross returns in fees over this five-year stretch.

Money market mutual funds, which invest in short-term paper, offer perhaps the most illustrative case of the dangers of fees. The average money fund's fees, according to the ICI, are 0.36 percent of total assets. Yet when short-term interest rates fell to 40-year lows at the start of the decade, the yield that some money funds generated through their investments was dangerously close to being eaten up entirely by fees. For the first time in recent memory, several money market funds threatened to show losses—something a money fund is not supposed to do. If you're shopping around for a bond or a money fund, make sure that you go to an established, *low-cost* leader, like Vanguard, TIAA-Cref, or T. Rowe Price.

Fees Are Predictive

There's another advantage to paying attention to fees. More so than Morningstar star ratings or popularity, fees are an accurate predictor of future mutual fund performance. In fact, a 2002 study by Financial Research Corp. found that fees are one of the few *consistent* predictors of future investment performance. The FRC study concluded: "John Bogle, the former chairman of Vanguard, is legendary for expressing his views on the importance of minimizing mutual fund expenses, and our tests on that factor appear to add credence to his strongly held beliefs. There is significant evidence that funds with [the lowest] total expense ratios do deliver above-average future performance across nearly all time periods."[33]

Among the study's specific findings:

- Expenses are an "exceptional" predictor of future performance of government bond funds, exhibiting the "highest possible predictive value score." In 100 percent of the cases measured by FRC, the lowest-fee government bond funds generated above-average returns over three- and five-year periods (see Figure 2-17).
- Expenses are a "moderate or good" predictor of future performance of corporate bond funds. Over one-, three-, and five-year periods, the lowest-fee corporate bond funds generated above-average returns about two-thirds of the time.
- Low fees are a "good to significant predictor" of the performance of domestic equity funds. This is especially true over long periods of time, because it is extremely difficult for money managers to beat the market over long periods of time (see "Mistake 7: Trying to Beat the Market with Funds"). According to the FRC study, more than 80 percent of the absolute lowest-cost stock funds posted above-average returns over one-year periods, but 100 percent of low-cost portfolios beat their peers over a five-year stretch.

The authors of the study concluded: "When advisers and investors screen domestic equity funds, they typically use statistics such as relative performance, alpha, beta, style consistency, and [fund manager] tenure. We believe that expenses should be added to the list, as a result of our testing."

So do I. In fact, given that most investors don't know what alpha, beta, and style consistency mean, there's a strong argument that individual investors should focus most of their attention on costs. You really can't go wrong by sticking with low-cost, low-turnover funds with strong, consistent, long-term performance records.

Bottom Line

Running a mutual fund is more art than science. Unlike banking services, money management is not a commodity. Or at least, it

Figure 2-17. Expenses as a Predictor of Returns

Funds with the lowest expense ratios tend to perform better than average. Financial Research Corp. studied five different categories of mutual funds. Each category was divided into 10 segments, based on the fees they charge. In the vast majority of cases, funds that ranked in the cheapest decile for fees performed better than average over time.

Source: Financial Research Corp.

Fund Categories	Percentage of Lowest-Cost Funds That Produced Better-Than-Average Returns		
	1-Yr. Returns	3-Yr. Returns	5-Yr. Returns
U.S. Stock Funds	83%	94%	100%
Government Bond Funds	89	100	100
Corporate Bond Funds	67	81	64
Tax-Free Bond Funds	78	88	100
International Funds	83	94	79

shouldn't be. While it's fairly easy to measure the performance of an ATM machine or a checking account—all you have to ask is, "Did my money come out?" and "Did my check clear?"—how do you measure the performance of a money manager? Is it by absolute returns? Or do you use risk-adjusted returns? Do you give more credit to a fund manager for beating the S&P 500 by a wide margin in some years? Or do you give more credit to a fund manager who never trounces the market but never loses to it either?

In the mutual fund industry, you'll sometimes hear the term "stewardship" tossed around. That's an old-fashioned word that refers to the fact that funds must act with the investors' interests foremost in mind. The Investment Company Act of 1940, which ushered in the modern mutual fund industry, explicitly states that funds must act in the best interest of shareholders, as opposed to, say, investment advisers. But what does stewardship mean? And more important, how much is good stewardship worth?

Let's say you invested money in a stock fund with an annual expense ratio of 4 percent—which is about three times more costly than the average fund. And assume that this fund lost 20 percent in the recent bear market. Though this is a sizable loss, let's say you're satisfied because you lost less than the broad stock market, measured by the S&P 500 index of blue chip stocks. The question some would ask is: Was the fund's "stewardship"—the fact that it steered you to smaller losses in a bad market—worth its steep fee?

This is the wrong question to ask. It's silly to wonder whether a fund's demonstration of stewardship earns it the right to demand steep fees. In my mind, it's just the opposite: You have to question whether a fund that charges steep fees to begin with is acting like a good steward. Stewardship doesn't just mean picking stocks that are in the best interest of shareholders. It means running the entire shop in the best interest of shareholders.

Similarly, we all have to be good stewards of our own affairs. In addition to demanding good service and advice from our financial institutions, consumers need to reduce the amount of money they lose every year to financial service fees. Wherever possible, strive to avoid fees that are clearly unnecessary, like late payment fees on credit cards and ATM charges. Moreover, avoid those costs that are detrimental to the long-term performance of your investments.

In the previous chapter, we noted that little amounts of money saved incrementally over time can add up to big savings. Similarly, little expenses like these—a late charge here, higher than necessary investment expenses there—can put us in the hole just as fast.

Checklist: Things to Do

❑ Reduce your banking expenses by sticking with no-frills checking accounts.

❑ Even better, if you're eligible to bank through a credit union, take advantage of the opportunity.

❑ Consider paying your bills electronically to avoid late payment fees.

❑ Call your fund companies and demand to know exactly how much you're paying every year in fees. Make sure you know exactly what your funds' expense ratios are.

❑ Stick with low-cost funds, even if you're investing with the help of a financial adviser. Remember: Low fees are probably the single biggest determinant of relative out-performance over time.

MONEY MISTAKE

3

NOT KNOWING
THE SCORE

Managing Your Credit— and Credit Score

So you want to do the right thing. You decide to attack your debt. You put your champagne wishes and caviar dreams on ice—at least for the moment. And with the proceeds of this crash diet, you manage to make ever larger monthly payments on your credit card balances until you eventually zero them out. Congratulations.

Now what? Some cardholders like to mark the occasion by taking scissors to plastic—a practical act, especially for those prone to falling off the wagon. It's also our generation's equivalent of an old-fashioned mortgage-burning party, symbolizing freedom from indebted servitude to our lenders. Still others listen to financial counselors and so-called experts and go one step further. They contact their credit card issuers to cancel their accounts outright. Good idea, right?

Not necessarily. Though closing out a credit card account that you don't use, don't need, and may entice you back into debt sounds like the responsible thing to do, it could end up being a big mistake—one that costs you thousands of dollars of interest payments down the road. This is especially true if the card you cut up has been tucked away in your wallet for a considerable amount of time.

It all has to do with four letters: F-I-C-O. Get to know them immediately, because the foibles of the FICO credit-scoring system will largely determine the terms of your credit cards, auto loans, home-equity loans, and mortgages for the rest of your life. In fact, "your FICO score is the no. 1 piece of data to determine how much you'll pay on a loan and whether you'll get credit," says Chris Larsen, chairman of the online lender E-Loan.[1]

What Is FICO?

In the late 1950s, engineer Bill Fair and mathematician Earl Isaac, founders of the company that would bear their names—Fair Isaac Corp., a somewhat obscure but publicly traded financial services firm based in California—created a mathematical scoring system to assess whether a person was a good enough "risk" for a company to do business with. Who would need such a system? Lenders maybe. Credit card issuers perhaps. Credit ratings were commonplace for corporate and government entities issuing bonds—Moody's, for instance, has been grading bonds since before the Great Depression—but the concept of *individual* credit ratings or scores was relatively new back then.

In the 1960s, Montgomery Ward, the department store chain, started using an iteration of the FICO system to extend credit to its customers. In the 1970s, Wells Fargo also began using the system, to manage its borrower base. By the 1990s, FICO's credit-scoring system had been adopted throughout the financial services industry, particularly after 1995, when Fannie Mae and Freddie Mac—the largest buyers of residential mortgages in the United States—recommended the use of FICO scores for evaluating the creditworthiness of home mortgage loan applicants.[2]

Today, FICO—sometimes referred to as *Fair Isaac*—scores are considered the gold standard for credit scoring. Roughly 70 percent of leading U.S. banks and 90 percent of credit card issuers worldwide use the system to weigh the risks of doing business with individual consumers.

Whenever you apply for a credit card, the issuing bank will punch up your credit score to see if you qualify for a card—and to determine what your credit limit and interest rate should be. If you're in the market for an auto loan, lenders won't let you sign on the dotted line or drive off the lot until they know your score. Indeed, whenever you see a car commercial advertising a special low rate, such as zero-percent financing, you will invariably see an asterisk. And in the fine print by that asterisk a note will tell you that the special low interest rate advertised is reserved only for "qualified buyers," pending credit check. That credit check will almost certainly involve your FICO (according to industry estimates, only about half of all car buyers end up qualifying for zero-percent auto-financing offers).

The rise of credit scoring isn't necessarily a bad thing. Because it is a quantitatively driven system, which relies on computers and algorithms rather than subjective loan officers, borrowers can get a fairly quick response to credit applications. This is why you can sign up and get approval for department store credit cards, auto loans, and in some cases even mortgages, within minutes. Furthermore, social factors such as race, religion, gender, age, and even profession are removed from the process, which is certainly a positive development.

The downside, of course, is that individuals are reduced to a single number. And you may not feel that your score adequately conveys your financial wherewithal to pay back a loan. Special circumstances, such as major illnesses that may have caused you to fall behind on past obligations, will not be reflected in your score. Meanwhile, incorrect or outdated information mistakenly included in your credit reports—from which FICO scores are derived—*will* be reflected in your score unless the credit bureaus correct those errors.

How FICO Affects You

Fair Isaac claims to be able to determine your creditworthiness by distilling data concerning your debt, your history of repaying debt, and your appetite for seeking out credit into a single three-digit number, which ranges from 300 to 850. The higher your score, the better off you are.

Nowhere is this score more important than when applying for a home mortgage. If you score below 500, which is considered very poor, it would be difficult to secure a home mortgage at all, especially a sizable one. At the very least, it would be hard to get approved by an A-list lender, and it would be difficult to get a good interest rate. In fact, you may be required to pay 2 or 3 percentage points more in interest, which could work out to a few hundred dollars more in monthly mortgage payments than top-scoring consumers pay. Conversely, if your FICO is 750 or higher, you'd easily qualify for a loan, and you'd probably get the lender's most favorable rate, because FICO scores correlate to a person's propensity to pay their lenders back on time.

Only 2 percent of consumers who score from 750 to 799, for example, have ever been 90 days or more past due with a credit card or loan payment, according to Fair Isaac. Only 1 in 100 people scoring 800 or higher have ever been that delinquent with a bill. On the other hand, 31 percent of borrowers scoring 600 to 649 have been that late at least once over the past two years. And nearly 9 out of 10 borrowers scoring under 500 have been late with their payments recently (see Figure 3-1).

During the mortgage-refinancing boom of 2002, when rates came tumbling down to 40-year lows and $2.5 trillion in mortgage loans were originated, borrowers with scores of 720 or higher easily obtained 30-year fixed-rate loans for as little as 6.1 percent interest. Had you scored slightly worse, 700 to 719 points, you probably got a rate of around 6.3 percent. With a marginal score of 620 to 675,

Figure 3-1. The Predictive Powers of FICO

Differing rates of credit card delinquencies, based on FICO scores. Consumers with FICO scores above 800 rarely are delinquent with even a single bill. On the other hand, the vast majority of those scoring 499 or below have been 90 days or more late with bills.

Source: Fair Isaac Corp.

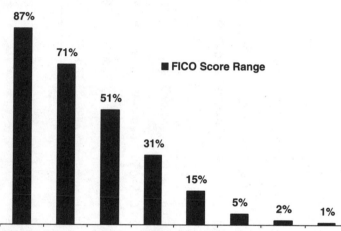

■ FICO Score Range

87% 71% 51% 31% 15% 5% 2% 1%

300-499 500-549 550-599 600-649 650-699 700-749 750-799 800-850

you'd have been lucky to get a mortgage charging around 7 percent (see Figure 3-2). And if you scored even worse, you were looking at an 8.5 or 8.9 percent mortgage.

The difference between having to pay 6.1 percent and 8.9 percent on a $100,000, 30-year fixed-rate mortgage works out to about $190 more a month, or about $67,000 more over the life of the loan.[3] What other single improvement can you make with your finances to save you $67,000 in one shot? Even if you were to become a decidedly better investor, there is no guarantee that the changes you make could lead to $67,000 in savings.

But it's not just your mortgage. If you scored below 660 in 2002, you probably qualified for a car loan charging about 11 percent. If you scored in the high 600s and low 700s, on the other hand, you could have found an auto loan for around 6 or 7 percent interest. The difference between a five-year, $20,000 car loan financed at 7 percent versus one at 11 percent works out to around $2000 over the life of the loan.[4]

Figure 3-2. FICO Scores and Interest Rates

Source: Fair Isaac Corp.

National Lending Rates Based On Fico Scores

	500–559	560–619	620–674	675–699	700–719	720–850
30-Year Fixed Mortgage	8.86%	8.50%	7.94%	6.79%	6.25%	6.12%

	500–559	560–639	640–659	660–679	680–719	720–850
Home Equity Loan	12.66%	11.41%	9.91%	9.14%	8.64%	8.34%
Home Equity Line of Credit	11.89%	10.39%	8.89%	7.51%	6.26%	5.89%

	500–589	590–624	625–659	660–689	690–719	720–850
48-Month New Auto Loan	18.36%	15.91%	11.86%	8.97%	6.82%	6.07%
60-Month New Auto Loan	18.42%	15.94%	11.89%	8.98%	6.84%	6.09%

As of October 2002

Low credit scores will also hamper your ability to access basic services. Individuals with extremely poor FICOs may find it difficult to open a checking account or establish service with a local utility. At the very least, a phone company or utility may require you to post a sizable deposit. Why? To protect itself from the "credit risk" you supposedly pose. Cellular phone companies often require deposits of as much as $100 or $200 for users with spotty credit histories. Some phone companies have even tried to levy extra service fees on customers with low credit scores, though it's unclear why consumers with low FICO scores deserve to be punished in this way.[5]

The FICO credit-scoring system represents either a virtuous or vicious cycle, depending on where you sit and what your score is. If you could save $200 a month in debt payments by improving your FICO score, and thus have $200 more to pay down other obligations—lowering your total required monthly interest payments—you'll probably like the FICO system. And paying down other debts could improve your FICO score even more, allowing you to refinance your mortgage once again and start the cycle all over.

On the other hand, a poor FICO score might cost you $200 more a month and leave you with $200 less to pay down other debts, potentially increasing your total debt load and worsening your FICO score. And it would put you at a further disadvantage to improving your financial circumstances.

Bear in mind too that your FICO affects more than your relationships with financial firms and service providers: It could affect your income. These days, a growing number of employers are looking at FICO scores as part of routine background checks to determine if a prospective employee is worthy of a job. The chances that you'd run into such a screen are greater if the job you're applying for gives you access to company cash or credit cards, according to employment experts.[6]

Though several states have begun to question or restrict the practice, an increasing number of insurers are also using credit scores to determine whether potential policyholders are good risks.[7] A low score, and your insurer may not renew a homeowner's policy or may hike your rates to compensate for what the company perceives to be greater risks in doing business with you. If your premiums were to rise 20 percent based on a low score, for example, it could easily amount to thousands of dollars during your stay in that home. To hear lenders tell it, there is a real, measurable correlation between how consumers treat certain responsibilities—like paying back credit cards on time—and driving carefully or taking care of a home.[8] Whether you believe this is in fact the case, about 80 percent of the nation's leading insurers utilize credit scores as if it is.

How Do You Stack Up?

The good news is, the majority of consumers score 690 or above, according to Fair Isaac (see Figure 3-3). This is important because 690 is typically the cusp between being able to obtain good and favorable interest rates on car loans, home mortgages, and the like. Better still, roughly four in 10 consumers score 750 or higher, which is considered a very good score.

Figure 3-3. Distribution of FICO Scores

A majority of consumers have FICO scores of 700 or better, which makes them good credit risks.
Source: Fair Isaac Corp.

Score	Percentage
800–850	11%
750–799	29
700–749	20
650–699	16
600–649	11
550–599	7
500–549	5
300–499	1

As we mentioned earlier, most Americans manage their finances quite well, despite all the horror stories you hear about consumer debt and irresponsibility. To be sure, the number of credit cards we carry and our balances on those cards are rising, on average. And both statistics—how many cards you have and how much money you owe—are reflected in an individual's FICO score. However, a lesser known but equally important fact is that a greater percentage of Americans are now paying off their card balances in full, and on time, than a decade ago: less than 29 percent of cardholders in 1990, compared to more than 40 percent today, according to Cardweb.com[9] (see Figure 3-4). Thus, the credit picture among consumers is split. Those having trouble with their finances are slipping into greater peril, while a growing number of households are doing just fine.

Still, even if your credit is good, it's important to know how Fair Isaac arrives at your score, so you can maintain your good standing.

Until recently, Fair Isaac actually hid scores from individual borrowers, making this confusing system even more frustrating. In fact,

Figure 3-4. Payback Time

A far greater percentage of credit card users pay their balances in full today than did at the start of the 1990s.
Source: CardWeb.com

Percent of Cardholders Paying Balances in Full Each Month	
1990: 28.6%	1996: 38.5%
1991: 29.2	1997: 40.2
1992: 31.3	1998: 42.0
1993: 33.7	1999: 43.4
1994: 35.1	2000: 44.4
1995: 37.9	2001: 42.1

consumers typically found out their scores through a friendly mortgage broker kind enough to share the information with them. Maybe if you scored poorly, your lender would feel obliged to show you your score, if only to explain why you didn't merit a better interest rate.

In 2001 Fair Isaac began to show borrowers their scores, for a fee.[10] Not only that, but through its consumer Web site (*www.myfico.com*), the company now offers to show you how your score might improve or worsen based on certain hypothetical changes in your finances. The company refers to this tool as its "FICO Score Simulator." You can find out how many points you'd gain if you paid down an additional $5000 in credit card balances, for example. Conversely, you could learn how many points you would lose, theoretically, if you filed for personal bankruptcy. Fair Isaac's Web site also has a loan savings calculator which shows you how much you could save, on average, on different types of loans by improving your score.

That being said, it is still extremely difficult to explain how Fair Isaac actually calculates these three-digit scores, since it involves mathematical formulas that would require a Ph.D. to fully understand. But suffice it to say, we do know more about how the scores are put together than we used to.

What FICO Does Not Consider

Before we get into what FICO considers, it's important to know what it does not (see Figure 3-5, below). For instance, you may feel that you're an excellent risk to lenders despite having $20,000 outstanding in credit card balances, $25,000 outstanding in car loans, and $40,000 outstanding in college debt. Perhaps you have an excellent job paying $200,000 a year. Maybe you're sitting on stock options that are potentially worth hundreds of thousands of dollars.

It doesn't matter one bit. FICO scores only consider one side of your personal financial ledger: your liabilities—and your history of dealing with those liabilities. As for your assets and income, none of it counts. In fact, your net worth doesn't even matter. If you've got a good-paying job and job security, it's unfortunate that FICO doesn't factor that in. But think of it this way: If you lose your job one day, you won't have to worry about your credit score being adversely affected. So long as you're able to keep up with your payments—maybe you were smart and established a sizable rainy-day fund (see *Mistake 1: Shortchanging Yourself*)—FICO won't penalize you for being unemployed.

In most cases, though, the lender will consider this information alongside your FICO score. So you're not totally out of the woods if your income picture is cloudy.

How much will your score matter vis-à-vis your income? That depends. As one lender put it to me: "If you're a first-time home-buyer putting only 5 percent down on a house and you have a low FICO score, that score will matter a lot. But if you're putting, say,

Figure 3-5. Calculating Your FICO

Source: Fair Isaac Corp.

Things That Count Toward Your FICO
1. Repayment History (35%)
2. Amount Owed (30%)
3. Length of Credit History (15%)
4. Whether You're Seeking New Credit (10%)
5. Your Mix of Credit (10%)
Things That Don't Count Toward Your FICO
1. Your Job History
2. Your Income
3. Your Stock Portfolio
4. Your Net Worth
5. Your Residence

50 percent down on a home and you have that same score—but earn a six-figure annual salary—it may not matter as much." As always, the devil is in the details.

What Else FICO Doesn't Consider

- *Interest rates on your credit cards.* You may think it's okay to have $10,000 on your credit card because your rate is an attractive 6 or 7 percent. But as far as FICO is concerned, that doesn't matter. To the FICO system, $10,000 is $10,000, whether it's on a 22-percent card or a 2-percent card.
- *Your residence.* You may live in a region where the cost of living is extremely low. So you might figure that carrying additional debt isn't as burdensome to you as to someone living in Manhattan. Think again.
- *Your age.* How old you are may be a factor in how long your credit history is, which is a factor that FICO considers. But your absolute age does not matter.
- *Information not found on your credit reports.* Remember, FICO scoring is a system that requires thousands of inputs. The inputted data comes from your credit reports, which are assembled by different companies known as credit bureaus. Anything not found in your credit file cannot be inputted, and therefore will not be a factor in calculating your score.

What FICO Does Consider

Your credit score will reflect how much credit has been extended to you, how much debt and the kinds of debt you have, how long you've managed that debt, and your overall record in managing it (see Figure 3-5, above).

The key, obviously, is to have a good track record in paying back your creditors. But implicit in this statement is that it's important to have a track record to begin with. A person who has five credit cards, an auto loan, and a home mortgage, but maintains low balances and has never been late with a payment is, all things being equal, a more favorable risk than a person who has never taken out a single loan or sought any credit in his or her life. At least lenders know what they're getting in the former. Who knows what a person who has no record with debt will do once he or she gets it?

Five basic categories of behavior are reflected in your score, which we'll go into. Get to know each of them.

MINI MISTAKE

NOT PAYING YOUR DEBTS ON TIME

The single most important determinant of your FICO, accounting for 35 percent of your score, is your track record of paying back debt. Do you pay your bills on time? Have you always paid your bills on time? Do you pay *all* your bills on time? All of this matters. As far as prospective lenders go, your past is prologue. Delinquencies in paying back debt in the past, especially the recent past, will raise concerns over your future ability and/or willingness and/or discipline to pay back creditors regularly and promptly. One or two late payments aren't necessarily going to wreck your score if your overall history with credit reflects timely repayments.

By the same token, because your entire history is factored into this portion of the score, it will take time—perhaps a year—for the ill effects of late payments to subside. So, if you're thinking of buying a house soon or taking out a home-equity loan, make sure you improve your payment history, and therefore your score, at least a year before you start applying for mortgages.

The reality is, a majority of consumers always make at least their minimum monthly payments on time. According to Fair, Isaac, less than 40 percent of all consumers have ever been 30 days or more past due on payments. Fewer than 20 percent have ever been more than 60 days past due. Fewer than 15 percent of all consumers have been more than three months late with their payments. And less than 10 percent have ever defaulted on a loan or credit account.

All in all, this is good news. But it still means that nearly 40 percent of the population has been late at least once—at least for a short period of time. And remember, it does not matter why you were late with a payment. You could have been sick. There could have been a glitch at your bank that caused your payment not to go out. The post office could have made an error. As long as it gets reported to the credit bureaus, it will affect your score.

Even if you're one of the 60 percent with an absolutely clean record, keep the following in mind:

- *The more accounts with no late payments, the better.* You don't have to pay back your debts quickly or in one fell swoop to score well. As long as you get your minimum monthly payments in on time for mortgages, car loans, credit cards, department store cards, and any installment loans, you should be fine. But be careful: As we discussed earlier, credit card issuers have quietly shortened grace periods between the time billing cycles end and when bills are due. The average card grace period is currently only 21 days.[11] So make sure you know exactly what day and time your lender requires monthly payments, and get those payments in beforehand.
- *Time and frequency matter.* The more days your payment is past due, the worse off you'll be. However, how recently that mistake occurred counts too. For instance, according to Fair Isaac: "A 60-day late payment made just a month ago will count more than a 90-day late payment from five years ago."
- *Collection accounts can be serious.* Bankruptcy filings, foreclosures, liens, and lawsuits may weigh heavily against your score, especially if the matters are big, recent, and unresolved.

MINI MISTAKE

OWING TOO MUCH

Your overall debt level is the second most important variable in determining your FICO, accounting for 30 percent of your score. Obviously, the more outstanding debt on your accounts, the more risk lenders will perceive in you. In addition, the more credit card accounts you have with balances, the worse off you'll be. According to Fair Isaac, "A large number [of accounts with balances] can indicate higher risk of overextension." And the more you owe on certain types of accounts—namely credit cards and installment loans versus mortgage debt—the worse your score will be.

In a previous chapter we noted that the average household has nearly $9000 outstanding in credit card balances. That's the average. The 10 percent of households with balances in excess of $10,000 are masking the generally responsible behavior of the majority. Indeed, 48 percent of cardholders have less than $1000 outstanding on their cards, according to Fair Isaac. Factoring in all obligations—minus home mortgage debt—the majority of consumers are carrying $5000 or less in credit obligations.

Still, as you go about managing your debt load, remember these somewhat counterintuitive rules:

- *Having some debt can be better than having none.* Owing money is not in and of itself a bad thing under the FICO system. You probably need a history of debt—and actually some debt on hand—to be considered a safe bet. This is a conundrum of sorts, but it's the reality. After all, the only way lenders can determine if you can manage credit in the future is to see how well you've done it in the past. That's why FICO admits that "in some cases, having a very small balance without missing a payment shows that you have managed credit responsibly, and may be slightly better than no balance at all."
- *Canceling credit cards can be harmful to your score.* One of the key factors that FICO considers is the *ratio* of your debt to your total credit limit. A person with, say, $20,000 in total outstanding balances may be considered safe if he or she has a total credit limit of $100,000. But another person with just $10,000 of debt may be considered a big risk with a credit limit of just $12,000. It is clearly a bad sign when a borrower burns through

all of his or her credit. According to Fair Isaac, more than 12 percent of cardholders are using 80 percent or more of their credit card limit. An important thing to remember is, whenever you close out a credit card account, you erase the credit limit that comes along with that card. Since FICO scores factor in your total balances against your *total* credit limit, closing out a zero-balance card can ultimately hurt your score—especially if it's a card with a big limit.

MINI MISTAKE

SHORTENING YOUR CREDIT HISTORY

The longer your track record of managing credit wisely, the more comfortable lenders will be extending credit to you. Fair Isaac says it considers both the age of your oldest account as well as the average age of all your accounts. In total, the length of your credit history will account for 15 percent of your score.

The good news: Most of us have a fairly lengthy history with credit. In fact, the average consumer's oldest credit relationship—be it an auto loan or credit card—is about 13 years. Roughly 20 percent of consumers have credit histories that extend beyond 20 years.

But canceling an old credit card could reduce that history. Let's say you carry three credit cards. One is 13 years old and the other two are five years old. But you're thinking about canceling your oldest card because you never use it. Closing out the 13-year-old card account would do two things to your credit history. First, it would shorten your oldest credit relationship to just five years. Plus, it would shorten your average credit history, which is currently 7.7 years, by more than two years. This is another reason why it would be a mistake to automatically close out an old credit card account.

Seeking out new card accounts could also hurt your score by shortening your average credit history. For instance, if you have two cards that are five years old, and all of a sudden you apply for and get five new cards, your average credit history would drop from five years down to just over two.

SEEKING TOO MUCH NEW CREDIT

Creditors are always fearful of someone going on a credit binge. Any indication that you're on the prowl for tons more credit is a clear-cut sign that you may be in financial trouble. That's why 10 percent of your FICO factors in whether you are seeking new credit, and how many new credit relationships you're seeking.

FICO also considers how long it's been since you last opened a new account. This is one reason why, contrary to popular belief, consumers need to be careful when flipping into and out of various credit cards in search of the absolute lowest interest rate. You may save a few bucks by moving to your seventh new card in two years, but you might damage your FICO score by bouncing around too much too often. Every new credit card is a request for new credit, even if your intent is simply to move your card balances to the lowest possible rate. (Remember that constantly opening new card accounts and closing old ones will also shorten your credit history.)

Having said that, FICO does recognize that *shopping* for the lowest rates when it comes to things like mortgages or auto loans is good consumer behavior. So if you're mortgage-rate shopping, and potential lenders make numerous inquiries about your credit score, don't worry. So long as you shop for rates in a fairly tight window of time— say, a month or so—FICO won't penalize you. "Also, the score does not count requests a lender has made for your credit report or score in order to make you a 'preapproved' credit offer," Fair, Isaac, points out. But just to play it safe, don't be too slow when it comes to researching rates. Don't stretch the process out over several months.

In case you're wondering if requesting your own credit report will hurt your score, don't be. You won't be penalized for making an inquiry on yourself as long as the report comes from an authorized credit reporting firm. In fact we urge you to check your credit report for errors, which we'll get to below.

MAINTAINING A POOR MIX OF CREDIT

The final 10 percent of your FICO is made up of the mix of your credit sources. Of all the variables that make up your score, this one really can't be "gamed." That's because it's difficult to say what an ideal mix is. But rely on common sense. Put yourself in the position of a lender.

For instance, let's say you're assessing the creditworthiness of two individuals, both of whom have $50,000 outstanding in loans. One person owes that $50,000 to eight different credit card companies, and the other owes that money on mortgages and auto loans. Who would you feel more comfortable lending money to? Mortgages and auto loans are investments inasmuch as they are loans. Plus, they can be secured by the underlying asset. Credit debt is unsecured.

The average consumer has about 11 credit relationships, of which seven are often credit cards, Fair Isaac research shows. Obviously, if you have 20 credit relationships and all 20 are credit cards, that wouldn't reflect positively on you. You'd have to wonder why an individual would require so many different card relationships.

NOT CHECKING YOUR CREDIT REPORTS

Even after you've taken every step you think you can to improve your score, your job isn't done. As you'll recall, the FICO system gathers data from your existing credit reports to generate your score. The problem is, there are at least three major credit bureaus that compile reports on your day-to-day credit activity. So you actually have three different FICO scores, something most consumers aren't aware of. And in fact you have even more scores, since some individual lenders have created their own credit scoring system that include FICO data.

The three major credit bureaus are Experian, TransUnion, and Equifax. The FICO generated with your Equifax information is sometimes referred to as your *Beacon* score; TransUnion's FICO is known as an *Empirica* score; and the Experian FICO is called the *Experian-Fair Isaac Risk Model* score.

Because information on each of your credit reports can—and do—contain errors, and because it takes each credit bureau time to update and correct your reports, it's important to routinely check each of your credit reports. If there is an error on even one of your three reports, you could find yourself in a situation where you have a high enough Beacon score to qualify for a favorable rate on a loan, but maybe a borderline Empirica score, or vice versa. And who knows which of your FICO scores a potential lender is looking at?

The Consumer Federation of America studied the credit scores of more than 500,000 Americans in 2002, and found that credit-score discrepancies are widespread. The scores of nearly one out of three consumers varied by as much as 50 points, depending on which credit bureau had generated the results. The range of scores was as wide as 100 points or more in one out of 25 cases. "This frequent huge discrepancy in scores reveals the importance of consumers being able to quickly learn and correct inaccuracies," says CFA Director of Insurance J. Robert Hunter.

Sadly, 40 percent of Americans have yet to check even one of their credit reports—ever, according to a recent survey by Quicken. Another 20 percent check their scores just once every three years or more. Yet the odds of an error showing up on your reports is quite high.

Studies have shown that 70 percent of all credit reports contain some inaccuracy, and that nearly one of every three has a serious error, be it false delinquencies or the existence of other people's credit accounts (see Figure 3-6). "Although credit reports contain vitally important information about most consumers, the accuracy of those reports is far from guaranteed," according to a study of credit reports by the U.S. Public Interest Research Group.[12] Indeed, in more than 40 percent of the cases studied by the CFA, different credit reports on a single consumer showed conflicting information about how often that person was more than 30 days late paying bills. And in 29 percent of the cases, the different credit bureaus had conflicting information about how many times the same consumer was more than 60 days late paying bills, an error that could be very damaging to your score.

Financial planners recommend that investors check all three of their credit reports routinely—at least once or twice a year. You can do this through the major credit bureau Web sites: *www.experian.com*, *www.transunion.com*, and *www.equifax.com*. All three agencies allow consumers to purchase individual credit reports on themselves for a small fee or to subscribe to a year's worth of reports. You can also obtain all three reports at *www.myfico.com*. Keep in mind that an innocent error could end up costing you thousands of dollars of interest payments if your FICO is adversely affected, so the fee is well worth it.

Remember too that not all errors are innocent. According to government officials, upward of $1.4 billion is lost each year to so-called "identity theft," where someone steals a person's identity, social security number, and address in order to open new credit accounts and obtains loans in their name[13] (see Figure 3-7). Obviously, thieves won't

Figure 3-6. Mistakes Happen

Recent studies have found that a surprisingly large number of credit reports contain errors, including significant ones.
Source: U.S. Public Interest Research Group

Percent of Credit Reports with . . .	
At least one error	70%
Wrong personal information	41
Serious errors, including false delinquencies	29
Incorrect information on closed accounts	26
Major credit accounts missing	20

Figure 3-7. Identity Theft

A big reason why financial planners recommend checking your credit reports is to make sure thieves haven't stolen your identity for the purposes of taking out loans in your name.
Source: U.S. News & World Report, Federal Trade Commission

Major Reasons Why Thieves Steal Financial Identities	
To obtain credit cards	43%
To obtain loans	20%
To purchase phone or utility service	20%
To obtain job	8%
To obtain documents or benefits	7%

alert you to the fact that they're using your identity. Since you don't know those bills exist and because the thieves won't pay them, the accounts rapidly fall into delinquency, ruining your credit score.

To prevent this from happening, you should routinely monitor your reports to see if accounts are being opened under your name. A simple way to do this is to sign up for new e-mail notification systems run by the three credit bureaus. These services, which can cost around $40 to $60 a year, alert consumers whenever their credit profiles change. Given that it takes victims of identity theft 200 hours and more than $1000 out of pocket to recover their names, it may be worth it.

Bottom Line

Throughout the 1990s we spent so much time worrying about two of our biggest assets—our homes and our portfolios—that we overlooked the third: our credit. Getting to know your FICO score and learning how to improve it isn't just an academic exercise. Your credit score is the single biggest determinant of whether you'll be approved for loans and the interest rates you'll be charged. In some cases, your score will be the *only* factor in making these decisions.

The difference between scoring well and scoring poorly could cost you tens of thousands of dollars in additional mortgage interest, thousands of dollars on a car loan, and hundreds of dollars in credit card rates. And the added interest expenses will make it that much harder for you to pay down other obligations.

Yet many of us aren't simply mismanaging our credit, we're ignoring it entirely. A majority of consumers haven't checked a single credit report, let alone their credit scores. Meanwhile, the vast majority of reports contain errors and omissions. In some cases our scores are hurt by accounts that don't belong to us or that were opened up by thieves using our names.

The good news is, all of this can be remedied. So long as you correct any errors on those reports and maintain good credit practices—paying your bills on time and not owing too much to lenders—you stand a good chance of improving your scores for the future.

Checklist: Things to Do

- ❏ Remember to pay all your bills on time.
- ❏ Pay close attention to the ratio of your debt to credit limit.
- ❏ Hang on to your oldest credit cards, even if you don't use them.
- ❏ Check each of your credit reports at least once a year.
- ❏ Get to know all three of your FICO scores.
- ❏ If you're in the market for a new home, start improving your credit behavior at least one year before applying for a mortgage.
- ❏ Protect your identity by signing up for e-mail alerts to changes in your credit profile.

OVERLOOKING RISKS

Understanding Key Investment Risks

All investments come with risks. Whether you buy a stake in a company by owning its stock or stake money to a business by purchasing its bonds, you run the risk that your original investment might not ever return, or might not return in full or might not return in full when you need it. Yet risk wasn't a four-letter word in the late 1990s. The only risk many of us perceived back then, if we perceived it at all, was the risk of not being aggressive enough. Every dollar that wasn't in the market was another dollar not earning 25 percent a year. Every dollar that wasn't in the technology sector was a dollar not earning 50 percent or more. And every dollar not invested in Internet stocks was perceived to be a dollar not doubling or tripling in value.

While we may have appreciated that risk and reward were related concepts, some of us had it backward. Instead of recognizing that high rewards come with high risk, we assumed that high-risk investments necessarily *lead to* high returns. (Of course, this makes no sense: If a high-risk investment always delivered high returns, why would someone sell it to you?) This explains why so much money poured into new economy stocks in 1999. That year, nearly 90 cents of every new dollar invested in mutual funds went into technology sector funds or large growth-oriented stock portfolios, which invest large amounts of money in technology and telecommunications companies. "That's just unheard of," said Carl Wittnebert, director of research for *TrimTabs.com*, which tracks trends in mutual fund investments.[1]

Yet this wasn't the first time fund investors threw caution to the wind in order to seek maximum returns. In the late '80s and early '90s, a similar though smaller mania formed around biotechnology stocks. Investors believed that many of these start-up companies, while still profitless, could tap into new and potentially lucrative scientific breakthroughs. In the early- to mid-'90s interest grew in the emerging markets—companies based in developing economies such as South Korea, Mexico, and Indonesia—after mutual funds that invested in those regions delivered returns of 75 percent or even higher in 1993. Yet in seven of the subsequent nine years, those funds lost money on average.

Similarly, reality struck for new economy investors in March 2000. When the bear market mauled the tech and telecom sectors at the start of the decade—from peak to trough, new economy stocks lost about three-quarters of their value—investors learned the hard way that there's no such thing as a free lunch. Those who put $100,000 into the Nasdaq at the start of the bear were left with only about $25,000 two and a half years later. Investors who played it slightly safer, by diversifying among a broader index of stocks, such as those found in the S&P 500, were left with slightly more: about $56,000. By comparison, had you considered market risks and invested only 60 percent of your money in equities, putting the remainder into bonds and cash for stability, you would have been left with about $80,000 two and a half years after the start of the bear market (see Figure 4-1). It's a painful but painfully important reminder of the importance of factoring risk into your investment strategy.

OVERLOOKING RISKS IN STOCKS

Despite the recent bear market, stocks are still the hands-down best performing asset for long-term investors—provided you have time. Between 1926 and 2001, the S&P 500 index of large, blue chip stocks has delivered average annual gains of nearly 11 percent, according to the financial research firm Ibbotson Associates. Smaller stocks have done even better, posting annual returns of nearly 13 percent. By

Figure 4-1. Risky Scenarios

How various portfolios with different risk profiles performed during the recent bear market.
Source: T. Rowe Price

Investment Mix	Bear Market Performance Between March 31, 2000, and Sept. 30, 2002	
	Total Return	Performance of $100,00
100% Nasdaq	−74.4%	$25,600
100% S&P 500	−43.8%	56,240
60% Stocks/30% Bonds/ 10% Cash	−20.8%	79,165
47% Stocks/37% Bonds/ 16% Cash	−12.9%	87,136
25% Stocks/40% Bonds/ 35% Cash	+2.8%	102,838

comparison, bonds have generated long-term total returns of less than 6 percent, while cash investments have grown by less than 4 percent a year over time (see Figure 4-2).

There's a simple explanation for the disparity in returns: Unlike a bond, which is a loan that investors extend to companies or governments in exchange for interest payments, stocks represent ownership of a company. As companies grow over time, the value of your shares are likely to appreciate. And there's no limit to how much or fast companies can grow.

Still, this doesn't mean that all individual investors should put all of their money into stocks. Nor does it mean that all individual investors should put *most* of their money in stocks. While equities are likely to return more in the long run, they're also more likely to lose more in the short run. This is the price (or risk) that stock investors pay for their long-term rewards. For every publicly traded company that grows from a small business to a "blue chip," there are countless others that fall by the wayside.

Between 1950 and 2002, the S&P lost money in 15 calendar years, or about 28 percent of the time (see Figure 4-3). On the other hand,

Figure 4-2. Stocks for the Long Run

Despite the recent bear market, stocks continue to outpace other asset classes over the long term. The figures below represent average annual returns for different assets between 1926 and 2001.
Source: Ibbotson Associates

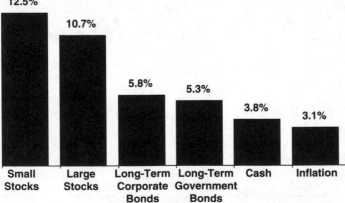

short-term T-bills, a cash equivalent, have never lost value in any calendar year during this stretch. When stocks fall, they're also likely to fall more than fixed-income investments ever will. Given this risk, stocks would seem to be an extremely dangerous place to invest if you absolutely need your money back in full in less than a year's time.

Figure 4-3. Stock Market Volatility

Though stocks outperform other asset classes in the long run, they can also lose more—and more often—than other asset classes in any given year. The annual performance of the S&P 500 from 1950 to 2001.
Source: Stock Trader's Almanac

Year	S&P 500 Return	Year	S&P 500 Return
1950	21.8%	**1966**	**−13.1**
1951	16.5	1967	20.1
1952	11.8	1968	7.7
1953	**−6.6**	**1969**	**−11.4**
1954	45.0	1970	0.1
1955	26.4	1971	10.8
1956	2.6	1972	15.6
1957	**−14.3**	**1973**	**−17.4**
1958	38.1	**1974**	**−29.7**
1959	8.5	1975	31.5
1960	**−3.0**	1976	19.1
1961	23.1	**1977**	**−11.5**
1962	**−11.8**	1978	1.1
1963	18.9	1979	12.3
1964	13.0	1980	25.8
1965	9.1	**1981**	**−9.7**

Figure 4-3. Stock Market Volatility (*Continued*)

Year:	S&P 500 Return:	Year:	S&P 500 Return:
1982	14.8	1993	7.1
1983	17.3	1994	–1.5
1984	1.4	1995	34.1
1985	26.3	1996	20.3
1986	14.6	1997	31.0
1987	2.0	1998	26.7
1988	12.4	1999	19.5
1989	27.3	2000	–10.1
1990	–6.6	2001	–13.0
1991	26.3	2002	–23.4
1992	4.5		

Since World War II stocks have experienced at least 11 major downturns, losing 32 percent of their value, on average, during these declines, according to The Leuthold Group, an investment research firm. (see Figure 4-4). In some cases, such as the most recent bear market, stock prices were literally cut in half. Equally important, it typically takes investors more than a year and a half to recoup their short-term losses from such slides. Often, it takes longer.

Following the 1973-74 bear market, for instance, when stock prices fell 48 percent, it took the market nearly four years to climb back to its previous peak set in January 1973. And stock prices didn't rise much above that peak until a new bull market started in 1982—nearly a decade later. Following the bear market in 1968, stocks didn't fully recover for more than two years. And three years after the start of the most recent bear, the Dow Jones industrial average was still about 3500 points below its previous bull market high. So, as an investor, you have to ask yourself: Can I afford to lose a quarter, a third, or even half of my money in the short term? And do I have enough time—perhaps several years—to recoup that money if my investments were to lose value?

The only way to calculate your ability to stomach this risk is to consider your time horizon. In other words, when do you need

Figure 4-4. Major Declines in the Stock Market Since World War II

Source: The Leuthold Group, T. Rowe Price

Date of Market Peak	Date of Market Trough	Decline	Time to Climb
March 24, 2000	Oct. 9, 2002*	−49%	?
July 17, 1998	Aug. 31, 1998	−19%	4 months
July 16, 1990	Oct. 11, 1990	−20%	9 months
Aug. 25, 1987	Dec. 24, 1987	−34%	1 year, 9 months
Nov. 28, 1980	Aug. 12, 1982	−27%	1 year, 11 months
Sept. 21, 1976	March 6, 1978	−20%	4 months
Jan. 11, 1973	Oct. 3, 1974	−48%	3 years, 9 months
Nov. 29, 1968	May 26, 1970	−36%	2 years, 3 months
Feb. 9, 1966	Oct. 7, 1966	−22%	1 year, 3 months
Dec. 12, 1961	June 26, 1962	−28%	1 year, 5 months
Aug. 2, 1956	Oct. 22, 1957	−22%	2 years
Average		**−32%**	**1 year, 7 months**

* As of publication, it was unclear if the market had hit on official "trough."

to spend the money that you're investing? The more time you have to invest, the greater tolerance you're likely to have for risk. Recently, researchers at T. Rowe Price studied the performance of the S&P 500 dating back to 1926. Instead of looking simply at calendar year returns, they analyzed the performance of stocks over rolling periods of time, on a quarterly basis, in an effort to be more thorough. Here's what they found: Between 1926 and 2002, the odds of losing money in the stock market in any given year was about 27 percent. That's not quite a coin flip, but it's close. Yet if you have a three-year window in which to invest, the chances of losing money in the market fall substantially: 14 percent. And if you have 10 years to invest, there's only about a 4 percent chance of losing money (see Figure 4-5). This explains why financial advisers say a majority of a person's retirement portfolio should be held in stocks as long as you're at least a decade or more from needing the money—the odds are simply in your favor.

Let's turn our attention to the factors that account for stock market risk.

Figure 4-5. More Time, Less Risk

The odds of losing money in stocks are significant in any one year but fall sharply over time.
Source: T. Rowe Price

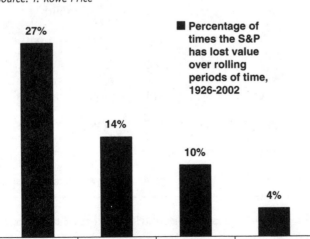

■ Percentage of times the S&P has lost value over rolling periods of time, 1926-2002

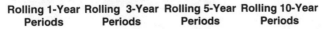

Company-Specific Risks

We all talk about bull markets and bear markets—and their impact on our portfolios. But at the end of the day, when we buy stocks, we're investing in the shares of a particular company, with a particular financial profile, led by a specific set of managers, at a specific moment in time. If we're smart and lucky, the company we invest in will be able to outmaneuver its competitors and dominate its peers. But the risk we face is that the company we're investing in runs into difficulties. This is referred to as "company risk."

Investors in Enron, Worldcom, Tyco, and other companies that came to symbolize Wall Street scandals at the start of this decade, know all too well the dangers of company risk. But it isn't limited to wrongdoing. Sometimes, a company's business model, as promising as it sounds, simply doesn't pan out. For example, there was a time not that long ago when Apple Computer rivaled IBM and Microsoft for dominance in the personal computer industry. But as competition in personal computing shook out, IBM's "Win-Tel" platform—using Intel microchips and Microsoft's operating system—won out as the industry standard, to the dismay of many consumers who to this day still think Apple's technology is superior.

Had you invested $10,000 in Apple on April 1, 1991, on the assumption that its user-friendly operating system would make it the dominant computer maker in the world, you would have seen your money shrink to about $4000 by December 31, 2002. Had you bet correctly and put that $10,000 into Microsoft shares instead, you'd have turned that money into nearly $175,000. That's the risk you run when you bet incorrectly on a single stock.

There's an easy way to avoid company risk. Instead of buying shares of just one stock, diversify your holdings. In a recent article, Harvard University economist John Campbell noted: "Finance theory does offer a free lunch: the reduction in risk that is obtainable through diversification." Yet, he added: "Many investors appear to ignore this free meal. They overinvest their retirement savings in the company they work for, in one or two favored sectors such as technology, and in companies that are based in the region where they live. An amusing example is the tendency of U.S. investors to buy the stock of their local telephone company."[2]

Campbell is an expert on this topic. He and three other scholars—Martin Lettau, Federal Reserve Bank of New York, Burton Malkiel, Princeton University, and Yexiao Xu, University of Texas at Dallas—have studied trends in company risk over the past four decades. They found that between 1962 and 1997 there was "a noticeable increase in firm-level volatility relative to market volatility."[3] In other words, company risk, relative to other risks in the stock market, is on the rise.

They discovered this by studying the so-called *standard deviation* of various securities. Standard deviation is an academic concept that measures an investment's volatility over a set period of time relative to its average performance during that same period of time.

For instance, let's say you invest in a stock that generates average returns of 10 percent over a three-year period. It rises 8 percent in year one, 10 percent in year two, and 12 percent in year three. By looking at how this stock achieved average annual gains of 10 percent, you'll notice that its performance has been quite stable. In year one the stock rose 2 percentage points less than its three-year average rate of return. In year two it gained exactly what it gained over its three-year average. And in year three it gained 2 percentage points above its average. Because the stock bounced 2 percentage points higher and lower than its three-year average, we can roughly estimate that its standard deviation over that period was about 2. (Technically, standard deviation is calculated by averaging various returns over time, subtracting each year's return from that average, squaring the resulting numbers, adding them back together, dividing that result by the number of years in the time period minus one, and then taking the square root of the final figure—but we don't need to be that precise for the purposes of our discussion.)

A stock that rises 40 percent in year one, falls 20 percent in year two, then gains 10 percent in year three would also have a 10 percent average annual rate of return. However, because the stock in years one and three bounced 30 percentage points above and below its average rate of return, its standard deviation would be around 30.

The higher the standard deviation, the more volatile an investment is considered to be.

Campbell, Lettau, Malkiel, and Xu looked at the standard deviation of single, randomly selected stocks versus the volatility of the broad stock market. A generation ago, the standard deviation of a single, randomly selected stock was about 35 percentage points higher than the volatility of the market as a whole, they determined. But during the past decade, the standard deviation for single stocks jumped to about 50 percentage points above the volatility of the overall market.

What does this mean? In the past, owning around 20 stocks could adequately diversify away most company-specific risk. But because individual stocks are that much more volatile today—you've seen it yourself, with stocks gaining or losing as much as 50 percent of their value in a single trading day—academic research shows that it now takes 50 stocks or more to adequately deal with company risk.

The good news is, you can easily gain exposure to 50 or 100 stocks in one fell swoop by simply investing in an S&P 500 or Wilshire 5000 index fund. In fact, if you invest in the Vanguard Total Stock Market Index fund or the Schwab Total Stock Market Index portfolio, you'll get exposure to more than 3000 different holdings. If you go with an actively managed stock portfolio, it might take two or three equity funds to reach 50 to 100 *distinct* stocks. Though the average large-cap growth fund tends to hold about 60 or 80 stocks, competing portfolios often own shares of the same companies. For instance, big, blue chip names like General Electric and Citigroup are found in countless large-cap stock portfolios.

An easy way to check if your funds have overlapping holdings is through the Web site of the mutual fund tracker Morningstar: *www.morningstar.com*. You can also check a fund's standard deviation through the site. For instance, while the Vanguard 500 fund, which simply buys and holds all of the stocks in the S&P 500 index, sports a three-year standard deviation of about 16 (as of May 2003), the WWW Internet Fund's standard deviation was more than twice that: nearly 37.

Market and Sector Risks

Sometimes a stock will fall because the overall market is trending down, not because of anything the underlying company is doing. This is referred to as "market risk," which is the investing equivalent of being in the wrong place (i.e., the stock market) at the wrong time. In 2002, for instance, the vast majority of stocks lost money as Wall Street accounting scandals shook investor confidence. Concerns over corporate fraud weighed down not only shares of companies accused of fraud, but the shares of all companies—including ethical ones with clean balance sheets. Indeed, virtually every single category of stocks and stock funds lost money that year, as investors lost faith in corporate America.

Similar to market risk is something called "sector risk," which can be thought of as being in the wrong *industry* at the wrong time. Sometimes, this risk involves real matters of dollars and cents specific to a particular sector of the economy. Should oil prices rise, for example, the transportation sector will likely suffer due to higher fuel costs, through no particular fault of any specific firm. Nevertheless, in this case, investors in companies like United Airlines, FedEx, and UPS would still suffer as company earnings would be adversely affected.

Often, a stock is punished not because there's a problem with the sector, but because some investors perceive trouble in a competitor. If Intel shares were to decline, for example, because the chip maker falls short of earnings or sales expectations, you'll likely see shares of competitors like Micron Technology also slump in the very short term—even if Intel's problems have nothing to do with the health of the overall sector. It could simply be a knee-jerk reaction of investors in a volatile market. Unfortunately, it might take days or longer for investors to correct their misjudgment of a stock.

While it's relatively easy to diversify away sector risk—again, by investing in a multitude of industries—how do you diversify away market risk while still being in the market? One option is to diversify among *different stock markets*, by investing overseas.

TIP: A simple way to avoid sector risk is to diversify among the 10 major sectors that make up the market: consumer cyclicals, consumer staples, energy, financials, health care, industrials, materials, technology, telecommunications, and utilities. This means being willing to invest in old economy names like Procter & Gamble alongside new economy leaders like Microsoft. It means being willing to invest in boring, basic materials stocks like Weyerhaeuser in addition to familiar retailers like Tiffany's. If you invest in a diversified portfolio of stock mutual funds, don't worry: You probably already have exposure to all 10 sectors (see Figure 4-6).

Figure 4-6. Major Market Sectors

One way to hedge against sector risk is to diversify your portfolio. The following table shows what percentage of the S&P 500 index is made up of the various sectors.
Source: Standard & Poor's

Sector	% of the S&P 500*
Consumer Discretionary	14.0%
Consumer Staples	9.0%
Energy	5.9
Financials	19.9
Health Care	15.0
Industrials	11.8
Technology	14.4
Basic Materials	2.9
Telecommunications	4.1
Utilities	3.0

* Market weightings as of November 2002

In 1980, U.S. stocks represented around two-thirds of the world's total stock market capitalization, or value. Today it's only about half, as equity markets in Europe, Asia, and Latin America have matured. Large European firms like Novartis, UBS, and Nokia, for instance, are now core holdings in many U.S. investors' portfolios alongside American counterparts such as Merck, Merrill Lynch, and Motorola. What's more, though U.S. stocks have been among the leaders in performance over time—and will continue to be—domestic stocks haven't been the absolute best performers in the world in more than 20 calendar years.

By putting some money to work overseas, then, you won't just lower your risk profile, you might improve your overall returns in certain years. But remember that your goal here is to reduce risk. Between September 1992 and September 2002, a 100 percent U.S. stock portfolio would have delivered annual returns of about 15.6 percent. Had you invested 40 percent of that money in foreign equities, you would have gained only slightly less, 14.5 percent—but with 7 percent *less* volatility, according to Ibbotson Associates.

Another way to hedge market risk is to diversify *when* you invest in equities. In this case, a strategy of *dollar-cost averaging* would do the trick. We'll talk about this at greater length in "Mistake 6: Trying to Beat the Market," but for now merely note that dollar-cost averaging means putting small amounts of money to work in the stock market at routine intervals of time—such as every month or every quarter—instead of buying all at once. In essence, you do this all the time through your 401(k), by putting small payroll contributions into your account with each paycheck.

This strategy won't result in the absolute highest returns, but will go a long way toward reducing your overall risk profile. How? If you invest small amounts of money each month, you'll end up paying different prices for stocks with each pot of money. By averaging out your cost basis over time, you'll ensure that you never pay the absolute highest price for your investments. That in turn lowers the risk of losses. Investors who dollar-cost-averaged into the stock market during the Great Depression, between 1929 and 1939, actually wound up making money when most others lost.

Political or Country Risk

In addition to risks associated with single stocks or sectors, there are geopolitical issues to consider. This is called "country risk." For instance, in the late 1990s, during the Asian currency crisis, you'd have lost about a third of your money had you invested in the Pacific Rim, not necessarily because individual companies were at fault, but because of the region's economic and currency troubles.

This is why it's important to invest in a diversity of regions and countries in addition to companies and sectors. But before you invest in foreign stocks or foreign stock funds to lower your exposure to this risk, it's important to keep a couple of things in mind, among them: You probably already invest in a multitude of foreign markets—you just don't realize it.

Microsoft and General Electric, for instance, the two largest companies in the United States based on market value, generate about a third of their sales overseas. Their fates and profits are thus tied to the politics and economy of more than one country. Citigroup, one of the nation's largest financial services firms, operates banks in more than 100 different countries. And while you can't get more American than Wal-Mart, more than a fourth of the discounter's 4,600 superstores are located outside the United States, a fact that not many people realize. "Just about any big, blue-chip company is going to give you exposure to a huge number of markets and economies outside the United States," according to Russel Kinnel, director of equity research for Morningstar.[4] This means that you probably don't need much more foreign exposure.

TIP: If you want or need additional exposure overseas, there are a plethora of choices. For instance, you can invest directly in foreign companies through their shares listed on U.S. exchanges. These arrangements are referred to as ADRs (American Depositary Receipts). Sony, Nokia, and Toyota are among hundreds of foreign companies with ADRs listed on U.S. exchanges. Another possibility is to invest in indexlike investments that give you broad exposure to foreign stock

(Continued)

markets. Barclays Global Investors offers such investments, known as exchange-traded funds or ETFs, which track stock markets in dozens of countries, including Germany, France, the United Kingdom, Hong Kong, South Korea, Brazil, Italy, Canada, and Sweden. (To learn more about these investments, you can go to *www.ishares.com.*)

But perhaps the easiest way to gain broad diversification overseas is to go with a diversified stock mutual fund that invests abroad. There are several major types: *foreign* or *international* funds, which invest all of their assets overseas; *global* or *world* funds, which invest in a mix of foreign and U.S. stocks; and *emerging markets stock funds*, which invest in companies based in underdeveloped nations (and are therefore considered the riskiest of the bunch). According to Morningstar, there are nearly 2000 mutual funds that invest most if not all of their money outside the U.S.

Currency Risk

Before you invest in a foreign or global fund, keep one more thing in mind: Whenever U.S. investors put money to work overseas, they trigger "currency risk," which has to be addressed.

When American investors buy foreign stocks either directly or indirectly (for instance, through a fund), they are in essence buying currency in addition to the shares. To purchase the stock of a Japanese company, for example, you would have to first buy Japanese yen to make the transaction. Similarly, when you sell a Japanese stock, you get back yen, which you must convert back into dollars to pocket the profit. If, between the time you purchase the stock and the time you sell it, the foreign currency weakens against the dollar, it will reduce your overall gains, or even produce losses in your portfolio.

Say you purchase one dollar's worth of Japanese stock when a dollar buys 100 yen. This means that you own 100 yen worth of stock. Let's assume that over the course of a year, the stock remains flat, at which point you sell. And let's say that during this time, the yen weakens against the dollar and it now takes 110 yen to buy back your original dollar. Since you only own 100 yen worth of stock, you would only get back around 91 cents on your original investment (based on the new exchange rate), even though the stock itself didn't lose money. A strengthening dollar, then, will always cut into the potential returns Americans enjoy in foreign stocks, while a falling dollar could add to American investors' gains overseas.

Tip: You can avoid currency risk, while still investing abroad, by buying shares of a fund that seeks foreign exposure exclusively through U.S.-based multinational corporations. John Hancock U.S. Global Leaders Growth and Fidelity Export & Multinational are examples of such funds that buy shares of big U.S. companies that do a substantial amount of their business overseas. By sticking with shares of U.S. companies, these funds never expose themselves to unnecessary currency risk.

Another option is to go with a foreign fund that "hedges" currency risk. Take Tweedy, Browne Global Value. Whenever the managers of Tweedy, Browne Global buy shares of a foreign stock—and therefore convert U.S. dollars into that foreign currency—they sell an equivalent amount of that foreign currency in the open market to hedge their bets. Conversely, whenever they sell a foreign holding, they buy an equivalent amount of that currency to even the score. This way, a particular currency's strength or weakness does not factor into their decision to buy or sell a given stock. Before investing in a foreign fund, it might be wise to find out if it hedges currency or not.

The Risk of Not Being in the Market

In addition to the myriad of risks involved in being in the stock market, there's the risk of *not* being in the market to consider. To be sure, if you weren't in equities during the recent bear market, your portfolio wouldn't have suffered severe losses for three consecutive years. Between 2000 and 2002, stocks lost about 10 percent, 12 percent, and 22 percent of their value, respectively. But failing to be in the market when it is rising, even for a few days or weeks, can be just as devastating to achieving your long-term goals (see Figure 4-7).

Figure 4-7. The Risk of Not Being in the Market

Missing out on only a few days of stock market gains can lead to the
loss of hundreds of thousands of dollars over time.
*Sources: The University of Michigan, and Crandall, Pierce & Company, Straight
Talk on Investing*

In the 1980s	S&P 500 Annualized Returns
August 1982 to August 1987	26.3%
Same period minus 10 best days	18.3
Same period minus 20 best days	13.1
Same period minus 30 best days	8.5
Same period minus 40 best days	4.3
In the 1990s	**S&P 500 Annualized Returns**
1992 to 2001	12.9%
Same period minus best month	12.2
Same period minus best 2 months	11.4
Same period minus best 3 months	10.5
Same period minus best 6 months	8.0

Consider this: Had you been in the market every day between
August 1982 and August 1987, you would have earned a stunning
26.3 percent a year on your money in the S&P 500. But if you were
on the sidelines for the 10 best days during this 1276-trading-day
stretch, you would have earned significantly less: 18.3 percent. And
if you missed out on 40 of the best days for the S&P during this
period, you would earned just 4.3 percent on your investments. At
that rate of return, you might as well have stuck your money in
bonds or cash—with far less risk. The difference between earning

26.3 percent and 4.3 percent on a $100,000 investment, for five years, is nearly $200,000.

Similarly, had you been in the market between 1992 and 2001, you would have earned close to 13 percent a year, on average, in the S&P 500. Had you missed out on just six of the best months for the S&P during this stretch, you would have earned only 8 percent on your money. The difference between earning 8 and 13 percent on a $100,000 investment over a decade works out to nearly $125,000 in potential gains.

Over even longer periods of time, lost opportunities in the stock market really add up. Had you invested $100,000 in the S&P 500 starting on December 31, 1969, that money would have grown to $1.2 million by December 31, 2001. Yet if you were out of the market for just 10 of its best days during this three-decade-long stretch, your account would only be worth about half as much. If you were out of the market for its 60 best days, you'd have earned only one-tenth as much. The problem for investors, of course, is that we never know in advance whether the market will rise or fall on any given day.

The risk of not being in the market is particularly dangerous during "inflection" points for stocks, when sentiment shifts dramatically. SEI Investments recently studied the performance of the S&P as it recovered from the dozen or so major bear markets since World War II. Emerging from those downturns, stocks gained 32.5 percent, on average, in the first 12 months of a market recovery. In other words, a $100,000 investment at the start of those rallies would have grown to $132,500 in just one year. But if you waited just one quarter into the rally to see if the recovery was "real," you'd have missed out on more than half of those gains (see Figure 4-8). Instead of turning $100,000 into $132,500, your money would have grown to less than $115,000.

Is that really a big price to pay, given how severe bear markets can be? Isn't it worth lower returns to reduce the risk of short-term losses? The answer depends on your time horizon. If you have less than a decade to invest, then the answer might very well be yes. That's because there might not be enough time to make up for those losses in your portfolio. But if you have 20 years or more to invest, the risk of not being in the market far outweighs the risks of being in it.

Figure 4-8. Waiting for the Recovery

Waiting to see if a market recovery is "real" can often hurt your returns, as stocks tend to surge strongly in the earliest stages of a rally. The figures below show the performance of the S&P 500 emerging from the 12 bear markets since World War II.

Source: SEI Investments

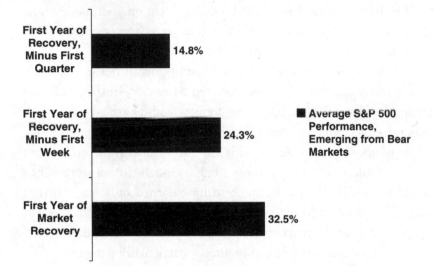

That's because time tends to heal most stock market wounds. Consider this interesting statistic: If you started investing money in the S&P 500 on December 31, 1972, just as the 1973–74 bear market was about to start—in other words, at the worst possible moment—you would have earned just 6.7 percent a year on average over the next decade. However, had you waited until after the bear market and started investing on November 30, 1974, your portfolio would have grown substantially more: 14.3 percent a year over the next 10 years. Clearly, being on the sidelines during that bear market made a huge difference.

But in reality, it's impossible to know exactly when a bear market is about to begin. In the above example, had you started investing exactly at the start of the 1973–74 bear market, you'd have earned less than 7 percent a year for the following decade. But over the next *two* decades, your average annual returns grew to 11.3 percent. If you waited until the bear market ended, you'd still have earned more over the next 20 years: 14.4 percent. But the difference in returns was substantially less (see Figure 4-9).

Figure 4-9. Time Heals Stock Market Wounds

The longer your time horizon, the less risk there is in being in the stock market. The figures shown here indicate the performance of investors who missed the 1973–1974 bear market versus those who didn't.
Source: Vanguard

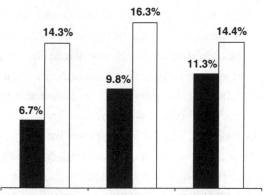

■ Starting 12/31/72
□ Starting 11/30/74

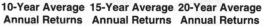

10-Year Average   15-Year Average   20-Year Average
Annual Returns   Annual Returns   Annual Returns

MINI MISTAKE

OVERLOOKING RISKS IN BONDS

Four out of 10 investors think that bonds can't lose money.[5] Yet the vast majority of bond funds did just that in 1994. Even more investors, two-thirds, think they can't lose money in *government* bonds. Yet in seven years since the 1970s, investments in long-term government bonds fell. Bonds might be safer on average than stocks, but they're by no means risk free. As investors shift money out of stocks and into bonds—more than $200 billion of new money poured into fixed-income funds in 2001 and 2002—this is an important point to keep in mind.

There are three basic types of risks associated with bonds: credit risk, interest rate risk, and inflation risk.

Credit Risk

A bond, like a stock, is an investment that reflects the health of the underlying issuer. In the case of stocks, you own a portion of the company that issues those shares. In other words, you're a part owner. When it comes to bonds, you're a lender. By buying a corporate or government bond, you lend that business or government entity money for a certain length of time.

Bondholders, then, face the same set of risks that a bank faces when it approves an auto loan or home mortgage: Will the borrower pay back the original loan amount in full at the agreed upon date, and will it make good on the interest payments it owes as compensation for the loan? The possibility that a bond issuer will default on its obligations, as Russia did in 1998—creating severe losses for its bondholders—is known as "credit risk."

You can gauge the credit risk that a bond issuer poses by looking up its credit rating, issued by agencies such as Standard & Poor's, Moody's, and Fitch. Just as FICO scores reflect the risk of doing business with an individual, bond ratings are supposed to reflect the risks associated with lending money to a business or government agency. Bonds issued by companies with strong balance sheets are often referred to as "investment grade" securities, while the debt of firms with questionable finances are considered "junk." Junk bonds are also referred to as high-yield debt because the issuers have to pay investors higher rates of interest to get them to buy the riskier debt. In the spring of 2003, for example, many junk bonds were yielding more than 10 percent while intermediate-term investment-grade corporate bonds were paying out only 5 to 6 percent and 10-year Treasury notes were paying out less than 4 percent.

Under S&P's credit-rating system, AAA-rated bonds are considered the safest, while bonds rated below BBB are considered junk (see Figure 4-10). Moody's, a competing credit-rating agency, uses a somewhat similar system, with Aaa the most creditworthy and Baa the lowest investment grade rating.

While a low credit rating doesn't necessarily mean that a bond issuer is going to default on its obligations, it implies that under poor economic conditions—such as a recession—there is a greater likelihood of

Figure 4-10. Credit Rating

Source: Standard & Poor's, Moody's

	Standard & Poor's	Moody's
Highest credit rating	AAA	Aaa
Small degree of risk	AA	Aa
Somewhat susceptible to risk	A	A
Vulnerable in bad economy	BBB	Baa
Start of "junk" status	BB	Ba
Major uncertainties exist	B	B
Vulnerable to nonpayment	CCC	Caa
Highly vulnerable to nonpayment	CC	Ca
Potentially in bankruptcy or default	C or D	C

default. The historic numbers bear this out. Between 1970 and 1995, for example, nearly 8 percent of bonds rated B defaulted within one year while virtually no bonds rated A or higher failed to meet their obligations. In fact, not a single bond rated Aaa defaulted during this stretch. Following bonds over longer periods of time, the results are even more pronounced. Between 1970 and 1997, only one-tenth of 1 percent of Aaa-rated bonds defaulted over five-year rolling periods of time, but nearly 31 percent of bonds rated B went bust (see Figure 4-11).

Yet this does not mean that investors can completely eliminate credit risk simply by sticking with high-grade debt. For example, between 1970 and 1995, 0.13 percent of bonds rated Baa—which is still considered investment grade—failed. And in recent years, there has been a noticeable pickup in the speed with which companies fall from investment-grade standing to junk. Consider this fact: Earlier this decade, bonds issued by the energy giant Enron were still rated investment-grade by Moody's and S&P one week before the company filed for bankruptcy.

Figure 4-11. Credit Ratings and Defaults

Historically, investment grade bonds (those rated Baa or higher) have rarely defaulted. But once you get into "junk" status (Ba or below), credit risk becomes a significantly bigger problem.
Source: Moody's

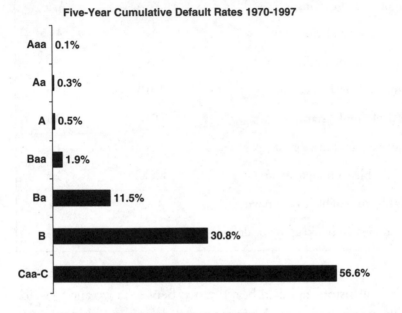

Five-Year Cumulative Default Rates 1970-1997

Rating	Default Rate
Aaa	0.1%
Aa	0.3%
A	0.5%
Baa	1.9%
Ba	11.5%
B	30.8%
Caa-C	56.6%

TIP: There are two simple ways to reduce credit risk. The first is to stick to investment-grade corporate bonds or U.S. Treasury bonds, which don't come with a rating because they don't need to. (Treasury securities are backed by the full faith and credit of the U.S. government. If the federal government ever gets into a financial bind, it can always print money to cover its obligations.) But by restricting yourself to only the highest quality bonds, you greatly limit what your portfolio can invest in and you lower your potential income.

An alternative is to invest in a diversified collection of bonds, just as you might do with stocks, through a mutual fund. Bond funds are particularly useful for investors who want to dabble in lower-quality fixed-income securities with higher yields. The average taxable bond fund, according to Morningstar, invests in roughly 240 different bonds. Should even a handful of those default, there would still be more than 200 other securities propping up the fund.

Interest Rate Risk

A second type of risk all bondholders face is "interest rate risk." It's important to remember that there are two ways to make money on a bond. There's the interest on the IOU, and there's the IOU itself—which, like a stock, can be bought and sold on the open market. Combined, a bond's yield plus or minus any changes in the underlying IOU's price make up the total return.

Changes in market interest rates affect bond *prices*. For instance, let's say you invest in a government bond that pays 5 percent interest, and let's assume that after you purchase the bond, market interest rates rise to 6 percent. If that happens, the price of your bond will automatically fall. After all, who would want to buy an older bond paying 5 percent interest when they can buy new bonds yielding 6 percent? This means that the riskiest time to invest in bond funds is when interest rates are rising dramatically, since the price of the underlying securities could fall. Unfortunately, 7 out of 10 investors don't understand this basic relationship, surveys show.

If a bond's price falls more than its yield, investors would suffer real losses. This happened in 1994. As market interest rates rose and bond prices fell that year, 88 percent of all bond funds lost money, and the average bond fund posted losses of 3.5 percent. It was even worse for long-term government bond funds. More than 97 percent of them lost money, with an average loss of more than 6 percent.

How can an individual investor measure interest rate risk? A term that all bond fund investors should become familiar with is "duration." You don't have to know what duration actually means—it has to do with the cash flow generated by a bond's interest payments over time. All you have to know is what duration means *to you*.

Let's say you invest in a bond fund whose duration is said to be seven years. Roughly speaking, this means if market interest rates rise 1 percentage point, your bond fund will lose about 7 percent of its value. If rates fall 1 percent, your fund will rise about 7 percent. The shorter your fund's duration, the less you have to worry about interest rate risk. If you were to invest in a bond fund with a duration of just two years, a 1 percentage point rise in rates would hurt

TIP: One way investors can avoid this type of interest rate risk is to buy *individual* bonds and hold them to maturity. Remember, at maturity—when the IOU comes due and you demand your money back—the bond issuer will pay back your principal in full. If that takes place, you don't have to worry about the price other investors place on your bonds.

Unfortunately, it's impossible for a bond *fund* investor to hold his or her investment to maturity because bond funds have no fixed maturity. Bond funds hold hundreds of different securities that mature on different dates. Moreover, bond fund managers often trade individual bonds before they mature. Bond fund investors, however, can reduce their exposure to interest-rate risk by sticking with short- and intermediate-term bond portfolios. According to Morningstar, the average bond in a long-term fixed-income fund matures in about 12 years. By comparison, the average maturity of an intermediate-term fund is less than eight years. And the average maturity of a short-term bond fund is only three years. If rates are rising, fixed-income funds holding short-maturity bonds will do better. That's in part because as bonds in short-term portfolios come due faster, the money can be reinvested more quickly at higher rates.

the fund's value by only 2 percent. The average short-term bond fund's duration is about 2.5 years, versus around seven years for the average long-term bond fund (see Figure 4-12). You can look up bond fund durations at *www.morningstar.com*.

What If Interest Rates Fall?

If interest rates fall, bond *fund* investors will profit as the price of older, higher-yielding debt in their portfolios rise. But *individual* bond investors who simply want to hold their securities to maturity would face a different type of interest rate risk altogether. That's the risk of having to reinvest money, as older bonds mature, into lower-yielding securities. If rates fall far enough, it could make

Figure 4-12. Bond Fund Durations*

The higher a fund's duration, the more vulnerable it is to losses if interest rates spike. Conversely, high duration funds will outperform when interest rates fall.
Source: Morningstar

Type of Bond Fund	Average Maturity	Average Duration
Long-Term Government	13.9 years	9.3 years
Intermediate-Term Government	7.5 years	4.4 years
Short-Term Government	3.9 years	2.4 years
Long-Term Corporate	12.6 years	7.0 years
Intermediate-Term Corporate	8.0 years	4.8 years
Short-Term Corporate	3.3 years	2.5 years
*As of June 2002		

it difficult to generate an adequate level of income. This is a particularly big risk for older investors who rely on the income their portfolios throw off to fund their retirement. Indeed, as Treasury yields fell to 40-year lows in 2002, retirees suffered billions of dollars in lost income.

One way to reduce this type of interest rate risk is to ladder your bonds. Laddering a bond portfolio is the fixed-income equivalent of dollar-cost averaging. A typical way to ladder your portfolio is to buy equal amounts of bonds with different maturities. Say you have $100,000 to invest. You buy $20,000 worth of bonds maturing in one year, $20,000 maturing in three years, $20,000 maturing in five years, $20,000 maturing in seven years, and $20,000 maturing in 9 or 10 years. The average maturity of your overall portfolio, in this scenario, would be about five years.

As time passes and the shorter-term bonds in your portfolio mature, you reinvest that money at the long end of the curve, to maintain your average maturity. So, for instance, once your one-year bond matures and pays you back your principal, you reinvest that sum in new 10-year bonds. Then, two years later, when that original three-year bond matures, reinvest that in new 10-year bonds. Doing this guarantees that you will never invest all of your bond money when rates are at their worst. Therefore, you reduce the risk of falling interest rates on your long-term portfolio. Savers can similarly ladder other income-generating investments, such as CDs.

Inflation Risk

There's one other major risk that all bond investors need to know about: the risk of not being able to meet one's long-term financial goals due to the harmful effects of inflation, an economic phenomenon in which the value of money falls as the price of goods and services rise over time.

We've lived through a recent period of unusually low inflation—in fact, in 2002 and 2003, economists started to worry about deflation, when prices for goods and services fall. But remember that it was only a little more than a decade ago when inflation was rising at around 4 percent. And more than two decades ago, the nation's inflation rate soared into the double digits.

No one is saying that inflation will return to 1970s and '80s levels. But if inflation rose to just 4 percent over the next 20 years, each dollar you save today would buy you less than 45 cents worth of goods and services two decades from now. In other words, even if you saved $1 million in your retirement portfolio, inflation would make sure it's worth less than half a million to you. If inflation kicked up to 5 percent a year, in 20 years that million-dollar portfolio would only buy you a retirement worth around $360,000. And if inflation rose to 7 percent, your account would really only be worth a quarter of a million dollars. (See Figure 4-13.)

Because stocks historically deliver greater total returns over the long run, inflation is less a concern to equity investors than it is to bond investors. But over the long run, inflation wreaks havoc on all portfolios.

Figure 4-13. Long-Term Effects of Inflation

What $100 would be worth at various rates of inflation over time

After...	Rate of Inflation					
	4%	5%	6%	7%	8%	10%
1 Year	$96.00	$95.00	$94.00	$93.00	$92.00	$90.00
3 Years	88.50	85.70	83.00	80.40	77.90	72.90
5 Years	81.50	77.40	73.40	69.50	65.90	59.00
10 Years	66.50	59.90	53.90	48.40	43.40	34.90
15 Years	54.20	46.30	39.50	33.70	28.60	20.60
20 Years	44.20	35.80	29.00	23.40	18.90	12.15

While common stocks delivered average annual returns of nearly 11 percent between 1926 and 2001, the real rate of return—after inflation, that is—was only 7.7 percent. And while long-term government bonds have returned 5.3 percent year throughout history, after inflation those returns shrunk to 2.18 percent (see Figure 4-14). At that rate, it would take about 33 years for your portfolio simply to double in value. This shows the ultimate risk of putting all of your money in bonds: You barely keep up with inflation.

MINI MISTAKE

Overlooking Risks in Mutual Funds

Investors can dramatically reduce the risks of owning stocks and bonds by purchasing well-diversified mutual funds. The typical U.S. stock fund, for instance, invests in more than 150 companies, while the average bond fund holds more than 200 securities. Should any single investment fall in value, it would have minimal impact on the portfolio as a whole.

Figure 4-14. Inflated Returns, 1926–2001

The effects of inflation on long-term investment returns.
Source: Ibbotson Associates

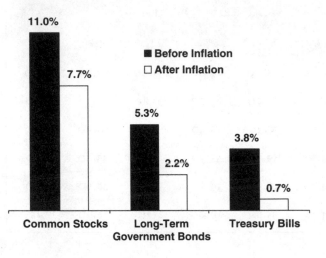

TIP: Bond investors today can deal with inflation risk by investing in so-called Treasury Inflation-Indexed Securities, sometimes called Treasury Inflation Protected Securities, or TIPs. These government bonds and notes pay a fixed rate of interest. However, your principal value is adjusted upward over time, based on the rate of inflation. So should inflation rise, your interest *payments* would rise too because they are applied to your inflation-adjusted principal. Plus, at maturity, you're likely to get more money back in principal then you originally invested since there's a greater likelihood of inflation, not deflation, over time. Still, if deflation does occur, the government guarantees that it will pay you back at least the original value of the bond. So you can't lose. There are several low-cost mutual funds that invest in these securities, including the Vanguard Inflation-Protected Securities Fund, the Fidelity Inflation-Protected Bond fund, and the American Century Inflation-Adjusted Bond fund. In 2002, the Vanguard and American Century funds delivered total returns of around 15 percent.

As an alternative, you can purchase inflation-indexed savings bonds, known as Series I Bonds, directly from the U.S. Treasury. I-Bonds, which mature in 30 years but can be redeemed much earlier,

(Continued)

are fairly easy to understand. Their yields are based on two components: a fixed rate of return set by the Treasury Department, and a variable rate of return based on the rate of inflation, as measured by the consumer price index, or CPI, for urban consumers. The variable rate is adjusted twice a year and is guaranteed to keep your total returns above the rate of inflation. Like Treasury notes, these savings bonds are backed by the full faith and credit of the federal government. Plus, their earnings are exempt from state and local income taxes. And what's especially nice is that I Bonds can be purchased for as little as $50.

However, mutual funds come with their own set of risks, "fund manager risk" chief among them. This comes about because, in addition to diversification, investors flock to funds for professional management. That is, an investor is buying the stock-picking or bond-picking skills of a fund manager in hopes of earning better-than-average returns. But fund managers are human and sometimes make wrong decisions. Indeed, in the long run the vast majority of stock pickers underperform broad stock market indexes that they're supposed to beat, like the S&P 500, as we'll discuss in "Mistake 7: Trying to Beat the Market with Funds."

William Sams was a legendary manager of the FPA Paramount fund until the late 1990s, when he made a big, but premature, bet on gold.[6] That mired the fund with losses in 1997 and 1998 while other stock funds were rocketing to double-digit gains. Indeed, the S&P 500 rose about 30 percent a year for both those years. Heiko Thieme, another manager, made a long and wrong bet on a single stock—Senetek, a British biotech company working on treatments for impotence—which led to five straight years of losses for his American Heritage fund shareholders between 1998 and 2002.

Your fellow shareholders in a mutual fund also expose you to risk, which we'll call "other shareholder risk."

While it's generally assumed that fund managers are in charge of their portfolios, they're sometimes forced to do things by investors that they wouldn't otherwise want to do. If half the shareholders of a fund leave all at once, for example, the manager might be forced

TIP: An easy way to avoid fund manager risk is to avoid fund managers. That is, invest in passively managed index funds, where there are no human stock pickers. Index funds simply buy and hold all of the stocks that comprise a particular stock market index. The Vanguard 500 fund, for instance, owns all 500 stocks in the S&P 500. And an index fund that tracks the Wilshire 5000 index would give you exposure to thousands of stocks of all sizes that comprise the total U.S. equity market. According to the Schwab Center for Investment Research, you can avoid fund manager risk while achieving adequate diversification by investing in one bond index fund, one small-cap stock index fund, one foreign index fund, and one large-cap stock index fund (see Figure 4-15).

Figure 4-15. Avoiding Fund Manager Risk

One way to avoid fund manager risk is to index your entire portfolio. The chart shown here represents a moderate-risk indexed portfolio.
Source: Schwab Center for Investment Research

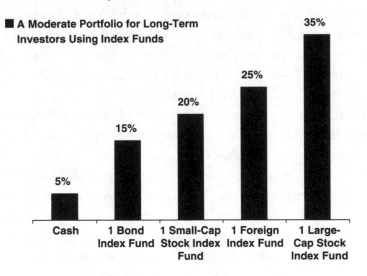

If, however, you prefer to stick with active fund managers, you'll need to invest in a *diversity* of actively managed portfolios. Research shows investors can achieve adequate fund diversification by owning three different funds *within* each asset class. Schwab researchers believe that a reasonably safe portfolio can be constructed

(Continued)

by investing in up to three different large-cap stock funds, three different small-cap stock funds, three different foreign funds, and one bond fund (see Figure 4-16). Owning just one fund per asset class allows investors the chance to beat the market, but does nothing to eliminate fund manager risk. On the other hand, investing in as many as 10 different funds within each asset class completely eliminates manager risk. But it also makes it virtually impossible to beat the market. Three funds, the Schwab researchers conclude: "can enable you to eliminate a substantial portion of the risk of underperforming the market, while retaining the opportunity to outperform it."[7]

Figure 4-16. Avoiding Fund Manager Risk

Another way to reduce fund manager risk is to invest in several different actively managed portfolios. Figures shown represent the percentage of assets to be invested in each investment class.
Source: Schwab Center for Investment Research

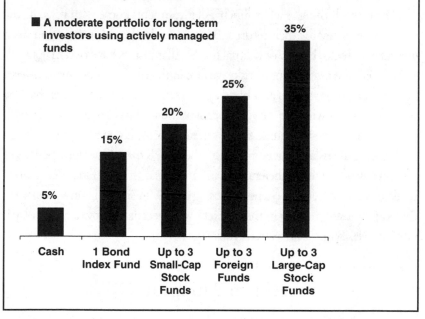

to sell stocks to redeem those investors, even though he or she might not have wanted to sell. And if, instead, the fund receives a torrent of cash, the manager could be forced to buy stocks in order to put all the incoming money to work in the market. In other words, volatile flows could cause the portfolio to miss out on opportunities in stocks when the market is rising, or conversely to be in the market when stocks are falling. Clearly, by forcing a fund manager's hand, fellow shareholders can pose potential risks to one another.

> **TIP**: You can avoid "other shareholder" risk by sticking with funds with stable assets. An easy way to do this is to check the total assets held by each of your funds once a quarter by going to your mutual fund company's Web site or to *www.morningstar.com.* If you find that your fund's assets rise or fall significantly from month to month—more significantly than the stock market is rising or falling—it may be a sign of a volatile shareholder base.

Bottom Line

There is no such thing as a free lunch: All investments come with risks. It's the price investors pay for their returns. But those risks shouldn't deter you from investing in stocks, bonds, or mutual funds. All investors have two major tools to deal with the assortment of risks we face in the market. The first is diversification. The more stocks and bonds you own, the less risk there is that any single investment will damage your overall portfolio. This is why mutual funds, which tend to invest in hundreds of different securities, are effective vehicles for reducing the risks of investing. Our other tool is *time.* Over long periods of time, many of the risks inherent in being an investor start to fade. Remember, while there's a 27 percent chance of losing money in stocks in any given year, the odds of losing money in the market over a decade—provided you play it safe by diversifying—are extremely slim.

> ## Checklist: Things to Do
>
> ❑ Avoid "company risk" by investing in at least 50 to 100 different stocks. You can do this easily by going with an S&P 500 index fund.
> ❑ Dollar-cost average into the stock market to diversify *when* you buy shares.

❑ See if your domestic stock funds give you foreign market exposure. If they don't, consider investing in a foreign fund, especially one that hedges currency risk.

❑ Remember that bonds are *not* risk free.

❑ Be careful investing in *bond funds* when interest rates are rising.

❑ Ladder a portfolio of *individual bonds* to reduce interest rate risk.

❑ If you invest through actively managed mutual funds, invest in at least three different funds to reduce "fund manager risk."

MONEY 5 MISTAKE

REARVIEW INVESTING

Taking a Diversified Approach
to Investing

In every era, without fail, investors glom onto a group of stocks that they say you *have to* own. Typically, these are among the best-performing investments of the recent past. What's more, conventional wisdom says you have to put a large chunk of your money into this group of stocks in order to beat the market. So many investors do. Invariably, these companies collapse under the weight of their own popularity—and hype. Which is why it's a huge mistake to fall into this trap of thinking you have to pile into any single group of stocks. Yet we fall for it, time and again.

In the 1990s, tech was "it." In the new economy, many investors knew only two types of investments: technology stocks and nontech stocks. And we all but ignored the latter. In fact, we were so enamored with the idea of getting in on the ground floor of the next new thing—the development of the Internet—that we shoveled more money into technology stock mutual funds—$17 billion—in the first 10 months of 1999 than we did in the previous 10 years combined.[1] Obviously, the fact that these funds were delivering historic returns helped. In 1999, a record 171 stock funds, mostly tech-only or tech-heavy portfolios, generated total returns of 100 percent or more. In other words, they doubled their investors' money in a single calendar year. Even in his best year, Peter Lynch, the famed former manager of the Fidelity Magellan fund (whom we will discuss more at length in *Mistake 8: Investing in What You Know*) generated returns of only about 70 percent.

Some of the most popular tech funds of the day did even better in 1999. The Kinetics Internet Fund, for example, delivered returns of more than 200 percent, tripling investors' money. Garrett Van Wagoner nearly quadrupled the money of shareholders in his Van Wagoner Emerging Growth fund. And the Nicholas-Applegate Global Technology portfolio turned a $10,000 investment at the start of 1999 into nearly $60,000 by the end of that year. While individual stocks do this from time to time, this was unheard of among mutual funds.

The performance of this sector of the economy was so great that even retirees were beginning to jump on this bandwagon. A 63-year-old investor I interviewed at the time told me how he had moved more than *half* of his retirement assets into tech-funds such as Janus Global Technology, Fidelity Aggressive Growth, Rydex OTC, Janus Olympus, and Fidelity Growth Company. In 1999 those funds delivered gains of 212, 103, 101, and 80 percent, respectively. Why did he abandon the more diversified, and therefore safer stock funds in his portfolio, such as Fidelity Value and the Fidelity Fund? "Who needs them when you look at Janus Global Technology?"[2]

That was certainly the way many of us felt. Indeed, there was a real sentiment among a cross section of investors that tech wasn't just leading the way, that it would *always* be the market's leader. After all, the products that these technology, telecommunications, and Internet companies were bringing to market were leading to huge productivity gains throughout the economy. Worker productivity soared more than 3 percent annually between 1998 and 2002, according to Labor Department statistics—fueling the bull market boom while keeping inflation largely in check. In the five prior years, productivity grew at only about half that pace. This fact alone justified higher, in some cases mind-boggling valuations for these stocks, some tech investors argued.

Yet this wasn't the first time this argument was made. In the late 1970s and early '80s, for instance, oil was the sector *du jour*. With energy sources stressed and oil prices rising, oil services giants like Exxon and Chevron were dominant stocks, the Microsofts and Intels of their day. Some of these big, blue-chip oil companies were considered such sure bets that they were bandied about as widows-and-orphan stocks, meaning you could feel comfortable putting your elderly mother's money in them. So much money poured into the sector that at one point oil represented nearly 25 percent of the total market capitalization, or value, of the S&P 500.

Back then, oil investors said these companies deserved to be that big because the product they brought to market literally fueled the economy. Sound familiar? But then energy prices fell and the sector hit a rough patch as the world entered into a global recession that sent demand for crude oil and energy plummeting. Eventually, the combined market value of the entire sector slid back down to around *5 percent* of the S&P, which is about where it is today.

The lesson? "Just because something is a large component of an index doesn't mean you have to own it," says Robert Rodriguez, manager of the FPA Capital Fund.[3] That was true for oil in the late '70s, and it was certainly the case for tech stocks in the late '90s. The tech sector at one point grew to around 40 percent of the S&P, but has since fallen back to its historic level of about 15 to 20 percent of the index. History, it seems, has a funny—or is it cruel?—way of repeating itself.

ANCHORING EXPECTATIONS TO THE PAST

While it's true that "those who forget the past are doomed to repeat it," investors who concentrate too much on the recent past are doomed to make some mistakes. In fact, a big mistake many of us continue to make is choosing our investments by looking at yesterday's stock tables. It's what's known as "rearview investing." And like rearview driving, looking over your shoulder instead of ahead at the road is fraught with danger.

Consider that between January 1990 and March 2000, the average stock fund's rolling three-year annualized rate of return was nearly 11 percent. But by chasing yesterday's winners—in many cases tech stocks—fund *investors* lost about a fifth of what they could have earned in the market had they simply taken a diversified, long-term approach. The average stock fund investor earned 20 percent less than the average stock fund, or just 8.7 percent a year during the 1990s bull market, according to a study by the Financial Research Corp.[4] The difference between earning 11 percent and 8.7 percent a year on your money could add up to hundreds of thousands of dollars in lost opportunities. A $50,000 investment earning close to 11 percent a year turns into $667,000 over 25 years. That same $50,000, earning just 8.7 percent a year for a quarter of a century, grows to $402,000, or about a quarter of a million dollars less.

FRC's study discovered an epidemic of rearview investing. For instance, in their rush to chase last year's winners, fund investors flipped into and out of funds at a significantly faster rate than in the past. The average investor's holding period—the time between buying and eventually selling an investment—for funds fell from 5.5 years in 1996 to less than 3 years by the end of the '90s. Meanwhile, the redemption rate for funds nearly doubled. This not only hurt overall performance, it ran up trading costs.

Furthermore, the vast majority of investors in the '90s put new money into stock funds immediately after those portfolios delivered their best quarterly gains, indicating that flows did chase performance. This confirms other research which indicates that the vast majority of investors tend to put money into funds only after they've been successful—not before. *The Wall Street Journal* reported that approximately $80 billion of new money was invested in 2002 in funds rated at four or five stars by Morningstar, while more than $100 billion was *yanked* from portfolios with lower ratings. Yet there's little evidence that funds already rated four or five stars perform better over time than lower-rated portfolios.

While it's a natural human impulse to buy a stock that's at its peak, it's the investing equivalent of buying concert tickets for a performance just as the band is about to play its finale. While that final song may be great, there's not much of a show left to enjoy.

Yet we continue to practice rearview investing. After the bull market ended, for example, shareholders, burned by equities at the start of this decade, plowed hundreds of billions of dollars into bond funds in 2002 and 2003, just as market interest rates were at record lows and bond prices were nearing record highs.

As human beings, it's hard not to be influenced by past performance. In fact, it's in our nature to base future decisions on what's taking place in the present and what took place in the past. What else do we have to go on? Some refer to this phenomenon as "representativeness." "People tend to put too much weight on recent experience," says Jay Ritter, a professor of behavioral finance at the University of Florida. "As an example, when equity returns have been high for many years, many people begin to believe that high equity returns are 'normal.'"[5] Similarly, when tech stocks were delivering 100-percent-plus returns in 1999, many just assumed that those gains could and would repeat.

Yet tech continued to fascinate investors well into the start of the bear market. Fund investors poured $52 billion into tech sector funds in 2000, with the majority of that money flowing into those portfolios well after the Nasdaq's slide had already begun. Why? Again, it may have to do with the way our brains are wired. Just as we base our future decisions on the past, our expectations for the future are colored by prior experiences. This phenomenon is referred to as "anchoring."

Let's say you invested in a tech stock when it was trading above $100 a share in early 2000. Three years later the stock tumbled to $10. Which price is closer to fair value? There's a tendency among investors, researchers have found, to think the initial price of a stock is closer to the "real" value because that's what we understood to be true in the past. In other words, first impressions do matter. Experts say this is why car salesmen always start negotiations by quoting an artificially high price—so the customer's determination of fair value will be "anchored" to his initial price, rather than some other measure.

Similarly, when tech stocks were trading at such high prices in the late 1990s, many investors grew to assume that they deserved to trade that high. Then, when tech shares fell, many of us kept investing in technology even after the start of the bear market because our opinions about the worth of those shares were anchored to late '90s prices. This would explain why so many investors—including professional money managers—hung on to shares of Cisco Systems after they tumbled from $80 a share in 2000 to $40 in 2001 to $20 in 2002 and to around $15 in early 2003.

Anchoring has been particularly problematic for investors who started out in the late '90s. For them, the tech boom wasn't just a recent experience, it was literally their first impression of the markets.

There's probably one more factor at work. "When buying a stock, investors are faced with a formidable search problem," finance professors Brad Barber and Terrance Odean say. "There are over 7000 U.S. common stocks from which to choose. Human beings have bounded rationality ... We are generally not able to rank hundreds, much less thousands, of alternatives." So we take some mental shortcuts. And one of those shortcuts is to focus on "attention-grabbing stocks." In their study on buying behavior, Barber and Odean discovered that individuals are "much more likely to be net buyers of stocks that are in the news than those that are not."[6] And tech stocks were certainly in the news in the late '90s.

The irony is, if investors paid attention to history—and not the news—they would see that market leadership rotates. While tech certainly dominated the market in the late '90s, only once in the past

15 years has there been an asset class that repeated as the *absolute* best-performing group for two years in a row.

In 1990 bonds were the best performers. The following year it was small-cap growth stocks. Then small-cap value stocks took the lead. That was followed by foreign stocks, which led for both 1993 and '94. In the late '90s large-cap growth stocks, large-cap value stocks, small-cap growth stocks, and even real estate investment trusts took turns leading the way (see Figure 5-1). This is part of the natural ebb and flow of the markets that is referred to as "reversion to the mean." No asset can continue to deliver above average returns forever. Over time, every asset class eventually falls back in line with its long-term average performance. As different investments gradually revert to their mean, other assets take turns leading the market.

Taking Turns: Stocks vs. Bonds

Take stocks and bonds. History shows that over long periods of time, stocks outperform bonds consistently and significantly. That's because when you buy a bond, you own a source of income limited by the terms of the loan. When you own a stock, you are a part-owner of a business whose earnings growth and market value are, theoretically, limitless. In a 2002 study, T. Rowe Price discovered that overrolling 5-year periods, stocks outperformed bonds 78 percent of the time throughout the past century. Over 10-year periods, stocks beat bonds 84 percent of the time. And over 30-year stretches, it wasn't even close: Equities outperformed fixed-income investments 100 percent of the time.

But as we discussed in *Mistake 4: Overlooking Risks,* the price we pay for the higher rewards that stocks provide is higher volatility. In the short term, stocks are more likely than bonds to lose money in any calendar year. This means that stocks and bonds take turns leading the market.

Typically, stocks outperform bonds during times of economic growth. That's because stock prices tend to rise or fall with corporate profits—and earnings are affected by the strength of the econ-

Figure 5-1. Change in Market Leadership

Throughout the past two decades, different investments have taken turns leading the stock market. This is why it's dangerous to chase last year's "winners."

Source: Frank Russell Company

	1994	1995	1996	1997	1998	1999	2000	2001
Best	Foreign	Large Val.	Real Estate	Large Val.	Large Grow.	Small Grow.	Real Estate	Small Val.
	Real Estate	Large Cap.	Large Grow.	Large Cap.	Large Cap.	Large Grow.	Small Val.	Real Estate
	Large Grow.	Large Grow.	Large Cap.	Small Val.	Foreign	Foreign	Bonds	Bonds
	Large Cap.	Small Grow.	Large Val.	Large Grow.	Large Val.	Small Cap.	Large Val.	Small Cap.
	Small Val.	Small Cap.	Small Val.	Small Cap.	Bonds	Large Cap.	Small Cap.	Large Val.
	Small Cap.	Small Val.	Small Cap.	Real Estate	Small Grow.	Large Val.	Large Cap.	Small Grow.
	Large Val.	Bonds	Small Grow.	Small Grow.	Small Cap.	Bonds	Foreign	Large Cap.
	Small Grow.	Real Estate	Foreign	Bonds	Small Val.	Small Val.	Large Grow.	Large Grow.
Worst	Bonds	Foreign	Bonds	Foreign	Real Estate	Real Estate	Small Grow.	Foreign

146

omy. We saw this in recent years, when stocks trounced bonds between 1995 and 1999, when the economy was growing at around 4 percent a year—but then were routed from 2000 to 2002, when GDP was rising just 2 percent on average. Another reason why stocks outperform bonds in good times is that inflation tends to kick up when the economy is strong. And as we discussed in the previous chapter, inflation is a major threat to bonds because it eats up a large chunk of their total returns.

Still, it's often difficult for investors to predict when market leadership will change hands. The Great Depression offers a perfect example. During the first four years of the Great Depression, when the economy was at its weakest, bonds led the market for an unprecedented four straight years. Between 1929 and 1932, government bonds delivered average annual gains of about 5 percent, while the stock market fell more than 20 percent a year. In the subsequent four years, between 1933 and 1936, government bonds did even better, posting average annual gains of nearly 6 percent. But stocks bounced back dramatically during this period, returning 30 percent a year and handily beating bonds. Was the economy that much better then? Not really. But this just goes to show how unpredictable the stock and bond markets can be. Sometimes, an asset has been beaten down so much that investors buy back into the market simply because the prices are so attractive on a relative basis.

Three years later, between 1939 and 1941, bonds retook market leadership, as the global economy was threatened by the start of the second world war. But once the nation entered World War II, stocks turned bullish again between 1942 and 1945, after the initial shock of the war subsided (see Figure 5-2).

Taking Turns: Growth vs. Value

The terms *growth* and *value* refer to the two competing schools of investing. There are those who believe that the best way to invest is to seek out the absolute strongest growers—companies with the fastest and most consistent profit growth over time. These are busi-

Figure 5-2. Taking Turns

Historically, stocks and bonds take turns leading the market. But it's difficult to tell when market leadership will change, as the Great Depression showed. Selected performance of the S&P 500 and Long-Term Treasury bonds, 1929–1945.
Source: Edward Jones

Year	S&P 500	Long-Term Treasuries
1929	−8.4%	**3.4%**
1930	−24.9	**4.7**
1931	−43.3	**−5.3**
1932	−8.2	**16.8**
1933	**54.0**	−0.1
1934	**−1.4**	10.0
1935	**47.7**	5.0
1936	**33.9**	7.5
1939	−0.4	**5.9**
1940	−9.8	**6.1**
1941	−11.6	**0.9**
1942	**20.3**	3.2
1943	**25.9**	2.1
1944	**19.8**	2.8
1945	**36.4**	10.7

nesses like Microsoft, which delivered double-digit earnings and revenue growth to shareholders throughout the 1990s. Because of their fixation with quality, growth investors are often willing to pay high prices for their stocks, on the assumption that the absolute best companies will continue to deliver the best returns.

Value-oriented investors, on the other hand, are fixated on discounts. Like bargain-bin shoppers, value investors don't mind if the companies they invest in aren't in vogue. All they care is that they're paying less for the shares than they think the stock is actually worth. Value stocks, then, tend to be beaten-down or overlooked companies that for whatever reason have fallen out of favor—and whose shares are therefore priced attractively. Recently, tobacco giant Altria Group (formerly known as Philip Morris) and old economy names like DuPont, which were largely forgotten in the late '90s, were examples of value stocks.

At varying times, investors tend to favor one group over the other. Typically, growth stocks tend to outperform when the economy is firing on all cylinders. For instance, in the late '90s bull market, growth investments dominated, as investors sought out companies with strong earnings momentum. In bear markets, however, investors tend to seek the relative safety of value stocks. After all, a stock that is undervalued by the market theoretically has less room to fall than a high flyer.

Remember too that stocks, like bonds, generate returns in a couple of different ways. When share prices rise, the value of shareholders' investments appreciate. This is referred to as capital appreciation. In addition, many stocks pay out dividends to entice investors to buy. Combined, a stock's capital appreciation and its dividend yield represent its total return.

In the '90s, fewer and fewer growth companies paid out dividends, preferring instead to reinvest the money in their businesses, in an effort to grow even faster. Many value stocks, however, still typically pay out dividends. At the start of 2003, the average dividend yield of value stocks in the S&P was slightly more than 2 percent, twice the payout of growth stocks.

When stock prices are soaring, dividends are often overlooked. If the market is rising 30 percent a year, what's another 2 percentage points? But there have been periods in history—in the 1970s, for instance—when the stock market simply inched along and a large percentage of equity returns came from dividends. In weaker times in the market, then, value stocks tend to outperform because of their higher yields.

Here again, it's often difficult to predict with absolute certainty when value or growth stocks will lead the way. Over the past 28 years, growth stocks and value stocks have each led the market 14 times (see Figure 5-3). Despite the absolute dominance of growth stocks in the late '90s, over long stretches of time, research indicates that value investing is superior. Between 1928 and 2001 the average value stock enjoyed around 13 percent annual returns, versus 9.4 percent gains for growth, according to Ibbotson Associates (see Figure 5-4).

Taking Turns: Large Versus Small

Large-company stocks and small-company stocks are fundamentally different types of investments. When you invest in small compa-

Figure 5-3. Growth Versus Value

Over the past 28 years, growth stocks have beaten value stocks 14 times, and value has beaten growth 14 times.
Source: Standard & Poor's.

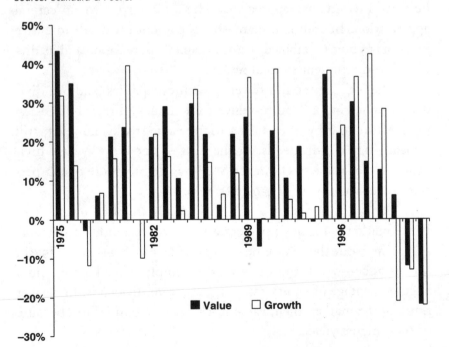

Figure 5-4. Virtue of Value Investing

Though growth and value stocks take turns leading the market, value delivers bigger gains over time. Between 1928 and 2001, value stocks delivered average annual returns of 13 percent, versus 9.4 percent for growth stocks. The figure below shows the performance of $10,000 in growth and value stocks over time.
Source: Ibbotson Associates

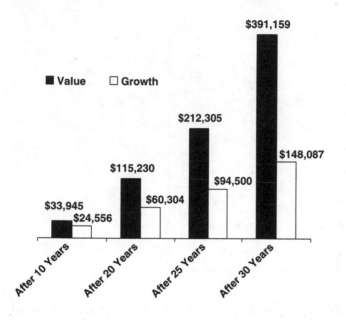

nies—those with market capitalizations (defined as a firm's stock price times its total number of shares outstanding) of $1 billion or less—you're buying fast and potential growth. You're also buying volatility. When you buy shares of big blue-chip companies, with market caps of $10 billion or more—you're buying stability and industry leadership. As with growth and value, large and small stocks take turns outperforming (sees Figure 5-5 and 5-6).

Typically, small companies are popular as the economy emerges from recession into a lengthy period of growth. Following the 1973–'74 bear market, for instance, small stocks beat the S&P 500 for seven consecutive years. In the early 1990s, emerging from the first Gulf War recession, small stocks dominated large ones again. But by the mid- to late 1990s, large-cap companies, like Cisco Systems,

Figure 5-5. Small Versus Large

Throughout the 1990s, small-cap funds and large-cap funds took turns leading the market.
Source: Morningstar

Year	Small-Cap Funds	Large-Cap Funds
1992	15.05%	8.52%
1993	16.41%	12.08%
1994	−0.37%	−1.06%
1995	29.68%	32.35%
1996	21.06%	20.17%
1997	23.4%	26.72%
1998	−0.91%	22.51%
1999	34.44%	22.71%
2000	5.51%	−4.96%
2001	1.58%	−14.24%

General Electric, and Coca-Cola—trounced the performance of smaller ones. Large stocks also tend to outperform on a relative basis as the economy heads *into* recession, as blue-chips typically have more financial strength to weather economic storms.

Over time, though, small stocks tend to outperform the overall market, delivering average annual returns of 12.5 percent between 1926 and 2001, versus 10.7 percent gains for large-company stocks.

MINI MISTAKE

IGNORING ASSET ALLOCATION

If you shouldn't look in the rearview mirror to spot tomorrow's winning stocks, where should you look? The answer is all over. For all of

Figure 5-6. Size and Style Matter

For the past decade, small-cap value funds, small-cap growth funds, large-cap value funds, and large-cap growth funds have taken turns on top.
Source: Morningstar

	Small Value	Small Growth	Large Value	Large Growth
1992	19.94%	11.93%	10.23%	6.78%
1993	16.69%	15.77%	14.09%	10.73%
1994	−1.08%	−0.16%	−0.48%	−2.24%
1995	24.65%	33.76%	32.37%	32.41%
1996	23.88%	19.63%	20.68%	18.47%
1997	31.21%	18.38%	27.09%	25.12%
1998	−6.27%	4.15%	12.58%	33.09%
1999	6.01%	59.27%	7.31%	41.26%
2000	18.28%	−3.67%	7.28%	−14.56%
2001	17.36%	−9.04%	−4.92%	−23.09%
Past 15 Yrs	11.70%	10.69%	10.77%	9.57%

the discussion about what hot stock will be the next Microsoft, the individual stocks' long-term investors pick will have less impact over the success of their portfolio than the *types* of investments they choose. In other words, deciding to put 5 percent of your money into Microsoft instead of Intel won't be as crucial over the next 20 or 30 years as how much of your total portfolio is invested in stocks versus bonds versus cash.

To be sure, if you were to put 100 percent of your money in one stock, say, Enron, then yes, that single stock would determine all of your long-term returns. But if you own a large portfolio of equities, perhaps through diversified mutual funds, over time that diversification will lead to *correlation* with the broader markets. As this occurs, stock selection diminishes in value and *asset allocation* grows in importance.

In recent years there's been much academic debate as to what role asset allocation really plays in an investor's portfolio. To determine this, Roger Ibbotson, Yale finance professor and chairman of Ibbotson Associates, studied the performance of "balanced" mutual funds with at least a 10-year track record. Because they invest in a mix of stocks and bonds, balanced funds can serve as a proxy for investor portfolios.

His research showed that nearly 100 percent of a balanced fund's total returns over a decade's time could be explained by its level of exposure to stocks versus bonds, as opposed to the individual stock-picking skills of the fund managers. He concluded that stock pickers were simply "not adding value ...[because of a] combination of timing, security selection, management fees, and expenses."[7] That's not to say that stockpicking can't or won't affect you in the short-term. Two investors can have virtually identical portfolios but have widely divergent results in any calendar year because of the performance of just one stock. But the role of stockpicking diminishes over time. And over long periods of time, the odds of adding value—i.e., beating the market—through stockpicking fall significantly, as we will discuss in the next two chapters: "Mistake 6: Trying to Beat the Market," and "Mistake 7: Trying to Beat the Market with Funds."

If you don't think asset allocation decisions are that consequential to your financial well-being, consider the historic performance of various types of portfolios.

First, let's consider the worst-case scenarios. Let's say, believing that you have a high tolerance for risk, you decide to invest 100 percent of your money in the stock market. Historically, the worst one-year performance of a 100 percent stock strategy based on the S&P 500 was a loss of more than 43 percent. That took place in 1931. However, even a minor allocation to bonds would have made a tremendous difference. The worst one-year performance of an 80 percent stock/20 percent bond allocation was a loss of 34.9 percent. And a slightly greater allocation to bonds produced even smaller losses. A

Figure 5-7. Worst-Case Scenarios, 1926–2001

Your asset allocation strategy can have a major short-term impact. The following table shows the worst one-year performance of different asset allocation strategies throughout the century.
Source: Ibbotson Associates, Vanguard Group, and Straight Talk on Investing.

Asset Allocation	Worst 1-Year Performance
100% Stocks	−43.1%
80% Stocks/20% Bonds	−34.9
60% Stocks/40% Bonds	−26.6
50% Stocks/50% Bonds	−22.5
40% Stocks/60% Bonds	−18.4
20% Stocks/80% Bonds	−10.1

50 percent stock/50 percent bond portfolio lost no more than 22.5 percent in a single year between 1926 and 2001 (see Figure 5-7).

What about in rising markets? The long-term average annual returns for equities between 1926 and 2001 was about 10.7 percent. By comparison, the historic average annual gain for an 80 percent stock/20 percent bond portfolio was about 10 percent. A 60 percent stock/40 percent bond portfolio historically delivered returns of about 9.1 percent. And a most conservative allocation—20 percent stocks/80 percent bonds—gained just 7 percent on average. The difference between earning 10.7 percent on a $100,000 investment and 7 percent on that same amount over 25 years works out to roughly $726,960 in lost potential gains (see Figure 5-8).

As we discussed earlier, you have to consider the trade-offs of short-term risks and long-term rewards that stocks and bonds deliver. For instance, while a 100 percent stock portfolio would earn significantly more over time, it would also subject you to much more short-term risks. This portfolio would have lost money in 22 years between 1926 and 2001. In comparison, the average conservative

Figure 5-8. Long-Term Performance of Different Allocation Strategies

The short-term dangers of being aggressive are clear, but in the long run the more aggressive you're willing to be, the more returns you can expect to earn.

Source: Ibbotson Associates, Vanguard Group, and Straight Talk on Investing

Asset Allocation	Historic Performance, 1926–2001		
	Avg. Ann. Total Ret.	Growth of $100,000 Over 25 Years	# of Losing Yrs. '26–'01
100% Stocks	10.7%	$1,269,700	22
80% Stocks/20% Bonds	10.0	1,083,470	21
60% Stocks/40% Bonds	9.1	882,300	19
50% Stocks/50% Bonds	8.7	804,900	17
40% Stocks/60% Bonds	8.1	700,880	16
20% Stocks/80% Bonds	7.0	542,740	13

portfolio, consisting of 20 percent stock and 80 percent bonds, fell in value only 13 years during this period.

Determining Asset Allocation

The question is: What's the appropriate mix of stocks and bonds for you? What should you invest in? The answer is, it depends on what you're investing *for*.

All too often, investors base their asset allocation strategy purely on age. A 20-something might put 100 percent of his or her investments in stocks, while a 40-something might put only 60 percent into equities. There used to be an old rule of thumb that said you should take your age and subtract it from 100 to determine how much of your portfolio belongs in stocks. So a 32-year-old might put 68 percent of her money in equities while a 65-year-old might invest 35 percent.

Others tweak their mix periodically, based on short-term opportunities they see in the stock or bond markets. For instance, if, based on the economy, they think bonds will outperform over the next 12 months, they might reverse a 60 percent stock/40 percent bond portfolio to overweight fixed income.

But at the end of the day, an asset allocation strategy must reflect the specific goals you have for your money. You might be saving toward a down payment on a house, two years away. You might be investing to send your kid to college, six years away. Or you might be saving for retirement, 25 years away. Meanwhile, your neighbor, who is exactly the same age, might not have kids to worry about and might already own a house. Determining your asset allocation, then, isn't just about how old you are or what you think is in store for the stock market so much as it's about sitting down and sorting out all of your buckets of money.

Here's a quick back-of-the-envelope way to determine your mix:

- *Step 1. What's the money for?* Sit down and figure out exactly how much of your total portfolio—your brokerage accounts, IRAs, 401(k)s, etc.—is dedicated for retirement; how much is dedicated for your children's needs; and how much is dedicated for other goals?

- *Step 2. When do you need the money?* Determine the time horizons for each of these goals. For instance, if your child is 12 and you want to send him to college, your time horizon is roughly five to eight years.
- *Step 3. When do you really need the money?* A common error people make in assessing their time horizon for retirement is assuming they'll need the money at 65. Or even that they'll need the money immediately once they quit. Your time horizon should reflect when you absolutely need to tap the account. If you plan on relying on Social Security and other sources of income before your investment accounts, for example, you might not need to tap your retirement accounts until you're 70. If you have a younger spouse who still plans to work when you retire, you might not need to tap your accounts for several more years.
- *Step 4. Separate the money into categories.* Put all of your short-term goals into one pile. These are goals that need to be funded in two years or less. Then put all of your intermediate-term goals (those that need to be funded in two to seven years) into another pile. Put all of your long-term goals (8 to 15 years) into a third pile. And finally, put your truly long-term needs (anything over 15 years) into a fourth.
- *Step 5. Match your investments with your needs.* Now that you have some rough numbers to work with, you'll recognize an approximate asset allocation strategy appropriate for your needs. Your short-term money represents your cash allocation; your intermediate term money represents your bond allocation; your long-term can be split between stocks and bonds (depending on your aversion to risk); and your really long-term money should be mostly invested in stocks.

Just remember: As each year passes, your time horizon shrinks. So you have to adjust your portfolio accordingly. Rebalancing your portfolio once a year to make sure it's in line with your ever-changing needs not only reduces your overall risk profile, in some cases it can even lead to higher returns, as we will discuss in "Money Mistake 9: Underfunding Your Pensions."

Bottom Line

In every era, we focus most of our attention on a single group of investments, usually the best performers of the previous era, as technology stocks were in the 1990s. It's a mental shortcut. Given all the complexities involved in predicting the future performance of investments, we simply find it easier to base our assumptions of tomorrow on real experiences from the past.

But what we often forget is that market leadership rotates. In fact, it rotates quite often. Rarely does one asset class repeat as the market's absolute leader for more than a year. This is why it's so important to be invested in both stocks and bonds—and among equities, growth, and value-oriented shares as well as large- and small-cap companies. The irony is that academic research indicates that over time, the individual stocks we pick have far less to do with our portfolio's long-term performance than our asset allocation strategy. Yet surveys show that only a minority of investors focus much if any attention on asset allocation.

Checklist: Things to Do

❑ Don't "anchor" your expectations of future returns to the past.

❑ Market leadership rotates. Diversify among stocks and bonds, growth and value stocks, and large- and small-cap stocks.

❑ Spend less time on stock selection and more time on asset allocation.

❑ Let what you're investing *for* determine your asset allocation strategy.

❑ Adjust your asset allocation once a year, to reflect changes in your time horizon.

MONEY MISTAKE 6

TRYING TO BEAT
THE MARKET

Taking What the Market
Gives You

If the stock market was our religion in the late 1990s, "beating the market" was our first and foremost commandment. The idea of just sitting back and accepting what the stock market gives you wasn't just considered stupid then, it was heresy. It was a sin. It went against the very principles that fomented the greatest bull market in history. If you could earn more than the overall market, whether it's measured by the S&P 500, the Dow Jones Industrial Average, or the Wilshire 5000 index, the cult of equity's mantra was: "Why not go for it?"

Many of us did. And we seemed to prosper, if only for a brief while. But then we found out the hard way why trying to beat the market over the long term is folly, and that trying to do so can end up costing us tens of thousands of dollars. Those of us who "went for it" by loading up on technology stocks in October 1999, just a few months before the peak of the dot.com bubble, ended up losing more than 30 percent a year in the subsequent three years (see Figure 6-1).

In real terms, that meant saying good-bye to about $6600 for every $10,000 we invested. If you "went for it" by investing in a single company's stock, like Lucent, which was once the most widely held stock in America, chances are you'd have lost considerably more. A $10,000 investment in Lucent on December 31, 1999 tumbled 75 percent a year on average for the next three years. In other words, the stock market turned your $10,000 into just $150.

We now know that "going for it" was the wrong thing to do, and that the question itself—"Why not go for it?"—was the wrong one to ask. A better question would have been: "Is it absolutely necessary to swing for the fences?"

At the very least, we should have considered the worst-case scenario of betting big in the market and losing. Yet studies indicate that less than 10 percent of investors spend significant time thinking

Figure 6-1. Trying to Beat the Market

In the bull market, conventional wisdom said you had to bet big on technology, telecommunications, and other growth stocks to beat the market. But had you done so in the fall of 1999, you'd have lost big in 2000 through 2002.
Source: Lipper Inc.

	1999 Total Return	Annualized Returns 9/30/99–9/30/02
Technology Stocks	133.3%	−30.7%
Telecom Stocks	63.9	−32.7
Large Growth Stocks	36.7	−17.5
Dow Jones Industrials	27.2	−9.8

about the dangers of investing.[1] Instead, the vast majority of us— nearly 75 percent, according to recent surveys—focus mostly on the potential gains. Investing in the stock market in the '90s was about as close to gambling as you could get, yet many of us never even considered the *odds* of placing bets on risky tech stocks and IPOs in that bull market.

Going forward, the most important question all investors should be asking is: "What do I need to earn to accomplish my goals?"

As with all things in life, it's helpful to know the rules of a game before taking the field. To win in basketball or football, all you have to do is beat your opponent by a single point. Winning by one point or 100 points makes no difference at the end of the day. It works sort of the same way when it comes to investing, though many of us don't understand this.

All too often we mistakenly think the goal of the stock market is to run up the score by earning the biggest gains possible, rather than meeting a predetermined goal—such as saving $50,000 within five years for a down payment on a house. That's because as investors we can enjoy the "extra" returns. We get to save or spend whatever money we make over and above what the stock market is returning or what we need to earn.

But this risky behavior can come back to bite us. In football, if you lose by one point or 20 points, you only lose a single game. In investing, the more you lose by, the more you lose. If you were to lose 1 percent on a $10,000 portfolio, you'd be out $100. If you were to lose 50 percent on $10,000, you would be out $5000.

What if, from now until the day you die, the stock market falls, say, 5 percent a year? If your portfolio was to lose 4 percent a year every year for the rest of your life, would you consider that victory? Of course you wouldn't. You can't buy a dream house or retire on losses of 4 percent a year.

What if, instead, you took all of your money out of the market and stuffed it into a bank account earning 2 percent a year? Would you feel good about having outsmarted the stock market? That depends. If you're Bill Gates, 2 percent interest on billions of dollars of wealth would be more than enough to get you by. If on the other hand you're Bill Middleclass, 2 percent probably won't cut it. As Jack Brennan, chairman of the mutual fund giant Vanguard Group, says in his book, *Straight Talk on Investing*: "As the saying goes, 'You can't eat relative performance.'" He adds: "Sensible investors don't put too much stock in a fund's relative performance."[2]

Setting Realistic Goals

As a long-term investor, it's important not to get distracted by arbitrary and relative things such as what the market is returning. Nor should you care how well your coworkers' 401(k)s are doing. Those are meaningless bogeys that at the end of the day flat out don't matter. The point of investing is not to get a trophy for being better than everyone else. It's not to beat the market year in and year out, which is a lot harder to do than many of us realize. The purpose of investing is to earn enough to meet a financial goal, be it buying a house, starting your own business, retiring early or retiring well. If you figure that you'll need to earn 5 percent a year for the next 20 years to get there, so be it. If you figure it's actually closer to 10 percent, so be that. The point is, what you need is an actual, ascertainable number.

Whatever your goal, you'll have to do a little math. Let's say your primary reason for investing is to retire comfortably. Based on your income, your lifestyle, your assets, your retirement benefits, and your health, you'll have to estimate how much you'll need to amass at retirement to retire well. Then you can work backward from that figure to determine how much you'll have to earn on your investments to get there.

Let's say you're a decade away from retiring. You currently have $100,000 invested, but you know you need to amass $200,000 within 10 years. This means you'll need to grow your money about 7.2 percent a year for the next decade (see Figure 6-2). That's less than the 10 percent historic annual rate of return for the broad stock market, which should tell you that you don't need to swing for the fences. If, on the other hand, you're trying to turn $50,000 into $75,000 within five years to pay for your daughter's tuition, you'll need to earn about 8.4 percent a year. If your goal is more short-term-oriented—for instance, if you're trying to save enough to put a down payment on a new home three years out—calculating how much you'll need to amass should be a lot easier.

Portfolio Envy

If you don't do the math, you'll fall into the trap of "financial relativism." That's the disease where you measure success not based on your specific needs, but relative to how the market is doing or how your friends are faring. It's peer pressure investing. It's portfolio envy. It's a sign of personal insecurity, which can often lead to personal *financial* insecurity.

The irony is, surveys indicate that Americans haven't a clue about their neighbors' real financial circumstances. A survey conducted by the Consumer Federation of America and Primerica in 1999 found that most investors overestimate, sometimes by as much as 25 times, the assets and wealth of their peers.[3] In other words, your neighbors

Figure 6-2. What It Takes to Reach Your Goals

The following table shows the annual rate of return needed to grow your portfolio by the various factors. For instance, to grow your investments three-fold, you'd have to earn 11.6 percent a year for the next 10 years.

	Annual Returns Needed to Grow Money by This Factor			
	1.5X	2X	2.5X	3X
3 years	14.5%	26.0%	35.7%	44.2%
5 years	8.4	14.9	20.1	24.6
7 years	6.0	10.4	14.0	17.0
10 years	4.1	7.2	9.6	11.6

aren't nearly as well off as you think—so don't worry. In the 1990s, as self-directed retirement accounts were burgeoning, a growing number of Americans also began to assume that the country was dotted with 401(k) millionaires. According to some surveys, many Americans thought that nearly one in six households was worth more than $1 million, when in fact the answer was closer to one in 25.

If you're susceptible to this kind of thinking, just remind yourself that beating your neighbor's portfolio is not your goal. Beating poverty is. The market is not your competition. Being able to retire comfortably is. Your goal is not to outpace the S&P 500. It is to outpace inflation so you can maintain a comfortable lifestyle in the future. The worst-case scenario isn't earning 5 percent when the Dow is rising 7 percent. Your worst-case scenario is betting the farm on a portfolio of speculative stocks in hopes of earning 20 percent—and losing the farm.

Not too long ago many of us were taking 10 percent and even 20 percent annual returns for granted. Between 1995 and 1999 the S&P 500 gained an average of around 28 percent a year. Given that some technology funds at the time were delivering 100-percent-plus returns, all of a sudden 28 percent looked downright miserable. How silly that all seems now.

I'm not saying it's impossible to beat the stock market. In any given year, many investors do. In the first calendar year of the bear market, for instance, a majority of stock funds beat the S&P 500 index. The question is, what are the odds that you'll be able to consistently beat the market, year in and year out, over the long term—over the next 20 or 25 years? Even professional money managers, who are backed by research analysts and who get paid handsome salaries and incentives to beat the market, have a miserable record doing so (as we'll discuss in the following chapter, *Mistake 7: Trying to Beat the Market with Funds*).

MINI MISTAKE

OVERESTIMATING YOUR ABILITIES

Of course, some of you may be thinking: "Just because the odds are stacked against me doesn't mean that I can't beat the market consistently over time." This is true. You may be among the minority of investors with the knack of outperforming your peers. But understand that most investors have a tendency to overestimate their capacity to manage money.

According to behavioral finance experts Terrance Odean, U.C. Berkeley, and Simon Gervais, University of Pennsylvania: "We tend to overestimate the degree to which we are responsible for our own successes."[4] Meanwhile, we underplay our responsibility for failures. We blame them on external forces. We saw this phenomenon play itself out during the bear market, when investors blamed stock market losses first on the Internet sector's meltdown and then on a wave of corporate scandals. Yet how many of us credited our bull market profits to those same factors—irrational exhuberance and accounting shenanigans that artificially pumped up profits—rather than our own skills?

It's not that we mean to be boastful. It's just the way our brains work. We're no more overconfident about our skills at investing as we are about our abilities to perform other tasks. Behavioral finance scholars often point to the fact that more than 80 percent of small business owners believe that their companies will succeed. Meanwhile, they give their peers only a two in five chance of surviving. The vast majority of us think we're good drivers when police accident reports would beg to differ. Similarly, research shows that about 90 percent of investors believe they're "above average" at managing their portfolios. Yet this defies the laws of mathematics. Eighty or 90 percent of any group cannot be better than the average of that group.

In 1999, two Northwestern University professors led a research study where they took aside a group of investors and provided them with ongoing information about how their mutual funds were performing over an extended period of time.[5] At the end of the study, reported on by *Money* magazine, the investors were asked how their portfolios fared relative to the overall stock market, as measured by the S&P 500. Nearly one in three said they beat the market by 5 percent or more—and one in six said they trounced the market by at least 10 percent. Yet when the scholars who ran the study went back and looked at the actual performance of those investors' portfolios, they discovered that 9 out of 10 investors who claimed that their funds beat the S&P 500 exaggerated their performance. More than 30 percent of those who said they outperformed the market actually trailed it by 5 percent. And 25 percent of the boasters lagged the market by 15 percent or more. This was remarkable, given that these investors were literally told how well their funds—and the market—were doing throughout the study.

Separately, *Money* discovered something interesting in its annual "Americans and Their Money" survey. In the fall of 1999 the magazine queried 500 investors and asked them whether their stock funds had beaten the S&P 500 and the Dow over the past year. Nearly 30 percent of the respondents said their portfolios had beaten the Dow, while nearly one-quarter said their funds had bested the S&P. But when the magazine asked the respondents how much their funds had returned, it discovered that the Dow and S&P had actually outperformed around 80 percent of those investors who claimed they were beating the market.[6]

Overconfidence

While we can chalk this up to innocent overconfidence, there is a potentially destructive consequence. Overconfident investors spend more time—in fact, most of their time—focusing on their potential gains rather than worrying about potential losses. That's what behavioral finance scholars Shlomo Benartzi, Richard Thaler, and Daniel Kahneman discovered in a recent study published by Morningstar. Nearly three quarters of investors they surveyed spent the majority of their time fixating on potential *gains,* while only 7 percent spent more time worrying about losses.[7] Overall, less than 20 percent of investors said they spend equal amounts of time worrying about gains and losses.

Overconfident investors also trade more often, which tends to lead to poor results. In a ground-breaking study published in the *Journal of Finance* in April 2000, Brad Barber and Terrance Odean studied the performance of 78,000 households with trading accounts at a large discount brokerage. They discovered that investors who traded stocks the least did the best, generating average returns of 18.5 percent a year between 1991 and 1996. That far exceeded the 16.4 percent gains for the average investor during this stretch. Meanwhile, investors who traded the most did the worst, earning just 11.4 percent a year during this period, badly trailing the S&P. As money manager Peter Lynch noted: "It's the rare investor who doesn't secretly harbor the conviction that he or she has a knack for divining stock prices or gold prices or interest rates, in spite of the fact that most of us have been proven wrong again and again."[8] (More about Peter Lynch in *Mistake 8: Investing in What You Know.*)

Again, one reason traders do so poorly, on average, has to do with psychology. In an earlier study, Barber and Odean looked at the trading behavior of 10,000 randomly selected investors at a major discount brokerage. They found that traders are more likely to sell stocks in their portfolio that are doing well than those that are performing poorly.[9] This seems counterintuitive, since investors who sell profitable stocks must pay taxes on their gains immediately. On the other hand, if you were to sell money-losing stocks, you could capture the losses and use them to offset gains elsewhere in your portfolio, thereby lowering your taxes while getting rid of your losers.

Barber and Odean found that traders hung on to losers due to a combination of overconfidence and pride. For example, they concluded that investors have a tendency to think that their money-losing stock picks will eventually turn around. So we hang on to our laggards, not wanting to admit that our original assessment of a stock was wrong. As part of their study, Barber and Odean tracked the stocks that these traders dumped for two more years. As it turns out, the winners that investors sold wound up continuing to outperform the losers that they hung on to throughout that period. They concluded: "Investors who sell winners and hold losers because they expect the losers to outperform the winners in the future are, on average, mistaken."

Missed Opportunities

For whatever reason, it's harder to beat the market over the long term than it sounds. At the start of this decade, Dalbar, a financial research

firm in Boston, studied the *actual* performance of mutual fund
investors between 1984 and 2000 by examining when investors
moved money into and out of mutual funds during this period of
time. What Dalbar discovered was that during the greatest bull market of this century, spanning those 17 years, the average stock fund
investor earned a meager 5.3 percent a year[10] (see Figure 6-3). Investors
could have easily earned more than 5 percent a year in a basic bond
mutual fund during this time—and with far less risk. In fact, they
did. According to Dalbar, the average fixed-income investor earned
6.1 percent a year between 1984 and 2000. Meanwhile, the S&P 500
generated annual returns of 16.3 percent for nearly two decades, and
the average stock fund gained about 13 percent a year, according to
Morningstar.

Figure 6-3. Market Underperformance

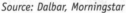

Between 1984 and 2000, the S&P 500 returned 16.3 percent a
year. But mutual fund investors earned just 5.3 percent a year, as
many flipped into and out of funds in a futile attempt to chase
yesterday's winners.
Source: Dalbar, Morningstar

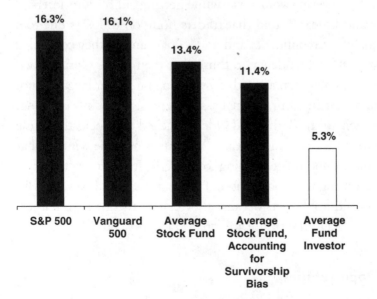

Dalbar wasn't the only research firm to discover our propensity to underperform the market. As you'll recall from the previous chapter, Financial Research Corp. studied the performance of fund investors between January 1990 and March 2000, and found that fund investors trailed the average fund by about 20 percent.[11] But that was over rolling three-year periods of time during the '90s. Over rolling one-year periods, FRC found the disparity was even greater. The average one-year performance for stock funds between 1990 and 2000 was nearly 12 percent, while the average mutual fund investor, chasing yesterday's winners, earned just 6.68 percent a year. That's about 40 percent less.

The Cost of Churning

In addition to lower returns, investors who trade often in an attempt to beat the market chase performance suffer other unintended costs. By flipping into and out of funds frequently, investors realize their capital gains sooner rather than later, leading to immediate and possibly higher tax bills.

Starting in 2003 capital gains on assets held for more than 12 months were taxed at 15 percent at most, thanks to the recent Bush tax cuts. But gains on assets held for 12 months or less were taxed at an individual's ordinary income tax rate, which could have been 30 percent or higher. In other words, your tax bill might have nearly doubled through impatience.

Moreover, frequent trading leads to higher brokerage and trading costs as you step into and out of various stocks. By one estimate, commissions and other expenses associated with trading wind up costing individual investors between 0.2 and 0.7 percent of the value of their transactions. So if investors traded $1 billion of shares, the tab would be between $2 million and $7 million.

Even no-load mutual fund investors, who aren't subject to commissions, risk higher fees by attempting to chase performance. According to a 2001 study by FRC, the number of mutual funds that now levy so-called redemption fees, assessed on traders in an effort to curtail short-term selling, has grown 82 percent since 1999.[12]

More funds charge redemption fees because more investors are bailing out of their funds so quickly. As we discussed, the average holding period for a fund is now only 2.9 years. Redemption fees typically cost investors 1 to 3 percent of the sale, so if you were to sell $10,000 worth of holdings prematurely, you could be charged $100 to $300.

Not only are a growing number of funds imposing such fees, but more funds are extending the length of the penalty period. In 1999 the typical fund with a redemption fee imposed it on investors who sold 7.5 months after purchasing those shares. Today, redemption fee periods typically last more than nine months.[13] Some last one year or more. And even if your fund company doesn't charge such fees, your broker might.

MINI MISTAKE

NOT DOLLAR-COST AVERAGING

The irony is, in a bear market there is one way to beat the overall market, especially through low-cost no-load mutual funds. Yet many investors overlook it. It's called dollar-cost averaging.

As we discussed earlier, dollar-cost averaging refers to investing incremental amounts of money in the market at routine intervals. We do this all the time with our 401(k)s, where a small percentage of our paychecks is automatically deducted and invested into our retirement accounts once a week or month—but we don't do it nearly enough outside of our employer-sponsored accounts.

Instead of investing a lump sum of $50,000, you might choose to put $4200 into the market each month over the course of an entire year, or $2100 a month over two years. By doing so, you *average* out the cost of shares you purchase over an extended period of time (hence the name). The idea is to ensure that you aren't investing all of your money at the absolute peak in the market.

Dollar-cost averaging works particularly well in an extended downturn. That's because with each monthly contribution, you would be buying stocks at ever lower prices. The hope is, you keep buying at lower and lower prices until the market eventually recovers and then soars prior to you tapping the account.

For instance, let's say you invested $100,000 on March 24, 2000, when the S&P 500 peaked at 1527. Two and a half years later the S&P had fallen to 819, turning your $100,000 to $54,000. But had you dollar-cost-averaged into the S&P starting at the end of March 2000, you would have purchased your shares at incrementally lower prices, reducing your losses. The average monthly closing value of the S&P 500 from March 24, 2000, to September 30, 2002, was around 1255, or 18 percent lower than the peak.

TrimTabs.com, a financial research firm in northern California, studied how an investor would have fared during the Great Depression had he or she dollar-cost-averaged into the market. It turns out that between December 1929 and December 1939, a person who dollar-cost-averaged would have made a decent amount of money despite the fact that the stock market, as measured by the S&P 200, declined 42 percent during this time. "If there had been an index fund during the 1930s and an investor bought $1000 worth of S&P stocks at the end of each month from 1929 through 1939, the $120,000 invested over 120 months would have grown by 12.7 percent over the decade," says TrimTabs president Charles Biderman. Moreover, had that investor continued to dollar-cost average through the 1940s and 1950s, he or she would have turned $360,000 into close to $1.5 million.[14]

Those of us who lived through the recent bear market would have loved earning 12.7 percent on our money. Hell, we would have loved just matching the market's returns.

Bottom Line

Emotions often get in the way of a sound investing strategy. It was true in the late 1990s. It's still true today. All too often we take unnecessary risks with our money in an attempt to achieve goals that don't need to be achieved—like beating the market. It's like that classic

Aesop's fable involving the dog and his shadow. One day, a dog walking home with a piece of meat in his mouth comes upon a bridge overlooking a stream. As he looks down, he happens to see another dog, carrying what looks like a bigger piece of meat. So he lunges for the food, only to discover that the other dog is simply a reflection of himself in the water. In the process, he ends up dropping his meal in the stream.

Similarly, overconfident investors who tried to beat the stock market in the 1980s and '90s lost their lunch, so to speak. Think about this: Had you invested $100,000 in the Vanguard 500 index fund between 1984 and 2000, and done nothing else, you'd be sitting on $1.2 million. Yet by trying to beat the market, the average fund investor managed to turn that same $100,000 into just $240,000. It was a costly lesson—but one we all need to learn.

Checklist: Things to Do

❏ Calculate your needs before deciding on an investment strategy.

❏ Weigh the potential cost of losing money when investing.

❏ Don't overestimate your ability to manage money successfully.

❏ Play the averages by investing through a broadly diversified index fund.

❏ Play the averages by "dollar-cost averaging" your investments over time.

MONEY MISTAKE 7

TRYING TO BEAT THE MARKET WITH FUNDS

The Triumph of Indexing

Since its creation 80 years ago, the mutual fund has played a vital role in millions of investors' portfolios. Funds offer their shareholders several attractive benefits, including convenience, professional management, and instant diversification. And thanks to their low minimum investment requirements—in many cases all it takes is $1000 to gain exposure to a diversified portfolio—funds have made it possible for a majority of Americans to be in the market. Today, more than 90 million Americans have nearly $7 trillion invested in stock, bond and money market mutual funds, either directly or through their retirement accounts.

Yet throughout the 1990s bull market, funds consistently let their shareholders down. Not only did the average "actively managed" stock portfolio fare worse than the S&P 500 in the late '90s, the majority of them lagged the major indexes they get paid to beat. Between 1994 and 1999, for example, actively managed stock funds that invest in large, blue-chip equities routinely trailed the Vanguard 500 index fund, which has no stock picker at the helm (see Figure 7-1).

At the time, there was serious debate within the investment community as to whether professional money managers could beat the market over the long term or whether indexing—simply owning all the stocks in the market through a passively managed index fund—might be a better bet. In 1999, *Business Week* asked: "Who needs a money manager? Index funds are cheap, easy, and they're changing

Figure 7-1. Bull Market Returns

Between 1994 and 1999, actively managed blue-chip stock funds routinely trailed the performance of the Vanguard 500, a fund that simply tracks the S&P 500 index of blue-chip stocks.
Source: Morningstar

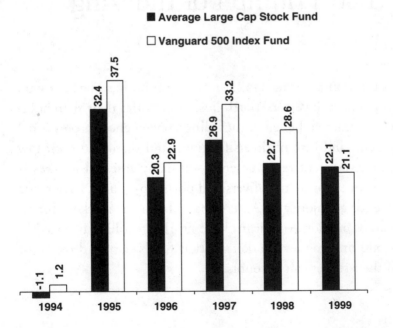

the way Americans invest."[1] *Fortune* magazine wondered out loud: "Who believes in mutual funds anymore? What used to be the fund industry's dirty little secret—the failure, year in and year out, of most actively managed funds to outperform the S&P 500—is no secret now."[2]

For their part, fund managers argued that it's difficult for stock pickers to consistently beat their respective indexes in roaring bull markets.[3] When the vast majority of stocks are rising, *stock selection* becomes less important on a relative basis, while other variables, such as a fund's costs, begin to matter more. They said actively managed funds would begin to beat the major indexes once the markets cooled off.

Stock pickers, after all, have more tools to protect shareholders when stock prices are meandering or falling. They can sidestep trouble by avoiding certain stocks or specific sectors altogether. They can move money into cash or buy safer assets like bonds or gold. They can also use options to hedge their bets. Index funds, on the other hand, are required to mirror a broad stock market index in good times and bad, and therefore cannot sell their holdings.

Funds in the Bear Market

Yet the record shows that during the recent bear market, when the S&P 500 lost nearly 50 percent of its value from peak to trough a majority of stock fund managers did worse than the broad market—again.

Between the market's peak on March 24, 2000, and September 30, 2002, the S&P fell about 21 percent a year. By comparison, the average large-cap stock fund fell nearly 23 percent, according to the mutual-fund tracking firm Lipper Inc. So much for being able to sidestep trouble in a bear market. In all, more than three out of five actively managed large-stock funds trailed the S&P.

Small-cap fund managers also underperformed—and by a wider margin. The average actively managed small-cap stock fund fell 12.5 percent a year between March 9, 2000, when small stocks peaked before entering the bear market, and September 30, 2002. The S&P

600 index of small stocks, on the other hand, lost only about 5 percent a year. And nearly 60 percent of small-cap stock fund managers failed to beat their respective benchmark (see Figure 7-2).

To be fair, the S&P 500 and S&P 600 are broad market indexes, perhaps too broad to serve as appropriate benchmarks for money managers. The mutual fund industry has become highly specialized since growing into a trillion-dollar business in 1990. By prospectus, some managers are only allowed to invest in stocks of a certain size and style. Some can only buy shares of large growth-oriented companies, for instance, while others are limited to small, value stocks. So-called sector fund managers can only invest in companies within a single industry.

Like pension funds, then, a growing number of mutual funds are being forced into increasingly restrictive "style boxes," in part so that fund-tracking services can compare funds within specific peer

Figure 7-2. Bear Market Returns

In the first two and a half years of the bear market, actively managed stock funds failed to beat their respective benchmarks. Average annualized small-cap fund returns are compared with the S&P 600 index of small stocks. Average annualized large-cap fund returns are
compared with the S&P 500 index of blue-chip stocks.
Source: Lipper Inc.

	3/9/00–9/30/02
Average Small-Cap Fund	−12.5%
S&P 600 Index	−5.2
Percent of Funds Trailing Index	*59.6*
	3/24/00–9/30/02
Average Large-Cap Fund	−22.8%
S&P 500 Index	−21.0
Percent of Funds Trailing Index	*60.4*

groups. Active managers thus argue it's unfair to compare their returns to these broad market indexes. They've got a point.

But style-specific versions of the S&P 500 and 600 exist. Starting in 1992, Standard & Poor's and the financial research firm Barra began to divide the major S&P indexes into their growth and value components for this very purpose. The S&P 500/Barra Growth Index, for instance, only includes those blue-chip companies in the S&P that exhibit growth characteristics. Therefore, it represents a fair benchmark for large-cap growth fund managers. Similarly, the S&P 500/Barra Value Index represents an appropriate yardstick for large-cap value funds.

When you compare actively managed funds against these style- and size-specific indexes, stock funds still had a difficult time beating their benchmarks in what was supposed to be a "stock picker's market." Consider the performance of funds in the first two and a half years of the bear market, between March 31, 2000, and September 30, 2002:

- The average large-cap growth fund lost about 30 percent a year on average. By comparison, the S&P 500/Barra Growth Index fell just 26 percent.
- The average large-cap "core" fund fell more than 21 percent. The S&P 500 index, which is a proxy for blended or core blue-chip stocks, fell 20.6 percent.
- The average small-cap growth fund tumbled nearly 26 percent annually, while the S&P 600/Barra Growth Index lost just 11.4 percent a year.
- The average small-cap "core" fund lost 6.4 percent of its value, versus the 3.5 percent annual losses for the S&P 600 index during this time.

The only group of actively managed portfolios that beat the indexes during this span, on average, were value-oriented funds. Large-cap value managers guided their funds to losses of 11.3 percent a year, while the S&P 500/Barra Value Index fell 14.7 percent. The average small-cap value fund returned more than 5 percent a year during this time, versus 3.4 percent for the S&P 600/Barra Value Index.

One possible explanation for the outperformance of value managers was that during the prior bull market, when stock prices were rising significantly, many value managers had a hard time finding attractively priced stocks they wanted to invest in. As a result, many chose to keep a greater-than-usual percentage of their assets in cash in 1999. And that cash cushioned their portfolios against severe losses during the subsequent downturn.

The performance of value managers notwithstanding, this wasn't the first time that stock pickers disappointed their shareholders in a lousy market. In the 1973–74 bear market, the average actively managed stock fund lost more than the Wilshire 5000: 47.9 percent versus 46.4 percent. In the 1987 market crash, the average stock fund lost 29 percent of its value, which was about the same as the Wilshire index. Equally noteworthy is the fact that active managers failed to beat their indexes in the subsequent rallies following these downturns. One year after the end of the 1973–74 bear, the Wilshire surged nearly 40 percent while actively managed portfolios gained only 35 percent. Twelve months after 1987's Black Monday, actively managed funds gained 21.9 percent—two percentage points *less* than the broad stock market.

Indexing: A Better Bet

A case can now be made that index funds are a better bet than actively managed portfolios in good, bad, and sideways markets. Here's a pretty amazing statistic: As of September 30, 2002, the S&P 500 had beaten the average large-cap stock fund over the prior one, three, five, 10, and 15 years (see Figure 7-3). This doesn't mean that the S&P beat *all* actively managed funds during these times. But over the past three years, it beat most of them: 56 percent. And over the past five, 10, and 15 years, the index beat more than 7 out of 10 large-cap funds.

Some argue that actively managed small-cap funds stand a better chance of consistently beating their benchmarks over time. There are

Figure 7-3. Large-Cap Funds Trail Index

In bull and bear markets, the average actively managed large-cap fund lags the S&P 500. (Figures are as of September 30, 2002.)
Source: Lipper Inc.

	1 YR	3 YR	5 YR	10 YR	15 YR
Large-Cap Stock Funds	−21.0%	−13.6%	−3.6%	7.3%	7.6%
S&P 500	−20.5	−12.9	−1.6	9.0	9.0
Percent of Funds Trailing Index	*57.2*	*56.1*	*71.1*	*78.1*	*76.0*

several reasons why. Part of it has to do with the relative "inefficiency" of the small-cap market. Large, blue-chip stocks tend to be covered by dozens of Wall Street analysts in addition to hundreds of mutual funds and hedge funds. This means a great deal of information about these companies is routinely disseminated to investors, allowing them to efficiently price these stocks. Small companies, on the other hand, enjoy little if any analyst coverage, meaning, in some cases, that investors might not know enough about a small business to properly value it. In theory, this gives skilled small-cap managers an opportunity to exploit situations where a company is undervalued by the market.

Another reason small-cap funds should outperform has to do with expenses. An advantage that index funds enjoy over actively managed portfolios is that they're cheaper to run. Actively managed funds will buy and sell stocks throughout the year, leading to trading costs in addition to other expenses, such as stock research. Index funds, because they simply hold all the stocks in the market, don't incur many of these costs. That's not to say index funds don't ever trade. Every year, the companies that oversee the major stock indexes— Standard & Poor's, Dow Jones, and the Frank Russell Co.—reconstitute those benchmarks as changes occur. If a member of the S&P 500 is acquired, for instance, a new company will have to be brought into the index to replace it. If a company's market capitalization changes dramatically in a given year, it could be moved into a different index. In still other cases, a company could simply go out of business.

In general, small-stock indexes like the S&P 600 or the Russell 2000 make more changes every year than the S&P 500. In some years, as many as 20 or 30 percent of the members of a small-cap index may be replaced, whereas the S&P 500's turnover rate is closer to 4 percent. This is largely due to the fact that so many small companies go out of business, get sold, merge, or grow in any given year.

Because they have to adjust their holdings more frequently to reflect these changes, small-cap index funds are typically more expensive to operate than large-cap index funds. While the Vanguard 500 fund charges annual fees of 0.18 percent of assets, the Vanguard Small Cap Index fund charges 0.27 percent. These higher costs would seemingly give small-cap stock pickers a better chance of beating small-cap index funds than large-cap funds have in beating the S&P 500.

Unfortunately, small-cap fund managers haven't been able to capitalize on these built-in advantages. Over the past one, three, five, 10, and 15 years (through September 30, 2002), you would have been better off investing in an S&P 600 Index fund than an actively managed small-cap portfolio (see Figure 7-4). Only 40 percent of

Figure 7-4. Small-Cap Funds Trail Index

In bull and bear markets, small stock funds lag the S&P 600. (Figures are through September 30, 2002.)
Source: Lipper Inc.

	1 YR	3 YR	5 YR	10 YR	15 YR
Small-Cap Stock Funds	−9.5%	−1.0%	−1.7%	8.3%	7.9%
S&P 600	−1.8	2.9	0.8	10.9	8.1
Percent of Funds Trailing Index	74.4	59.2	65.3	71.8	47.5

small-cap funds beat the S&P 600 over the past three years; only 35 percent beat the index over the past five years; and only 28 percent did it over the past decade. And over the past 10 years, the S&P 600 outpaced the average small-cap fund by more than two and a half percentage points annually.

Survivorship Bias

The situation is actually much worse for active management than the numbers would indicate. Every year, the mutual fund industry launches hundreds of new portfolios while liquidating others as different types of investments come into and out of fashion. In 2002, for example, nearly 1000 funds were merged or liquidated out of existence, while hundreds more were created. Many of the new funds launched that year were fixed-income portfolios, as the industry sought to capitalize on the growing demand for bond investments during the bear market.

Similarly, in the late 1990s the industry launched hundreds of new "new economy" funds, including dozens of portfolios that only invested in Internet stocks—only to shutter many of them when the tech sector fell out of favor at the start of this decade. It's the same thing that takes place in other businesses. Automakers routinely design new cars while jettisoning older, less popular models, and clothing designers are always paying attention to the latest fashions.

Funds are liquidated for essentially one of three reasons:

1. *The fund turns out to be a lemon.* There's a saying in the mutual fund industry: Flows follow performance. Investors rarely put money into portfolios with bad track records. One reason why so many technology funds were liquidated at the start of the decade was that the tech sector was hit so hard that it would have taken years—and a miracle—for many of those portfolios to look appealing again. By June 2003 the average tech fund was still down about 30 percent a year for the prior three years despite a major rally. Try putting that in an ad in *Money* magazine and see how many people invest in your fund.

2. *The fund isn't popular.* In a sea of thousands of funds, some portfolios just don't attract enough assets to justify the costs of keeping them open. As Jack Bogle says: "In this business, you bring out a fund not because you think it will make money for individuals but because you think it will make money for you." If the fund isn't turning a profit for the fund company, why keep it open?[4]

3. *The fund company operating the portfolio merges with another fund company.* Often when this happens, the merged company decides to shutter some funds to avoid duplication. For instance, if both of the companies operated health-care sector funds prior to the merger, there might not be a need to maintain both after the deal.

During the bear market, a record number of funds—about 2700 out of more than 13,000—were liquidated or merged out of existence, according to Morningstar (see Figure 7-5). And over the past five years through 2002, about 30 percent of the funds that existed in the late-1990s were erased from history.

The problem of fund liquidations is only growing worse. In a study of mutual fund survivorship rates in 1997, Mark Carhart, then a professor at the University of Southern California, discovered that one-third of the funds that existed in 1962 ceased to exist by 1993.[5] Yet between 1995 and the end of the third quarter of 2002, more than 5000 funds were liquidated or merged out of existence, according to Morningstar. That's about as many funds as existed in 1995.

You might ask: What's the big deal? The answer is that it's a matter of being able to keep track of performance.

When a fund ceases to exist, so does the need to maintain records on it. Every time a fund is liquidated, its long-term performance records are expunged by the major fund-tracking firms such as Morningstar or Lipper.[6] Fund performance records, then, have a built-in bias: They only care about portfolios that have survived to this point. In the industry, it's referred to as "survivorship bias." But isn't calculating historic performance data based only on surviving

Figure 7-5. Survivorship Bias

Since 1995, approximately 5,200 mutual funds have been merged or liquidated out of existence—and their poor performance records have been expunged from the official records.
Source: Morningstar

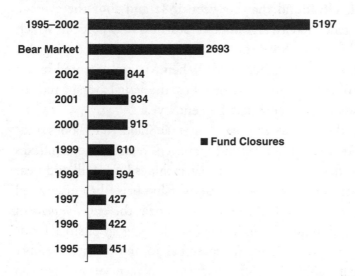

funds like showing your report card to your parents after erasing all the D's and F's?

Because funds that are liquidated tend to be among the worst-performing portfolios, the long-term performance of actively managed funds is actually worse than the numbers cited earlier. If you were to add back the long-term records of every actively managed portfolio that ever existed, it would be no contest. Index funds are a far better bet than most active managers.

Adjusting for Survivorship Bias

A recent study by Bing Liang of Case Western Reserve University in 1999 found that "survivorship bias" among hedge funds, which are diversified portfolios available to high-net-worth investors, resulted in more than 2 percentage points of annual performance bias.[7] If that's the case, the average mutual fund may have done about 2 percentage points worse over time, annually, than Morningstar or Lipper figures would indicate. "It's certainly something investors should be aware of," says Morningstar analyst Russell Kinnel.[8]

In an earlier study, Princeton's Burton Malkiel looked at the performance of stock funds in the 1980s bull market with survivorship bias in mind. He found that between 1982 and 1991 the average mutual fund generated average annual returns of 17.1 percent, which was comparable to the S&P 500's 17.5 percent gains. Yet during this period one in six funds disappeared. When Malkiel factored in the performance of those liquidated portfolios, the actual average returns for stock funds was closer to 15.7 percent a year.[9]

More recently, in October 2002, analysts at Standard & Poor's studied the performance of active fund managers versus various indexes over the prior five years—a period that includes both bull and bear markets. When they corrected for survivorship bias, they discovered what we already know: The major indexes beat the *vast majority* of actively managed mutual funds in every single category of stock funds over the past five years. Between September 30, 1997, and September 30, 2002, for instance, the S&P 500 beat 63 percent of all large-cap funds. The S&P 400 index of medium-sized companies beat 93 percent of all mid-cap stock funds. The S&P 600 beat 67 percent of small stock funds. And the so-called S&P 1500 supercomposite index—which, like the Wilshire 5000, represents the total U.S. stock market—beat two-thirds of all domestic equity portfolios.

Active fund managers also trailed their *style-specific* indexes. The S&P 500/Barra Growth Index beat 65 percent of all large-cap growth funds, the S&P 400/Barra Value Index beat 84 percent of all mid-cap value funds, and the S&P 600/Barra Growth Index beat 69 percent of all small-cap growth portfolios (see Figure 7-6). Even in much shorter time periods—over the past one to three years—most actively managed funds lagged the indexes they get paid to beat.

To be sure, a number of professional fund managers have beaten their indexes consistently over extended periods of time. Bill Miller of the Legg Mason Value fund, for one, beat the S&P 500 for 12 straight years, finding a way to outpace the index in both bull and bear markets. David Williams, manager of the

Figure 7-6. Indexes Versus Funds

When liquidated funds are added back to the equation, the majority of actively managed mutual funds lag behind their respective indexes. (Figures are through September 30, 2002.)

Source: Standard & Poor's

Fund Category	Appropriate Index	Percent of Funds Beaten by Their Respective Indexes		
		Past 1 Yr	Past 3 Yrs	Past 5 Yrs
All Large-Cap Funds	S&P 500	46.9%	46%	62.9%
Large-Cap Growth Funds	S&P 500/Barra Growth	65.9	41	65.4
Large-Cap Value Funds	S&P 500/Barra Value	20.3	37	50.8
All Mid-Cap Funds	S&P 400	83.6%	83.2%	93.2%
Mid-Cap Growth Funds	S&P 400/Barra Growth	94.3	88.8	97.2
Mid-Cap Value Funds	S&P 400/Barra Value	73.8	93.5	84.2
All Small-Cap Funds	S&P 600	78%	71.2%	67.3%
Small-Cap Growth Funds	S&P 600/Barra Growth	93.4	82.8	68.7
Small-Cap Value Funds	S&P 600/Barra Value	54.5	55.4	54.3

Excelsior Value & Restructuring Fund, outperformed the S&P by about 5 percent a year between May 1993 and May 2003. And according to Lipper, over the past 30 years, between October 31, 1972, and October 31, 2002, Fidelity Magellan posted average annual returns of more than 16 percent, while the S&P's performance was closer to 10 percent (in recent years, however, Magellan and the S&P have performed about equally).

The question is: Can the Bill Millers, David Williams, and Magellans of the world continue to outperform the market for another decade or more? And what are the odds that you can identify the next market-beating fund manager *before* he or she starts his or her market-beating run?

If mutual fund assets are an indicator, the majority of investors think the odds aren't that bad. Only about $200 billion of the $2.8 trillion invested in stock funds is currently held in S&P 500 index portfolios. And more than a third of that is invested in a single fund: Vanguard 500.

Still, if you decide to go with active management, ask yourself the following questions before turning your back on indexing:

1. What are the odds that a stock fund will be able to beat the market over the long term; for instance, over the next 15 to 25 years? Let's be generous and say the answer is 50-50.

2. What are the odds that the funds you select will consistently beat the market over the next 15 to 25 years? Now your ability to beat the market becomes less than a 50-50 proposition, because you have two variables at work: your ability to select above-average funds, and your fund managers' abilities to pick above-average stocks.

3. What are the odds, even if you're able to successfully select winning funds, that those funds will continue to exist in their current form over the next 15 to 25 years? Even if your fund survives, there is still the chance that it will change. Quite possibly, another fund might be merged into it, potentially changing the nature of the portfolio.

4. Even if you consistently pick funds that consistently beat the market—and those funds continue to exist over the long term— what are the odds that the fund manager responsible for those long-term returns will stick around? According to Morningstar, nearly 2500 funds experienced a manager change between the start of 2000 and the end of the third quarter of 2002 (see Figure 7-7). This means that roughly one out of every six mutual funds has a different manager today than it did at the start of the bear market. Yet, as we'll discuss in a moment, experience matters a great deal.

Once you go through these questions, it becomes clear that the odds of beating the market with actively managed funds, over time, aren't good at all. In fact, the evidence would seem to point to an unavoidable conclusion: Indexing is the best bet for most long-term investors.

Figure 7-7. Manager Changes

Since the start of 2000, nearly 2,500 funds have experienced managerial changes, a troublesome trend since studies show managers with more experience perform better—especially in bear markets.

Source: Morningstar

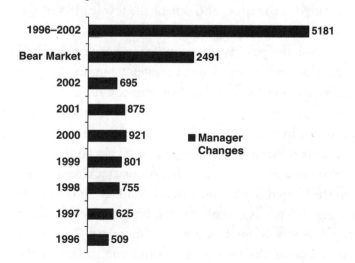

MINI MISTAKE

REFUSING TO BE AVERAGE

The Dow Jones Industrial Average, the first broad market index, was created in 1896. But it wasn't until the 1970s that the first indexed portfolios were conceived. In fact, mirroring an index and maintaining precise weightings for hundreds of stocks is surprisingly difficult to do, and it required certain technological developments to create a reliable index fund.[10] Even then, however—three-quarters of a century after the Dow's creation—the concept of simply buying and holding all the stocks in the market, without trying to beat the market, was ridiculed by Wall Street and the investment establishment.

In 1972, for instance, *Pensions & Investments* magazine awarded its "Dubious Achievement Award" to the money management firm Batterymarch Financial for even espousing indexing's virtues.[11] While Batterymarch began work on an S&P 500 portfolio for institutional investors, the first *retail* index fund, the Vanguard 500, wasn't created until Aug. 31, 1976.[12] At the time, one Boston newspaper called the notion of indexing "conceding defeat,"[13] and opponents of the strategy said it was a sure path to mediocrity. Some even referred to the Vanguard 500 as "Bogle's Folly," referring to Jack Bogle, Vanguard's chief executive at the time, and one of the few leaders of the fund industry who saw indexing's potential.[14]

Folly indeed. Over the past 25 years, indexing has proven itself not only a viable, mainstream investment strategy, but an effective one. Had you invested $1 million in the Vanguard 500 fund at inception, it would have grown to nearly $23 million by October 2001. That same $1 million, in contrast, would have become just $14 million in the average stock fund accounting for survivorship bias.

Today, there are nearly 500 stock index funds tracking myriad markets both in the United States and abroad. With around $75 billion in assets, Vanguard 500 is one of the two biggest stock funds in the world, alongside only Magellan, and the Vanguard Group has grown to become one of the two biggest fund companies in the world, alongside Fidelity.

Why has indexing triumphed? Part of it has to do with the simplicity of the concept. The surest way to own the best stocks is to own a stake in all stocks. Or as Bogle puts it: "Why look for the needle in the haystack when you can simply buy the haystack?"[15]

To be sure, index funds will *never* be the absolute best-performing portfolios over any given period of time. Since they buy and hold all the stocks in a given index, by definition index funds give you the *average* returns of all the stocks in the market. And as we noted, many actively managed stock funds have managed to beat the Vanguard 500 over the past 30 years. Among them are some of the most respected names in the mutual fund business: The Sequoia Fund, Mutual Shares, Magellan, Liberty Acorn, Davis New York Venture, Dodge & Cox Stock, and the Janus Fund. Had you invested your money in these portfolios on October 31, 1972, you'd be significantly richer.

But again the odds that a mutual fund will beat the market over the long term are slim. So too are the odds that fund investors will find those market-beating portfolios. Perhaps the best argument for indexing is that active fund management is easier said than done. There are a variety of reasons why.

The Hazards of Stock Picking

If we're to believe the argument that active fund managers add value in bear markets through superior stock selection, there should be some evidence that trading led to better returns in the recent downturn. For instance, active traders—those who turn over stocks in their portfolio more often than their peers—should have done better in recent years than less active traders. And extremely active traders should have performed even better than that. Yet it was just the opposite.

Recently, I divided Morningstar's database of domestic stock funds into four groups, based on their turnover rates. The term *turnover* refers to the speed with which funds sell their holdings. The average equity fund's turnover is about 111 percent, which means it tends to hold on to stocks for less than one year. I looked at funds with extremely low turnover rates (less than 50 percent), below-average turnover, above-average turnover, and those with extremely high turnover (more than 200 percent).

Over the past one, three, five, 10, and 15 years (through June 2002), the less a stock fund traded, the better it did. Conversely, funds that traded the most did the worst in each of those time periods (this is similar to what Barber and Odean found in their study of individual investors, discussed in the previous chapter). In fact, over the past three years through June 2002, funds with the lowest turnover made money on average, while those with highest did not (see Figure 7-8). Over the past five years, funds with turnover rates below 50 percent gained nearly 7 percent annually, a full percentage point more than funds with 200-percent-plus turnover. And over the past 15 years, funds with the lowest turnover returned 11.1 percent a year, versus 9.6 percent returns for funds that trade the most.

Experience Matters

This much can be said for active managers: The more experience they have, the better their chances of outperforming their respective indexes.

Morningstar ran an interesting study in the midst of the recent bear market. The firm's analysts examined the performance of fund

Figures 7-8. The More They Trade, the Less You Make

Stock fund performance based on turnover rates.
Source: Morningstar

Turnover Rate	1 Yr Total Return	3 Yr Ann. Return	5 Yr Ann. Return	10 Yr Ann. Return	15 Yr Ann. Return
< 50%	−8.7%	0.7%	6.7%	11.6%	11.1%
Below Average*	−9.2	0.5	6.4	11.1	10.8
Above Average*	−13.5	−0.5	5.6	9.8	9.7
> 200%	−15.2	−0.6	5.4	9.2	9.6

Data through June 2002
* Average tenure approximately 111%

managers in four groups: those who'd been with their funds for 20 years or more, those with tenures of 10 years or more, managers with above average tenure (the average is around 4 years), and managers with below average tenures.

They found that in the first 12 months of the bear market, between March 2000 and March 2001, fund managers with 20 or more years experience lost the least. Those with tenures of at least 10 years did slightly worse. And those with below average tenure did the absolute worst (see Figure 7-9). Fund managers with the most tenure lost only 5.4 percent in the first 12 months of the bear market, while the least experienced managers lost more than 20 percent. For the full calendar year 2000, the most experienced managers made money for their investors—nearly 5 percent—while the least experienced lost money.

Unfortunately for fund investors, as we noted, a large percentage of actively managed portfolios went through managerial changes in the bear market. According to Morningstar, nearly 2500 funds out of more than 13,000 replaced managers in recent years (because the stock picker left the fund, retired, or got fired). This means nearly 20 percent of mutual funds got a new manager precisely at a time when experience and tenure mattered the most.

The experience of having managed money in previous bear markets certainly helped older managers cope with the recent downturn.

Figure 7-9. Experience Matters

Fund managers with longer tenures did better during the first year of the bear market than less experienced stock pickers.
Source: Morningstar

Manager Tenure	March 2000–March 2001	2000
20 years or more	−5.4%	4.5%
10 years or more	−8.1%	4.1%
Above average*	−14.9%	0.6%
Below average*	−20.1%	−1.4%

* Average tenure is approximately 4 years.

But there could be another explanation for the outperformance of more seasoned stock pickers. According to Morningstar, managers with more tenure tend to trade stocks less frequently than newbies do. The average fund manager with 10 or more years of tenure exhibits a turnover rate of just 68 percent. In contrast, managers with less than four years of tenure tend to trade almost twice as frequently. Again, the more investors trade, the worse they tend to do.

Trading Costs Matter

A major reason why funds that trade frequently fare poorly has to do with expenses. Just as individual investors must pay commissions whenever they buy and sell stocks, mutual funds incur trading costs whenever they make a transaction. In some cases involving extremely high-turnover funds, those and other related costs, including brokerage expenses, could amount to 1 percent or even more of the fund's assets.[16] This means trading costs, in extreme cases, can be as expensive as a fund's total management fees. (Trading costs, like other expenses, are ultimately paid by fund investors.)

Keep in mind that commissions and brokerage expenses are only one component of a fund's total trading costs. Investors should also be aware of a hidden expense that funds incur when they execute their trades, which some refer to as the "market impact" cost. What it means is, a mutual fund can literally move the market in a stock as it makes a transaction, as other investors take note of what it's doing. While incrementally buying shares of a stock, a fund might inadvertently push the price of that stock higher, for example. Or, conversely, a fund might drive the price of a stock lower as it begins to sell its shares and influences the market. If a fund cannot completely and efficiently execute its buys and sells ahead of this "market impact," it could end up paying substantially more for a stock than it intended to.

Studies show that total trading costs and related expenses for large blue-chip stock funds can sometimes reduce returns by about 2 percent a year. Trading costs associated with less efficiently traded stocks, including small stocks and foreign equities, could be even higher.

At the end of the 1990s, the financial consulting firm Barra studied the impact of market costs, trading costs, commissions, and the like and determined that the so-called hurdle rate for an average actively managed fund ranges from about 1 to 4 percent. In other words, an active fund manager would have to beat the market by as much as 4 percentage points a year simply to keep up with the indexes.

Expenses Matter

Basic management fees are another reason active managers have such a hard time beating the market, as we discussed in *Mistake 2: Getting Fee'd Up*. Because a fund's expenses are deducted from its returns, high fees make it that much harder for an actively managed portfolio to beat the index. In fact, academic research shows that management expenses, for this very reason, are one of the biggest determinants of a fund's long-term relative performance.

Recently, I studied the performance of actively managed funds with different expense ratios, using Morningstar's database of domestic stock portfolios. I divided U.S. stock funds into four groups: those with extremely low expense ratios (less than 0.5 percent of assets), funds with expense ratios between 0.5 and 1 percent, funds with expense ratios between 1 and 2 percent, and funds with expense ratios of 2 percent or higher. Over the past one, three, five, 10, and 15 years (through June 2002), the lowest-cost funds (those with expense ratios of less than 0.5 percent) consistently did the best. Meanwhile, the most expensive funds—those that charge 2 percent of assets or more—did the worst in each of those time periods.

Over the past three years, stock funds charging less than 0.5 percent fell 7.2 percent a year on average. But funds charging more than 2 percent in fees tumbled nearly 9 percent a year during that stretch. Over the past decade, low-cost funds have returned 9.1 percent a year, while high-cost funds delivered less than 5 percent. And over the past 15 years, low-cost funds gained 9.4 percent, more than double what high-cost funds returned (see Figure 7-10).

Figure 7-10. Pay for Performance

The lower a stock fund's expenses, the better its performance tends to be over time. (Figures are through June 2002.)
Source: Morningstar

Expense Ratio	1 YR	3 YR	5 YR	10 YR	15 YR
<0.5%	–13.3%	–7.2%	–0.4%	9.1%	9.4%
>0.5% to <1%	–15.1	–7.5	–1.0	8.5	8.6
>1% to <2%	–15.5	–7.2	–1.5	7.9	8.0
>2%	–17.0	–8.7	–3.6	4.6	4.1

Clearly, cheaper funds tend to do better. This is a big reason why index funds do so well so often. The average equity fund's annual expense ratio, according to the Investment Company Institute, is 1.28 percent of assets. By comparison, the average index fund, which doesn't trade as often and doesn't have to pay for research, is just 0.75 percent, according to Morningstar. Better still, many index funds are significantly cheaper than that. As we discussed, Vanguard 500's expense ratio is only 0.18 percent, which means that instead of paying $128 a year for every $10,000 you invest in an actively managed fund, you only pay $18 a year. If you invest in the Vanguard 500 fund through its so-called admiral shares (which require a $250,000 minimum investment), your expense ratio would drop even further—to 0.12 percent.

Taxes Matter

While fees are one of the biggest determinants of a fund's performance, taxes are the single largest expense for mutual fund investors. They eat up as much as 2.5 percentage points of a fund's returns, according to a recent study by the Vanguard Group.[17] It's another reason investors should consider indexing.

There are two basic ways that taxes are triggered in a fund: (1) whenever individual investors sell their shares of the fund at a profit, and (2) whenever fund managers realize capital gains by selling stocks within the portfolio at a profit. Either way, the investor pays the tax bill.

By law, funds must distribute to their shareholders all of the capital gains they realize within that year. Funds typically pass along those gains between October and December, which is one reason why many fund investors wait until the start of a new year to buy a fund—that way, they don't step into an immediate tax bill.

Taxable distributions are a significantly larger problem for actively managed funds than index portfolios, because of their higher turnover rates. A generation ago, the average actively managed stock fund used to turn over less than a third of its portfolio each year—that is, funds used to hold stocks for three years or more. Today, the average turnover rate is more than 100 percent, which means the typical fund manager holds stocks for less than a year. In contrast, an S&P 500 index fund has a turnover rate of just 4 percent. The more a fund trades, the more likely it is to realize capital gains. Though capital gains taxes have become less of an issue in the bear market—since many funds are sitting on huge losses and because the capital gains tax was recently lowered—taxes should still be a huge concern for fund investors.

How big? Bogle notes that in the 15 years through June 30, 1998, the average actively managed portfolio earned annualized returns of 13.6 percent. But *after* taxes, the real return enjoyed by fund investors was just 10.8 percent. Because index funds don't trade in and out of stocks, their after-tax returns were considerably higher (see Figure 7-11). In fact, after taxes, the average index fund delivered annual returns of *15 percent* during this same time period. Had you invested $100,000 in an index fund for these 15 years, you would have turned your original investment into $813,000 after taxes, fees, and expenses. In comparison, after taxes, fees, and expenses, a $100,000 investment in the average actively managed stock fund would have grown to just $465,000.

The longer the time horizon, the worse the case for active management. Between 1950 and 1999, a $1000 investment in an S&P 500 fund would have grown to $471,000 after expenses, and $276,000 after expenses and taxes. By comparison, that same $1000 would have become just $65,000, after taxes and fees, in an average actively managed fund[18] (see Figures 7-12 and 7-13).

Figure 7-11. Tax-Advantaged Investing

Because index funds rarely trade stocks, their after-tax
returns are significantly better than those of actively
managed stock funds, which frequently realize capital
gains as they flip their holdings. Figures shown represent
annual returns for 15 years ended June 1998.
Source: John Bogle, Common Sense on Mutual Funds

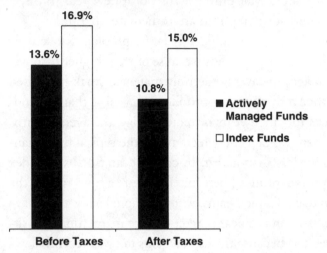

Figure 7-12. The Index Advantage, 1950–1999

For the past half century, actively managed stock funds
have badly trailed the overall stock market, largely due
to expenses.
*Source: John Bogle, Vanguard Group, The Bogle Financial Markets
Research Center*

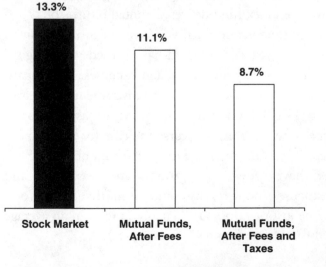

Figure 7-13. The Index Advantage, 1950–1999

The growth of $1000 invested in index funds and actively managed stock mutual funds over the past half century.
Source: John Bogle, Vanguard Group, The Bogle Financial Markets Research Center

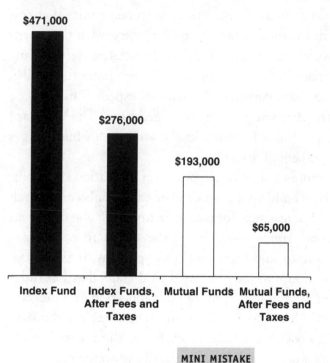

$471,000 — Index Fund

$276,000 — Index Funds, After Fees and Taxes

$193,000 — Mutual Funds

$65,000 — Mutual Funds, After Fees and Taxes

MINI MISTAKE

INDEXING ONLY THE S&P 500

So the smartest thing to do would be to go with an S&P 500 fund, right? Not necessarily. Though an S&P 500 index fund would be a better bet than an actively managed portfolio, the S&P 500 is a *large stock* index. It represents only the 500 biggest and most established companies in the U.S. market.

To be sure, those 500 large companies make up about three-quarters of the total capitalization of the U.S. stock market. But the index excludes the remaining 25 percent, made up of medium-sized companies (such as the Washington Post Co. and Coach) and small stocks (like Western Digital or Del Monte Foods). And as we discussed, there are times in the market when smaller companies outperform large ones, sometimes for long stretches. Small stocks, for instance, beat large-caps throughout the mid-1970s, in the early 1990s, and in the recent bear market.

An alternative would be to go with a single fund that tracks a total U.S. stock market index such as the Wilshire 5000. Despite its name, the Wilshire 5000 consists of more than 6500 companies that collectively represent the total domestic stock market, with the exception of penny stocks and the like. Wilshire Associates, the company that created the index in the 1970s, oversees its own index fund called the Wilshire 5000 Index Portfolio. But with an expense ratio of 0.64 percent, it isn't the cheapest passively managed fund. The Vanguard Total Stock Market Index fund tracks the same index but charges fees of only 0.2 percent of assets.

If you want more control over your asset allocation decisions, another option is to build your own diversified portfolio using multiple index funds. For instance, for your core holdings, you can invest the majority of your equity allocation in the Vanguard 500. If you then want exposure to mid-caps, you could put, say, 15 percent of your equity allocation into the Vanguard Mid Capitalization Index fund. Finally, you can put 10 percent of your allocation into the Vanguard Small Cap Index fund. In effect, this would achieve the same goal as owning the Vanguard Total Stock Market Index, but would give you more control over rebalancing decisions over time.

If you want even more control, you can now index specific styles, such as growth and value, as well as specific sectors of the economy. Barclays Global Investors has created so-called exchange-traded funds, or ETFs, which index the energy, financial services, health care, real estate, technology, telecommunications, and utilities sectors, among others. Barclays also offers ETFs, under the brandname iShares, which track broader and more traditional benchmarks like the S&P 500, the S&P 600, the Russell 2000, and the Dow Jones total market index.

An ETF is a hybrid investment that is part stock and part fund. Like a mutual fund, an ETF allows shareholders to invest in a basket of companies all at once. However, unlike a traditional fund, ETF shares are traded on an exchange (primarily the American Stock

Exchange) like an individual stock and therefore can be bought and sold in the middle of the trading day. Mutual fund shares, by contrast, can only be purchased or redeemed through the fund company at the day's closing price.

Because you'll have to pay brokerage commissions everytime you buy and sell an ETF like you would a stock, ETFs are *not* a good vehicle for dollar-cost averaging. However, because many exchange-traded funds come with relatively low annual fees—Barclays' S&P 500 ETF, for example, charges annual expenses of just 0.09 percent of assets, or half the cost of the Vanguard 500—they are an attractive alternative for investors who want to put a lump sum of money to work in the market all at once.

You can also use index funds—traditional ones and ETFs—to gain exposure to foreign and fixed-income markets as well. There are dozens of fixed-income index funds available to individual investors, and their big advantage is costs. While the average bond fund charges annual expenses of 0.90 percent of assets, the typical bond index portfolio charges about a third as much in annual fees. And the Vanguard Total Bond Market Index fund sports an expense ratio of only 0.22 percent. This might explain why $1 million invested in an average bond fund in 1986 grew to $2.7 million by October 2001, according to Vanguard research. But that same $1 million invested in a bond *index* fund swelled to $3.1 million.

Bottom Line

If there's any doubt about the relative advantages of indexing, consider this fact: Had you invested $10,000 in an index fund that tracks the Wilshire 5000 in 1981, you would have amassed nearly $153,000 by 2001. Had you invested that same $10,000 in the average actively managed mutual fund, you'd have earned almost $100,000 less.

For some investors, the idea of simply settling for average returns is unappealing. Who wants to think of themselves as *average*? But when you crunch the numbers, what's truly unappealing is the performance of actively managed funds over long periods of time. Though it is entirely possible to find actively managed portfolios that beat the market over the long term, the odds of identifying such funds are stacked against you because so much is stacked against active management. Actively managed funds are expensive to run. They incur steep trading costs. They trade more frequently than index portfolios, and high-turnover funds are inefficient when it comes to fees and taxes. Index funds, on the other hand, are cheap, tax-efficient, and simple to understand.

Even if you think you can beat the market with your actively managed funds this year, ask yourself this: What are the odds your funds can beat the market consistently over time? And what are the odds that you can consistently pick such funds over time? Even if you have several above-average funds in your portfolio, chances are you own other funds that are doing worse than average. In the end, it all cancels out. Again, to borrow a phrase from Bogle: "Why look for a needle in the haystack when you can simply own the haystack?"

Checklist: Things to Do

❑   Don't assume actively managed funds can beat the indexes in downturns.

❑   Even if you go with an active manager, stick with low-cost, low-turnover funds.

❑   Play the averages by indexing your portfolio.

❑   Consider a Wilshire 5000 fund over an S&P 500 portfolio.

❑   Even if you choose an index fund, don't pay more than you have to in fees.

MONEY MISTAKE 8

INVESTING IN
WHAT YOU KNOW

Taking an Arm's Length Approach

In the late 1980s, Peter Lynch, former manager of the Fidelity Magellan fund, popularized the notion of "investing in what you know." And given his credentials—Lynch generated returns of 2740 percent for his shareholders between May 1, 1977, and June 1, 1990, versus the S&P's 556-percent rise —this notion of using "what you already know to make money in the market" had tremendous credibility. It was the literal inspiration for the investment club craze of the 1990s. It was the oft-repeated mantra of the do-it-yourself investor movement.

It helped that this populist strategy was simple to understand. It also helped that investing in what you know became popular during the biggest bull market in modern history, a market in which a monkey throwing darts at stock tables could often pick better investments than professional money managers.[1] But taking this seemingly innocuous piece of advice *too much* to heart—or misinterpreting it, which many of us have done—has proven a big mistake. In fact, it's one that tens of thousands of investors learned the hard way at the end of the bull market, as many of the bluest of blue-chip companies—like Lucent, Cisco Systems, General Electric, Intel, and McDonald's—fell on hard times.

The theory itself goes something like this: As investors, we're faced with hundreds if not thousands of choices of where to put our money to work. There are about 10,000 publicly traded stocks in the U.S. market alone, and even more mutual funds—more than 13,000—to choose from. So where to begin? Why not start from your own experiences? That is, start investigating those companies that produce the goods and services you buy and use every day.

If you take your kids to McDonald's every week, use your investigative skills to determine whether the company is doing well. How was business when you were last in the restaurant? Was it cleaner than you expected? Were the lines longer than before? Ask yourself why you're taking your kids to that particular fast-food restaurant in the first place, instead of to Burger King or to Wendy's. Turn what you and all other Americans are good at—being a consumer—from a liability into an asset.

"The best place to begin looking for the tenbagger is close to home—if not in the backyard then down at the shopping mall, and especially wherever you happen to work," Lynch wrote in his bestselling book, *One Up on Wall Street*. He added:

> ... people who make things, sell things, clean things, or analyze things encounter numerous stock-picking opportunities ... You don't have to be Steven Spielberg to know that some new blockbuster, or string of blockbusters, is going to give a significant boost to the earnings of Paramount or Orion Pictures. You could be an actor, an extra, a director, a stuntman, a lawyer, a gaffer, the makeup person, or the usher at a local cinema, where the

standing-room-only crowds six weeks in a row inspire you to investigate the pros and cons of investing in Orion's stock. Maybe you're a teacher and the school board chooses your school to test a new gizmo that takes attendance, saving the teachers thousands of wasted hours counting heads. "Who makes this gizmo?" is the first question I'd ask.[2]

A few years later, in his follow-up bestseller, *Beating the Street*, Lynch noted that his favorite source for new investing ideas was the Burlington Mall. He talked about how a number of popular retailers, like Home Depot, the Limited, the Gap, and Wal-Mart, were among the biggest winners in the stock market in the late 1980s— and that shoppers could easily have spotted them years before, if only they were paying attention. "As an investment strategy," he wrote, "hanging out at the mall is far superior to taking a stockbroker's advice on faith or combing the financial press for the latest tips. Many of the biggest gainers of all time come from the places that millions of consumers visit all the time."[3]

On paper, this strategy makes a lot of sense. After all, why invest in a company whose business model you don't quite understand when you can invest in a more familiar firm whose products you use and whose "story" you already know? Is it any wonder, then, that some of the biggest holdings among the nation's investment clubs are companies that produce goods and services Main Street America has fallen in love with? According to the National Association of Investors Corporation, the most popular stocks among investment club portfolios have been familiar names like Intel, Home Depot, Dell Computer, Starbucks, Wal-Mart, and PepsiCo.

MINI MISTAKE

OVERESTIMATING YOUR CIRCLE OF COMPETENCE

The reality, unfortunately, isn't that simple. There's a huge difference between what we *think* we know about a company and what we actually know. Indeed, there's a real question as to whether we can ever know everything we need to know about a stock, as the Wall Street accounting scandals in recent years demonstrated.

Take Enron. At the start of the decade, the energy giant was a favored holding of many growth stock funds and was among the top 100 stocks held by investment clubs nationwide (along with other controversial companies including Qwest and Tyco). Yet even professional equity analysts and money managers didn't know what was going on at the company, despite having access to its books and its executives, until it was too late. If you recall, the majority of Wall Street analysts who covered Enron had either a "strong buy," or a "buy" rating on the troubled energy firm's shares just months before the company filed for bankruptcy. Many analysts maintained their positive outlook on the stock even after discovering the firm's off-balance sheet entities, which were used to hide the company's debt. Meanwhile, the major credit-rating agencies didn't downgrade Enron's bonds to "junk" status until *days* before the company sought bankruptcy protection in December 2001.

"Rarely have so many analysts liked a stock they concede they know so little about," the *Wall Street Journal* wrote in October 2001.[4] *Business Week* summed it up this way: "In hindsight, it sure looks as though Enron's top management was asleep at the wheel or had little supervision, as they crafted private partnerships that allowed the company to move millions of dollars of debt off its balance sheet. But truth is, this sad saga has no shortage of culprits—accountants, the company's board, stock analysts, shareholders, and the press all bear some of the responsibility for not realizing sooner that something untoward was going on at Enron."[5]

Yet it wasn't just Enron. Tyco International, which owns ADT, a popular home-security business, was another company that professionals and amateurs alike professed to know. But as with Enron, investors didn't learn what was really going on at the conglomerate until state and federal regulators got involved. Eventually, the Securities and Exchange Commission and the Manhattan district attorney filed charges against Tyco's former executives, accusing them of stealing tens of millions of dollars from the company. But by then it was too late. Many investors rode the stock down from its high of $60 in late 2001 to $15 a share in early 2002.[6]

The natural human tendency is to think we know more about a stock than we really do—and to think that this supposed knowledge is the reason for our success. Once again, optimism is the culprit. According to Mark Riepe, vice president for investment research at Charles Schwab, and Princeton psychology professor Daniel Kahneman, overly optimistic investors are "prone to an illusion of control. They tend to underestimate the role of chance in human affairs and to misperceive games of chance as games of skill. The combination of overconfidence and optimism is a potent brew, which causes people to overestimate their knowledge, underestimate risks, and exaggerate their ability to control events."[7]

Knowing What You Don't Know

Often, investors are successful not because they know so much, but because they realize the limitations of their knowledge, time, and analytical skills. Warren Buffett, arguably the most successful investor in American history, and the second-richest man in the country, has a saying: The size of your "circle of competence" is not very important. "Knowing its boundaries, however, is vital."[8]

For instance, Buffett purposefully avoided technology stocks in general and Internet stocks in particular during the new economy bubble of the late 1990s because, he says, he simply didn't understand the underlying technology. "It's beyond me," he said at the time.[9] Instead, he stuck with companies whose business models he thought he could understand, old economy names like Dairy Queen, Geico, and See's Candies, which propelled his portfolio for years.

This strategy seemed to betray Buffet in 1999, when his company, Berkshire Hathaway, saw its investments *lose* 22 percent of their value. Meanwhile, the average domestic stock fund soared more than 20 percent and the average technology fund rose 134 percent. Some wondered whether Buffett's old-fashioned ways could work in the new economy. The media even began to question whether he had lost his Midas touch.[10]

He hadn't. The following years proved that Buffett's discipline and patience had been warranted. Berkshire Hathaway beat its peers and the overall stock market throughout the bear market, posting solid gains in 2000 and 2001. In fact, Berkshire shares rose nearly 30 percent in 2000 when the S&P lost around 9 percent. By being patient with his stocks and by sticking to those companies within his "circle of competence," Buffett managed to make money during the bear market when the vast majority of investors did not.

The questions we should all ask ourselves are: Do I have the same kind of discipline and self-awareness that Buffett has? Do I have his stock-picking skills? And most important, do I know the boundaries of *my* circle of competence?

Clearly, some of us have the skills and resources to be very successful stock pickers. But there's no shame in leaving those decisions up to professionals, be it investment planners or mutual funds. An easy option, as we discussed, is to simply play the averages by investing in a diversified basket of stocks that mirror a broad stock index. By choosing this option, you don't have to worry about what you know or don't. You simply invest in a cross section of companies and industries with the hope that more stocks will succeed than fail.

In the best of all possible worlds, "investing in what you know" not only makes good investment sense, it's common sense. Given the choice between investing in something you're familiar with and something you're not, of course it makes more sense to go with the former. But we don't live in the best of all possible worlds. We live in the real world, where we have to deal with our own emotional shortcomings. And in the real world, we are far more likely to be dispassionate—and therefore objective and disciplined—about a company we don't have emotional ties to. Yet every year, tens of thousands of us take Lynch's notion to heart and take the strategy to its natural though dangerous conclusion: by loading up on company stock.

LOADING UP ON COMPANY STOCK

If in theory it makes sense to invest in what we know, and the company most of us know best is the firm we work for, logic would dictate that we should invest most of our money in our employer's stock. That's certainly the conclusion many 401(k) investors came to in recent years—with disastrous consequences.

We may shop at Wal-Mart, hang out at Starbucks, and buy Procter & Gamble products. But as employees, we're privy to information about our own companies that outsiders aren't. We receive memos announcing new ventures and investments. We talk to supervisors who in theory know the financial health and trends of the firm. We know when our employer is hiring and when it's firing. We know if the Christmas bonuses are larger than expected or if they're smaller. We can tell if the company is wasteful or efficient based on the little things, like whether employees are docked for making long distance phone calls or whether the company supplies the staff with free coffee.

Indeed, Lynch argued that top executives of a company aren't the only ones who should be able to spot such opportunities. For instance, in describing the success of Pep Boys, an auto parts retailer, he wrote: "Executives at Pep Boys, clerks at Pep Boys, lawyers and accountants, suppliers of Pep Boys, the firm that did the advertising, sign painters, building contractors for the new stores, and even the people who washed the floors all must have observed Pep Boys' success."[11]

Yet how much do workers actually know? Throughout the corporate scandals of 2001 and 2002, the chairmen and chief executive officers at troubled firms like Enron and WorldCom pleaded ignorance when it came to key facts, such as the accounting practices that roiled their own companies. They blamed those instead on their financial officers, their auditors, or the auditing committees. If these CEOs were in fact telling the truth, and didn't know what was going on at the companies they ran, how can low- and mid-level workers ever know what's going on at their firms? And if the CEOs were lying, how can workers trust information about their employers, whether the information comes in the form of a memo, an e-mail, or in government filings?

The fact is, workers don't know nearly as much about their own companies as they think they know. Surveys indicate that three-quarters of us don't even know what kind of insurance coverage we get through our employers. Most of us don't know who the chief financial officer is at our company. So what's the likelihood that we know what's going on with our company's financials? "Investors who chant this mantra ['invest in what you know'] don't research a stock anywhere near as thoroughly as would a Lynch or a Buffett," argues John Rekenthaler, director of research for the fund-tracking firm Morningstar. "They may know a little bit about the product and industry, but in general they don't have a clue about buyer/supplier power, competitive restraints, the financials, and so forth."[12]

Lynch himself stressed the importance of doing some old-fashioned shoe-leather research. He noted that "however a stock has come to your attention, whether via the office, the shopping mall, something you ate, something you bought, or something you heard from your broker, your mother-in-law, or even from Ivan Boesky's parole officer, the discovery is not a buy signal."[13]

You have to dig deeper. You have to pore over the company's financials: its balance sheet, income statement, and statement of cash flows, all of which are now easily available on the Web. And in addition to its growth characteristics, you have to assess a stock's valuation: whether a promising stock is cheap or expensive at its current price. Depending on the company or industry, investors can do this by comparing a stock's price relative to the underlying firm's earnings per share or assets per share. "Investing without research," Lynch says, "is like playing stud poker and never looking at the cards."[14]

Forgetting the Lessons of Enron

Unfortunately, hundreds of thousands of workers are in fact investing large amounts of their wealth into their companies without doing much homework. If the Enron scandal showed us anything, it was the danger of putting too much 401(k) money into company stock. Thousands of Enron employees lost hundreds of millions of dollars starting in 2001, when the energy company's shares plummeted from about $85 at its peak to less than 10 cents. A $1 million retirement account in Enron stock shrunk to around $1000 virtually overnight. What's more, these same workers also lost their jobs, their health insurance, and even their life insurance coverage—which is a big reason why you shouldn't have so many of your financial eggs in one basket.

Yet little has changed on this front.[15] Though financial planners had hoped that the Enron collapse would scare 401(k) investors straight, workers continue to be overly optimistic about their companies' fortunes. How else can you explain the fact that 401(k) investors continue to rate company stock as a "safer" investment option than diversified domestic stock funds or diversified foreign stock funds?

Over the past decade, John Hancock Financial Services has conducted routine surveys of participants in 401(k)s and other "defined contribution" retirement plans. In seven such surveys since the early 1990s, company stock was perceived by investors to be safer than *diversified* equity funds, which often hold more than 100 different securities. Even more startling is the fact that while 401(k) investors think equity funds are riskier now than they were in the late 1990s, many of us think company stock is actually *safer* today than it was in 2001, before the Enron scandal.

Plan participants surveyed by John Hancock in 2002 were asked to rate different types of investment options within their 401(k) on a scale of 1 to 5, with 1 meaning the investment has no risk and 5 meaning very high risk. Foreign stock funds were rated 4.1. Domestic stock funds were rated 3.6. Meanwhile, investors rated company stock 3.1, down from 3.2 in 2001 (see Figure 8-1).

Investors believe owning company stock is barely riskier than investing in a balanced fund—a type of fund that invests nearly half of its money in *bonds*. Yet many individual stocks lost half or even 75 percent of their value during the recent bear market. Some

Figure 8-1. Understanding Risk of Company Stock

Despite recent disasters in company stock, investors today actually perceive company shares to be a safer investment than they did in 2001. Risk levels are on a scale of 1 to 5, with 1 meaning "no risk" and 5 meaning "very high risk."
Source: John Hancock

Year	Company Stock	Domestic Stock Fund	Foreign Stock Fund	Balanced Funds
1995	3.2	3.5	3.8	2.7
1997	3.2	3.4	3.8	2.7
1999	3.1	3.7	4.0	2.7
2001	3.2	3.6	4.0	2.8
2002	3.1	3.6	4.1	2.8

dropped more than 99 percent. In contrast, the average balanced fund lost only about 2.5 percent of its value a year over the past three years ended May 2003. "There appears to be the attitude, 'That may have happened at Enron, but it wouldn't happen at my company,'" says Wayne Gates, who runs the survey for John Hancock.[16] This is an example, he adds, of what's often termed the "halo effect of company stock."

At the start of the bear market, in March 2000, about 24 cents of every dollar in a 401(k) was invested in company stock, according to Hewitt Associates, an employee benefits consulting firm that tracks 401(k) behavior. Two and a half years later, in September 2002, nearly 25 cents of every 401(k) dollar was held in company stock (see Figures 8-2 and 8-3). While overall equity allocations fell, investments in company stock ironically rose after Enron blew up.

The Hewitt numbers reflect an estimate of the overall 401(k) marketplace. But not all 401(k)s offer company stock. Some companies are privately held, with no publicly traded shares to dole out to workers. In other cases, a firm may choose not to make company stock available to employees as an investment option, believing that

Figure 8-2. 401(k) Asset Allocation, March 2000

401(k) investors are still investing roughly the same percentage of their retirement accounts in company stock than they did at the start of the bear market. The average asset allocation of 401(k) investors before the bear market.
Source: Hewitt Associates

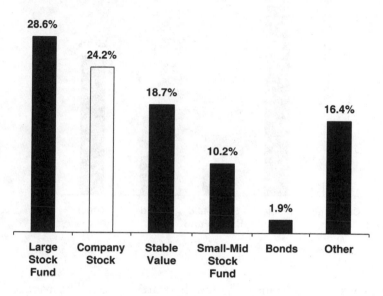

workers can simply purchase it on their own. Recently, a number of firms like AMR, parent company of American Airlines, stopped letting 401(k) participants invest in company stock, because they considered it too risky for retirement investors.[17] AMR officials started to restrict employees from investing in company shares in February 2003, as the carrier was struggling to avoid bankruptcy.

But in 401(k) plans that allow workers to invest in company stock and that also make matching contributions to workers' accounts in the form of company stock, the situation is much more dire. According to the Investment Company Institute and the Employee Benefit Research Institute, workers with such 401(k)s are investing nearly 53 percent of their retirement accounts in their employer's stock.[18] The average 30-something in these plans had more than 58 percent of his or her money tied up in company stock at the start of the decade. Even among 60-somethings, who have a shorter time horizon to invest and

Figure 8-3. 401(k) Asset Allocation, September 2002

Retirement investors' asset allocation two and a half years into the bear market.
Source: Hewitt Associates

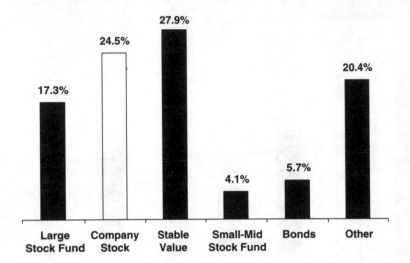

thus a far lower risk tolerance, the numbers aren't good. The average 60-something in this type of 401(k) had more than 41 cents of every dollar invested in his or her employer. That's nearly twice as much money as they had in investments designed to preserve assets, such as bond funds and guaranteed investment contracts (see Figure 8-4).

At some of the nation's largest corporations, like Procter & Gamble, Coca-Cola, Pfizer, Anheuser-Busch, Sherwin-Williams, and Abbott Laboratories, more than 70 cents of every dollar invested in company-sponsored 401(k) plans in 2001 and 2002 was invested in company stock, according to *DC Plan Investing*, a trade publication[19] (see Figure 8-5). This seems to be consistent with a recent Hewitt study, which found that 29 percent of all 401(k) participants held more than 75 percent of their retirement assets in their company stock and that 15 percent held *all* of their nest eggs in shares of their employers. Even more troubling, a third of retirement savers age 60 or older held three-quarters or more of their savings in company stock and nearly 20 percent of older workers put all their savings in those shares.

Figure 8-4. Company Stock Time Bomb

Asset allocation strategies of 401(k) investors in 2000 by age.*
Source: Employee Benefit Research Institute and Investment Company Institute

	Co. Stock	Stock Fund	Balanced Fund	Bond Fund	Money Fund	GICs**
20s	**53.7**	31.8	5.0	0.6	3.1	3.6
30s	**58.4**	27.9	4.7	0.6	1.8	4.9
40s	**56.9**	26.0	4.7	0.9	2.8	6.4
50s	**50.9**	26.2	5.5	1.4	3.6	10.1
60s	**41.4**	25.0	6.3	2.3	7.2	15.3
Total	**52.9**	26.2	5.2	1.2	3.5	8.8

*Among plans that allow both employee and employer contributions, and among plans that have company stock as an investment option
** GICs are guaranteed investment contracts (debt that comes with an insurance contract that promises a set rate of interest).

To be sure, no one complained when blue-chip stocks like Coke or Pfizer were skyrocketing in the 1990s. But as we discussed in an earlier chapter, it's important not to "anchor" your expectations to past performance.

General Electric employees, who held more than two-thirds of their 401(k) in company stock in 2001, found this out the hard way. After soaring 41 percent in 1998 and 54 percent in '99, GE shares fell 6 percent in 2000, 15 percent in 2001, and nearly 38 percent in 2002. In another example, McDonald's employees, who had almost 75 percent of their retirement assets in company stock in 2001, saw the value of the stock nearly cut in half in the bear market. And it was worse at Sprint. The long-distance giant saw its stock fall around 70 percent in the first year of the bear market. Yet in that year, about half of Sprint workers' 401(k)s were invested in company stock.

Ironically, federal law prohibits old-fashioned traditional pensions—where *employers* are responsible for managing investments—from investing more than 10 percent of their money in company shares. But at the time of this writing, there was no such restriction for company stock in 401(k) plans.

401(k) Risks

For some of us, the risk of company stock in our 401(k)s is heightened by the fact that our employers make matching contributions to

Figure 8-5. 401(k) Plans Drowning in Company Stock

Source: DC Plan Investing

Company	% of Plan Assets in Co. Stock*
Procter & Gamble	96.2%
Sherwin-Williams	91.6
Abbott Laboratories	90.2
Pfizer	89.0
Dell Computer	88.2
Anheuser-Busch	81.6
Coca-Cola	80.8
BB&T	80.6
Progressive Corp.	80.4
May Department Stores	78.0
McDonald's	74.3
McKesson HBOC	72.0
Marsh & McLennan	72.0
Duke Energy	71.3
Kroger	70.5

*Data as of February 20, 2001

our accounts using those same shares. In addition to the money workers put into their 401(k)s through payroll deductions, many companies contribute their own money into these accounts, often as an incentive to get workers to participate. Studies show that the vast majority of companies that sponsor 401(k)s make matching contributions. According to a survey by the consulting firm Buck Consultants, 91 percent of companies with 401(k) plans matched employee contributions in 2002. There are myriad ways employers design this match, but the typical arrangement works out to around 50 cents for every dollar workers contribute, up to around 6 percent of salary deferral.

Hundreds of companies make matching contributions not with cash, but with their stock. There are a variety of reasons why they do this. Matching with stock allows the firm to free up more of its cash for other purposes. It also gives the firm more say as to who owns its shares. In plans where company stock is an investment option, one-third of those firms make matching contributions using their own shares.[20] The problem is, the vast majority of these plans—85 percent by one count—place some restrictions on the worker's ability to sell out of those shares.[21] In some cases, only workers 50 or older can sell out of company stock that was given to them via a 401(k) match. Other plans say you have to be 55 years old to sell. And still others specify a set number of years that have to pass before workers are eligible to transfer their stake into other, safer investments.

And yet, some workers don't even realize that matching contributions are being made in company stock. Of course, if you don't know this and you invest even more money in company stock through your own 401(k) contributions, you could find yourself dangerously overloaded not just in equities, but in shares of a single firm. Investing your contributions in company stock in a plan that matches with company shares is doubling up on an already dangerous bet.

Company stock is all the more dangerous in a 401(k) for another reason: Investors are not allowed to "harvest" losses inside tax-deferred investment accounts such as 401(k)s and IRAs because those accounts are already tax-favored. In comparison, if you invest in company stock outside your tax-deferred retirement account, you at least have a safety net to fall back on. Any losses suffered in a taxable account can be realized and used to offset capital gains elsewhere in your portfolio, thereby lowering your tax bill. In effect, the IRS assumes some of the risk of investing in the stock in an outside account.

Financial planners counsel against putting more than 20 percent of your investments in any single stock. It's even more dangerous to invest such a large percentage of your portfolio in your employer's stock. Why? Diversification is the secret to a sound personal financial plan, just as it's key to solid investment returns. Most workers already owe their salaries, life insurance, medical insurance, dental care, disability coverage, and tuition benefits to the company they work for. Why add investment success and retirement savings to that list?

The strange thing is that when it comes to other aspects of our financial lives, we know not to put all our eggs in one basket. Most households, as we discussed in "Mistake 2: Getting Fee'd Up," have relationships with three or more banks largely because they don't feel

---

TIP: If you participate in a 401(k) where matching contributions are made with company stock, don't invest your own payroll deductions in employer shares. At the very least, limit the amount you proactively invest in the stock. This is what got so many Enron workers in trouble.

While what happened at Enron was tragic, many workers could have easily avoided their fate. Some who lost their life savings were old enough to sell out of their Enron stock. I recall one such employee who retired with more than $900,000 in his account. No one forced him to invest any of his own money in Enron, yet he chose to put 100 percent of his nest egg in the stock, only to see it collapse to less than $10,000. "Enron was doing so much better than most other stocks that it looked like a much better investment," he said.[22]

comfortable entrusting all of their assets to a single company.[23] Yet many of us feel perfectly comfortable entrusting virtually everything—our salaries, our benefits, our retiree health insurance, and our retirement savings—to companies that have absolutely no compunction about laying us off at the first sign of trouble.

Bottom Line

Why do we have such a fascination with company stock? Academic research shows that workers are far more likely to invest in company stock if their employers match their 401(k)s with it. "Employees view this as implicit advice and guidance from the company" that the investment is safe, says UCLA's Shlomo Benartzi.[24]

In other words, investors feel even more confident about investing in "what they know" because the company's decision to match with the stock is viewed as an endorsement of it. In the case of Enron, company executives told their workers that it was not only safe to invest more of their 401(k) money in company stock, but to invest *all* of their 401(k) assets in Enron. What those workers didn't know at the time, and that we of course know now, was that some of the same corporate executives recommending this investment were selling their own holdings.

Investing in what you know may seem a relatively safe strategy, but it's only safe insofar as you do your homework. Peter Lynch never argued that workers should invest all of their money in any company, let alone their employer stock. Paying attention to trends at the shopping mall, at the grocery store, or at your own company can be useful, he said, in creating a short list of investments to consider. But as he said in his book, even if a particular company you spot seems like a good investment, it still doesn't mean you should buy it. It's a lesson all of us should heed.

Checklist: Things to Do

❑   Investigate companies you know.

❑   But do your homework. Don't just buy a stock because you "know" a company's products.

❑   Invest no more than 20 percent of your total portfolio in company stock.

❑   Find out if your employer makes matching contributions to your 401(k) using company stock.

❑   If you work for such a company, find out exactly when and how you can diversify out of those holdings.

❑   Avoid investing your 401(k) contributions in company stock if your employer matches with company stock.

9

UNDERFUNDING
YOUR PENSIONS

Taking Full Advantage of
Your Retirement Accounts

A few years ago, before the onset of the bear market, Wall Street watchers and retirement experts began to worry. What if the stock market, which at that time had never lost money since the first 401(k) plan was created in 1981, fell? And what if stock prices didn't just fall for a week or a month or a quarter, but fell month in and month out, year in and year out, for an extended period of time?

In late 1997, William Arnone, a retirement plan expert at Ernst & Young, described the financial community's concerns this way: "Most 401(k) plan participants have no recollection of the bear prowl of 1973–74. Many were not even exposed to the bear growl of late 1987. Most only know the good times of the recent past, where stock prices keep going higher and corrections end quickly."[1] How would investors react to a real, and really long, bear market?

Three years into this bear market, we found out the answer. It turns out that the 45 million Americans who participate in company-sponsored 401(k) retirement accounts largely did *not* react. The vast majority of us who were contributing to our 401(k)s before the bear market continue to contribute to them today.

To be sure, there is ample anecdotal evidence that some workers have begun to cut back— or turn their backs—on their retirement plans.[2] A study by the consulting firm Spectrem Group found that workers on average were contributing about 7 percent of their paychecks into their plans in 2002, down from more than 8 percent in 1999.[3] But among working class and middle class workers, contribution rates have fallen only slightly.[4]

And while one recent survey of 401(k) plans showed that the average participation rate—the percentage of workers eligible to contribute to a 401(k) who do—had fallen to the lowest levels in more than a decade,[5] a separate survey by the Profit Sharing/401(k) Council of America showed that participation rates stood at around 78 percent.[6] Though that's still down from late-'90s levels, it still means that the vast majority of all workers eligible to participate in self-directed retirement accounts take advantage of them. As one industry official said to me: "If ten years ago you would have told people that three-quarters of participants would still be in their 401(k) plans, at this point, after this kind of bear market, they would have been astounded. There was a real consensus that this type of bad news would have led to a complete collapse in the system."

The big fear in the late '90s was that a bear market would send retirement investors heading for the exits, fleeing or possibly even liquidating their tax-advantaged investment accounts just when they needed them the most. Yet only a minority of retirement investors— 19.5 percent, to be exact—made even one trade in their 401(k) accounts in 2001, according to Hewitt Associates. That was fewer than in 2000, when 30 percent of all 401(k) participants shifted their investments at least once.[7] And in 2002, even fewer investors—one in six—did anything with their accounts. The fact of the matter is, most of us did not react to the bear market in 2000. We didn't react following the September 11, 2001, terrorist attacks, and we didn't react to the wave of corporate scandals that plagued Wall Street in 2002.

This provides some comfort to those who feared the worst, but many individual investors are making a big mistake by not doing *more* with their accounts. "While it is gratifying to see that . . . 401(k) participants did not panic, the fact that less than one in five participants proactively interacted with their 401(k) plan is telling," says Lori Lucas, a 401(k) consultant with Hewitt Associates. "People basically disconnected from the investment process."[8]

Many of us are still disconnected from our accounts, having our 401(k)s on autopilot even though the bear market has dramatically changed the trajectory of our retirement plans. For the first time ever, 401(k) balances have shrunk, from an average of about $61,100 in 1999 to $58,800 in 2001, according to an ongoing study of plan participants by the Employee Benefit Research Institute and the Investment Company Institute.[9] A separate study by the Vanguard Group found that average account balances fell again in 2002. Vanguard took a random sampling of 50,000 of its 401(k) participants and found that average balances among its customers fell from $50,230 in 1999 to $48,718 in 2000 to $47,513 in 2001 to $45,634 in 2002.[10]

What does this all mean? Of all the errors we make with our 401(k)s, how we invest the money isn't the biggest problem. The biggest mistake many of us make with our retirement plans is that we still don't save enough. The good news is, this problem can be fixed.

MINI MISTAKE

NOT PUTTING ENOUGH INTO YOUR 401(K)S

With all the talk about the significance of 401(k) plans—including that they democratized Wall Street in the '90s—they aren't that *financially* significant. At least not yet. According to the Vanguard study, the average 401(k) account is worth only around $45,000. To be sure, smaller balances of younger workers who haven't had as much time to contribute could be distorting this figure. But even among 40-somethings, the average balance is only $62,900 (see Figure 9-1). The average balance for 50-somethings, many of whom are less than a decade away from retiring, is a modest $92,500. And the average 60-something has slightly less than $109,000 saved up in his or her account. So much for the myth of the 401(k) millionaire.

While account balances actually increased among workers in their 20s and 30s during the bear market as more of them started to contribute—in fact, average balances for 20-somethings increased 47 percent—balances for 50- and 60-year olds took a noticeable hit. Between 1999 and 2001, for example, the average 50-year-old's 401(k) declined nearly 8 percent in value, and 60-year-olds lost more than 14 percent of their nest eggs.[11] And keep in mind that throughout this period, workers were continuing to put new money into their plans. So their market losses were much more severe.

Figure 9-1. Average 401(k) Account Balances, by Age

Source: Employee Benefit Research Institute and Investment Company Institute

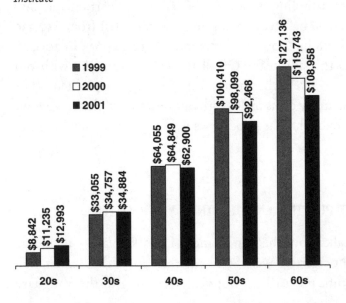

This couldn't have occurred at a worse time. History has shown that sustaining considerable losses at or just before retirement can turn a sizable nest egg into one that's insufficient to meet your long-term needs.[12] In all, eight out of 10 workers who participate in 401(k)s have less than $50,000 saved up, roughly seven out of 10 have less than $40,000, and six out of 10 have less than $20,000 in their retirement accounts (see Figure 9-2).

But the situation is actually much worse. These figures reflect *average* account balances. Averages can be skewed by a small number of investors with sizable savings. The average balance of two workers, one with $900,000 saved and another with $2000, would be $451,000. But that figure wouldn't reflect the significant shortfall of the poorer employee.

A better number to consider is the *median* 401(k) balance, which would reflect the balance of the typical saver. Here, the situation is quite worrisome. According to Vanguard, the median 401(k) balance in 2002 was just $15,474, down from $15,736 in 1999 (see Figure 9-3). This means that roughly half of all 401(k) participants have less than $15,500 saved.

Figure 9-2. The Majority of 401(k) Investors Undersave

The vast majority of retirement investors had less than
$20,000 saved in their 401(k)s as of 2001.
Source: Employee Benefit Research Institute

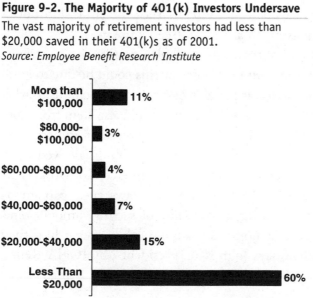

Figure 9-3. Average and Median 401(k) Balances

Retirement account balances have fallen for three straight years during the bear market, the first time that's happened in the history of the 401(k).
Source: Vanguard

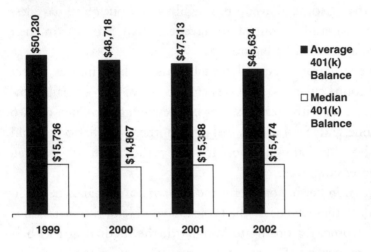

401(k) Shortfall

While the rate of 401(k) participation slipped modestly during the bear market—78 percent of workers eligible to contribute in 2001 did so, down from 82.5 percent in 1999—the problem is, most of us aren't contributing as much as we can (see Figure 9-4).

Studies show that less than half of all plan participants contribute the maximum allowed each year. Some of this could be due to ignorance, since as many as a third of all workers haven't a clue as to what their annual contribution limit is. Part of it could also stem from confusion. One recent survey by CIGNA discovered that 47 percent of Americans *think* they are contributing the maximum allowed when in fact, government records show that only 11 percent of workers are maxing out their 401(k)s. "There is clearly an awareness gap among U.S. workers that is creating a false sense of security among some, and a growing sense of confusion among others, regarding their retirement planning," says John Kim, president of CIGNA Retirement & Investment Services.[13]

Another point of confusion: The federal cap on pretax contri-butions to 401(k)s has risen in recent years and will continue to rise about $1000 a year until 2006, thanks to recent tax law changes in effect at the time of this writing. While rising contri-bution limits is good news for savers, changes to 401(k) laws tend to add to confusion in the short term.

Moreover, while the federal government increased the annual limit for pretax contributions from $11,000 in 2002 to $12,000 in 2003 and $13,000 in 2004, individual company plans come with their own specific caps that may be much lower than the federal limit. (Many company plans must meet a nondiscrimination test demon-strating that highly paid workers aren't disproportionately benefiting. If executives are contributing a far greater percentage of their salaries than average workers are putting in, then the company may be forced to lower the amount that managers and other highly paid workers can save.)

More than likely, the real problem is inertia. Studies show that once 401(k) participants select a rate of contribution, they often stick with it for years, even if they can afford to contribute much more as their incomes grow. Again quoting from Benartzi and Thaler: Iner-tia can "lower the savings rates of those who do participate."[14] Yet it would be a big mistake to let this happen.

Figure 9-4. 401(k) Participation Rates
Source: Profit Sharing/401(k) Council of America

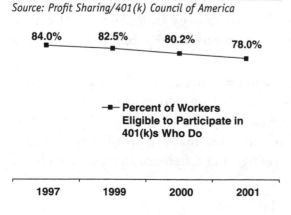

84.0% 82.5% 80.2% 78.0%

—■— **Percent of Workers Eligible to Participate in 401(k)s Who Do**

1997 1999 2000 2001

Whatever the reason, 401(k) contribution rates have reached a plateau. In 2001 workers, excluding highly paid managers, contributed 5.3 percent of their pretax salaries into their 401(k)s. In 1999 the average rate was 5.4 percent. The contribution rate for non-highly-paid workers has hovered in the low 5 percent range since the mid- to late 1990s (see Figure 9-5).

Yet the single most effective way to repair your 401(k) is to put more money into it. "The average worker contributes about 5 percent to a 401(k) plan, but this will most likely not be enough to retire on," says Peter Syslack, manager of retirement and college planning for the Strong Financial Corp.

Syslack offers this telling example: Say you're a 40-year-old earning $50,000 a year and contributing 5 percent of your salary to your 401(k). And assume that your company matches your contributions dollar for dollar up to 3 percent of your payroll deductions. And further assume that your salary grows an average of 3 percent a year through bonuses, raises, and cost-of-living adjustments. By the time you retire at 65, assuming an 8 percent annual return, your account will have grown to $413,700.

But if you were to save just 1 percentage point more each year—in other words, if you were to increase your contribution rate to 6 percent—your 401(k) would grow to $465,400, or 12 percent more. If you were to increase your contribution rate from 5 to 7 percent, your account would mushroom to $517,100, or 25 percent more. What this means is that saving a tiny bit more each year in your 401(k) can be a more effective strategy in building wealth than spending weeks and months searching for the absolute hottest stock or mutual fund to invest in.

What's more, for a person earning $50,000 a year to increase his 401(k) contributions from 5 to 6 percent would be virtually painless. Your take-home pay would only be reduced by around $7 a week. "The 401(k) tax deduction makes increasing your contributions easier without feeling a big difference in the pocketbook," says Syslack.

Figure 9-5. 401(k) Contribution Rates

Source: Profit Sharing/401(k) Council of America

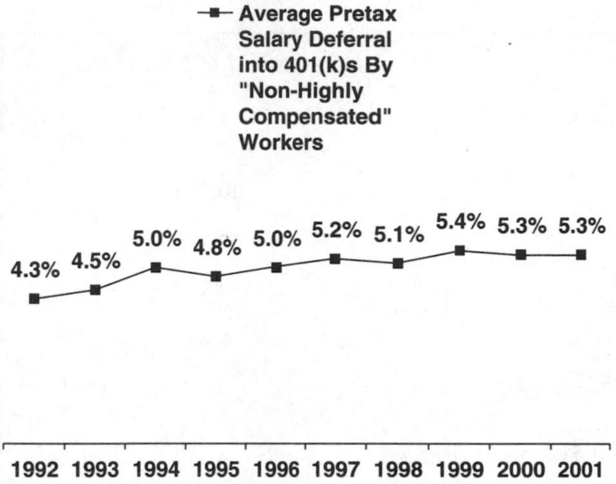

```
—■— Average Pretax
    Salary Deferral
    into 401(k)s By
    "Non-Highly
    Compensated"
    Workers
```

```
                                                5.4%  5.3%  5.3%
            5.0%  4.8%  5.0%  5.2%  5.1%
4.3%  4.5%
```

```
1992  1993  1994  1995  1996  1997  1998  1999  2000  2001
```

Perhaps what's most troubling is the fact that many investors still aren't even taking full advantage of their company matches. Despite the recent downturn in the economy and recent moves by influential companies to temporarily suspend their 401(k) matches, the majority of plans—close to 9 out of 10—still offer a match of some sort. Different plans use different matching formulas. Under a typical scenario, a company may contribute as much as 50 cents for every dollar that a worker contributes to his or her plan, up to about 6 percent of that worker's salary deferral (see Figure 9-6).

A company match is free money. If your employer kicks in 25 cents on every dollar you contribute, you've just earned 25 percent on your money, risk free. If the company matches 50 cents on the dollar, that's a 50 percent gain, again risk free. Nearly one out of four companies that offer a fixed match actually matches dollar for dollar. If you're lucky enough to be eligible for such a plan, you would be doubling your money immediately. Yet a study by Hewitt in 2001 found that 59 percent of employees are still not taking full advantage of these matches.

Figure 9-6. Common 401(k) Matching Formulas Used by 401(k) Plans with Fixed Matches

Source: Profit Sharing/401(k) Council of America

	Percent of 401(k) Plans
Less than $0.25 per $1.00	2.7%
$0.25 per $1.00	16.1%
on first 4%	3.5
on first 5%	2.5
on first 6%	7.6
other	2.5
Between $0.25 and $0.50 per $1.00	4.5%
$0.50 per $1.00	45.6%
on first 3%	3.3
on first 4%	8.0
on first 5%	4.9
on first 6%	26.0
on first 7–10%	2.4
other	0.8
Between $0.50 and $1.00 per $1.00	6.2%
$1.00 per $1.00	23.1%
on first 2%	0.8
on first 3%	4.3
on first 4%	4.5
on first 5%	4.1
on first 6%	7.2
other	2.1
More than $1.00 per $1.00	1.9%

> **TIP**: Everyone who is eligible for a 401(k) should not only consider participating, but take full advantage of it. At the very least, take full advantage of the company match. Your 401(k) may not offer the best investment options, but as long as the plan matches, you're likely to earn double-digit gains. If you can't afford to max out now, take incremental steps. Do what we discussed in the first chapter: automatically increase your 401(k) contribution rate the next time you get a raise. This is a simple but effective way to save more for retirement—without feeling as if you're making a huge sacrifice.

If you're wary of contributing more to your retirement account because of concerns about the stock market, remember that you don't have to *invest* 401(k) money. At the very least, you don't have to invest the money in equities. The average 401(k) offers workers a choice of more than 14 different options, according to a survey by the Profit Sharing/401(k) Council of America. And nearly one in three plans offers more than 15 options. Generally included among those choices, in addition to several diversified stock funds, are: at least one bond mutual fund, a money market mutual fund, a so-called "stable value" fund (which promises to pay a set amount of interest every year and is backed by an insurance policy), and at least one "balanced fund"—a mutual fund that invests in a mix of bonds and stocks.

Yet many workers who quit their 401(k)s in recent years did so because they feared losing even more money in the stock market. If you're that worried, instead of quitting your 401(k) altogether, and putting that money in a bank CD or money market fund outside your plan, why not simply invest the money in a fixed-income or cash vehicle *inside* your 401(k)? Why walk away from the tax break?

Finally, remember how inexpensive it is to contribute to a 401(k), as Peter Syslack mentioned earlier. Because 401(k) contributions are made largely with *pretax dollars*, it takes only about 70 or 72 cents to contribute the equivalent of one dollar into your account. In plans that offer a company match, it could cost substantially less.

IRA Shortfall

While it's true that a majority who are eligible to contribute to a 401(k) do, most of the nation's 100-million-plus workers aren't eligible for these employer-sponsored plans (see Figure 9-7). Some workers are employed by companies that still rely on traditional pensions. Others work for firms that don't offer any retirement benefits. A large number of small businesses, which have been a big engine of job growth in this country for the past two decades, say they can't afford to run 401(k) plans.

An alternative for these workers, then, is to take full advantage of their individual retirement accounts, or IRAs. The federal government has begun talking about changing and simplifying rules for tax-deferred investing, but in the meanwhile, there are still two primary individual retirement accounts for most households: the traditional IRA and the Roth IRA.

In a traditional account, those with earned income—and who earn a modest salary or who don't participate in employer-sponsored retirement accounts—can make annual deductible contributions. In 2003 and 2004, for instance, they could contribute as much as $3000 annually, though this figure is set to rise throughout the decade. As in a 401(k), money invested in a traditional IRA is deductible and earnings withdrawn at retirement are taxed as normal income. By comparison, money contributed to a Roth is not deductible, but withdrawals are tax free.

The problem here is the same: Many of us aren't taking full advantage of our IRAs. For all the recent talk about increasing the annual contribution limits for individual retirement accounts—including allowing investors to contribute as much as $7500 a year—the fact is, the majority of households aren't currently utilizing these plans. To be sure, about 39.5 percent of all households (about 42 million families) had at least one IRA account in 2002, according to the Investment Company Institute. But that's down from 2001, when 39.7 percent of households had an active IRA, and

Figure 9-7. The 401(k) Minority

Source: Department of Labor and Cerulli Associates

	Total # of 401(k) Participants	Total # of Workers	Participation Rate
1990	19,500,000	91,100,000	21.4%
1991	19,100,000	89,800,000	21.3
1992	22,400,000	90,000,000	24.9
1993	23,100,000	91,900,000	25.1
1994	25,200,000	95,000,000	26.5
1995	28,100,000	97,900,000	28.7
1996	30,700,000	100,200,000	30.6
1997	33,500,000	103,100,000	32.5
1998	36,700,000	106,000,000	34.6
1999	39,900,000	108,500,000	36.8

2000, when 41 percent did (see Figure 9-8). What's more, the average traditional IRA investor has less than $40,000 in his or her accounts, a modest sum, given that the average traditional IRA owner is 50. The average household with Roth IRAs has even less in those accounts: only about $12,000.

Adding to the concern is the fact that for about half of all households with a traditional IRA, accounts include money rolled over from a previous 401(k). This means a good many IRA investors aren't contributing new money into their plans so much as they're shifting money from other retirement accounts. The sad truth is, only about 7 percent of individuals eligible to contribute new money every year into a traditional IRA do so, and only about 4 percent sock away the maximum amount allowed each year.[15]

Figure 9-8. IRA Ownership in America

Source: Investment Company Institute

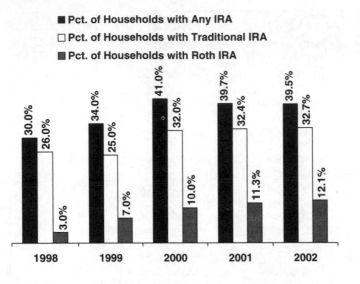

■ Pct. of Households with Any IRA
☐ Pct. of Households with Traditional IRA
■ Pct. of Households with Roth IRA

TIP: Even if you've fallen behind in your IRA contributions, it's not too late to start. New "catch-up" provisions approved by the federal government allow workers 50 and older to put even more money into their accounts to make up for lost time. From 2003 to 2005, IRA investors 50 or older will be allowed to put an additional $500 a year into their plans, over and above the normal contribution caps. This means that older workers in 2003 can actually contribute $3500. Starting in 2006, older workers will be allowed to invest an additional $1000 each year through catch-up contributions (instead of the current $500). There are similar catch-up provisions for 401(k) investors. In 2003, 401(k) participants 50 or older could kick in an additional $2000. That goes up to $3000 in 2004, $4000 in 2005, and $5000 in 2006.

MINI MISTAKE

TAKING TOO MUCH MONEY OUT OF YOUR 401(K)S

At a time when investors should be putting more money into their retirement accounts, many workers are pulling large sums out. Some of them are borrowing money against the accounts strategically, figuring it's better to borrow from themselves than from a bank. Yet this isn't always true. Still others are cashing out of their retirement accounts as they switch jobs, even though there are several ways to keep the money tax sheltered.

401(k) Loans

Surveys show that one out of six 401(k) investors has a loan outstanding against his or her account. Thirty- and 40-somethings are the most likely to borrow. According to recent studies, 19 percent of 40-year-olds and 17 percent of 30-year-olds have outstanding loans against their retirement plans (see Figure 9-9). Meanwhile, 15 percent of 50-year-olds continue to borrow. The danger isn't just that workers are taking out loans against their plans—it's how much they're borrowing. The typical 30-something, for instance, has tapped about 20 cents of every dollar saved in his or her 401(k) while the typical 40-year-old is borrowing 15 percent. (see Figure 9-10).

You might ask: Is borrowing from a 401(k) so wrong? Why should you pay a bank interest when you could loan yourself the money?

While it is indeed true that you would be paying yourself back on a 401(k) loan, there are several considerations to factor into your decision. When you're borrowing from your 401(k), you are actually

Figure 9-9. Percentage of Eligible 401(k) Investors with Loans

Source: Employee Benefit Research Institute and the Investment Company Institute

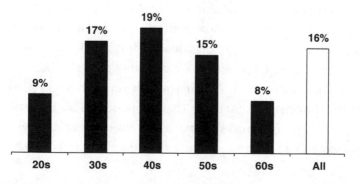

Figure 9-10. Loan Balances as a Percentage of 401(k) Balances

Source: Employee Benefit Research Institute and the Investment Company Institute

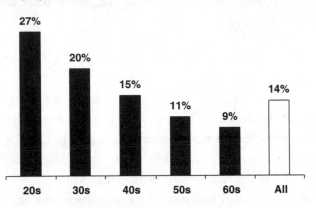

making two separate investment calculations: one as the lender and the other as the borrower.[16]

As the lender, you have to ask yourself: Could I put the money to better use? Given the recent downturn in stocks, you could argue that taking 401(k) money out of the market and lending it to yourself isn't that bad. After all, if stocks continue to drop, you'd be taking money out of the market just as prices are falling. Then, over time, as the market heals, you'd be paying yourself back incrementally—with interest (the typical loan charges about 5 or 6 percent interest).

But what if stock prices climb higher? If stocks simply revert to their long-term average annual returns of about 10 percent, you might end up losing money by loaning it out at only 5 or 6 percent.

As the borrower, you have to ask yourself a different question: Are these the best terms I can get on a loan? Most 401(k) loans, for instance, have to be paid back within a reasonably quick amount of time—typically under five years. And if you quit your job or get fired while you're in repayment (something that happened to an increasing number of plan participants during the recent economic downturn), you'll have to pay the money back all at once. Otherwise, the

IRS will deem the loan an "early withdrawal" subject to a 10 percent penalty in addition to income taxes.

What's more, if your loan requires large monthly payments, preventing you from repaying it while simultaneously continuing to make new contributions, then the cost of the loan will be significantly higher than just the interest rate charged. There would be the opportunity cost of not being able to invest new money in your 401(k). And even if you can afford to pay back the loan and invest more, some plans place restrictions on a borrower's ability to contribute new money.

There is another disadvantage to borrowing that often gets overlooked. When you contribute money to a 401(k), you do so with *pretax* dollars. But when you take it out in the form of a loan, you have to repay it with *after-tax* money. This means that by borrowing from your 401(k), you are turning a tax-advantaged account into a tax-*disadvantaged* plan. Whenever you borrow from a 401(k), you are in effect double-taxed. You're taxed once when repaying pretax dollars with after-tax currency. Then you're taxed again when you withdraw the money at retirement.

Cashing Out

Another way 401(k) investors pull money out of their plans is by actually pulling money directly out of their accounts. The average American worker changes jobs at least eight times in his or her career. And a disturbingly large percentage of job changers cash out their 401(k)s when they leave their firms.

A recent study by Hewitt Associates found that nearly 70 percent of 401(k) participants who leave their positions cash out their retirement accounts.[17] Yet doing so before you turn $59^1/2$ often subjects you not only to a 10 percent early withdrawal penalty, it forces you to pay income taxes on your money now. On a $25,000 account, you could easily lose $7500 or more in taxes and penalties, depending on your income tax rate. Overall, a separate study by Putnam Investments estimated that Americans lose as much as $8 billion a year to unnecessary penalties and taxes by withdrawing money from their 401(k)s too early.

Clearly, among younger workers with smaller balances, the law of small numbers is at work. If you have less than $10,000 in your account, you might think that taxes and penalties won't be that bad. But by cashing out early, you destroy your ability to compound money, tax deferred, over time. You also lose money unnecessarily to taxes and penalties, which is always a big mistake.

Bear in mind also that every time you pull money out of your 401(k) when you quit a job, you set yourself up for the same exact excuse down the road. The second time you quit your job and cash out a 401(k), you might tell yourself again that it's only $10,000. But had you left your original account intact, at your first job, it wouldn't be just $10,000 at your second one. It could have been $20,000 or more.

> **TIP**: About 19 percent of job-hoppers who quit a company leave their 401(k) assets in their old employer's plan, according to Putnam Investments. And another 10 percent or so transfer their money into their new employer's 401(k). A better solution might be to roll your 401(k) money into an IRA, where it can remain tax-sheltered—with some added flexibility. While your old employer's 401(k) may be great, it still has a limited number of investment options from which to choose. In an IRA, on the other hand, you can select any investment you want simply by choosing which mutual fund company or brokerage to open the account at. Also, as you move from job to job throughout your career, it will be easier to keep track of all your retirement assets if you roll them into one or two financial institutions.

MINI MISTAKE

NOT REBALANCING YOUR RETIREMENT ACCOUNTS

In the late 1990s the big concern was that 401(k) investors would trade too often and too aggressively in their accounts. If you recall, this was the era of the day trader, and 401(k) plans had just started letting investors switch into and out of their investment options on a daily basis. Some 401(k)s even started offering a so-called brokerage window, through which workers could not only trade funds, but individual stocks as well.

As it turns out, we don't trade nearly enough. A recent study of 401(k) investors uncovered a troubling statistic. Roughly three out of five plan participants have never made a single change in asset allocation strategy since enrolling.[18] In other words, many of us haven't sold out of a single investment since we started participating. Nor have we adjusted or "rebalanced" our accounts.

Rebalancing is a term often used by financial planners referring to routine adjustments that need to be made to one's portfolio, once or twice a year, to make sure the money is appropriately invested. For instance, let's say you decide that the optimal asset allocation strategy for you, given your risk tolerance, is 50 percent stocks and 50 percent bonds. In a $100,000 portfolio this means investing $50,000 in equity funds and another $50,000 in fixed-income portfolios.

Just to make this simple, let's say you put all of your stock money into the Vanguard 500 fund and all of your bond money into the Vanguard Total Bond Market Index portfolio. In a short period of time, market movements can dramatically skew your original investment plan, as in 2000, for instance, when the Vanguard 500 fund fell 9.1 percent, while the Total Bond Market Index rose 11.4 percent. In 2001, Vanguard 500 lost another 12 percent, while the Total Bond Market Index fund rose 8.4 percent. As a result of stock and bond market movements, the $50,000 you invested in Vanguard 500 at the start of 2000 was worth only $40,000 by the end of 2001, and your $50,000 stake in the Vanguard bond fund grew to $60,400. This means that your 50 percent stock/50 percent bond allocation became a 40 percent stock/60 percent bond portfolio. But what if a 40/60 asset allocation strategy is too conservative for your longer-term needs?

This is why financial planners say it is necessary, at least once a year, to readjust or "rebalance" your investments to reflect your longer-term approach. In our example, it would require selling a bit of your bond allocation and shifting the money back into stocks to get closer to your original 50/50 split.

When you rebalance, you are essentially selling a portion of an asset that has grown disproportionately, and moving the money into a competing asset that has fallen disproportionately (or at the very least hasn't kept up). By selling a sliver of the rising investment and reallocating that money into a falling one, you ensure that you always sell one asset when it's trading at high prices to buy another asset that's relatively inexpensive. This is the essence of sound, long-term investing—buying low and selling high. In the short run you might not see the benefits of this approach, but over time, studies have shown, rebalancing works in your favor.

T. Rowe Price recently crunched the numbers and discovered something worth commenting on. Let's say you entered 1995 with an asset allocation strategy that called for investing 60 percent of your money in stocks, 30 percent in bonds, and 10 percent in cash. And let's say you had $100,000 in your portfolio. A little more than five years later, at the peak of the bull market in March 2000, your portfolio would have grown to $271,400—if you did *not* rebalance along the way—and your original 60-30-10 portfolio would have turned into one with 78 percent stocks, 17 percent bonds, and 5 percent cash.[19]

In comparison, had you rebalanced your portfolio annually between 1995 and 2000, your portfolio would have grown to about $255,300 by the bull market peak. You might ask: Since that's less than you would have had without rebalancing, why rebalance?

The answer has to do with the changed allocation, and because rebalancing would have protected you in the subsequent bear market. The T. Rowe Price analysis showed that had you rebalanced your portfolio in 2000 back to its original 60-30-10 split, by selling stocks and buying bonds, the additional fixed-income exposure would have cushioned your investments when stocks turned down that year. While the rebalanced portfolio in this example fell to around $215,200 by July 2002, the *un*-rebalanced portfolio dropped below $204,000 (see Figure 9-11). Rebalancing, in effect, allowed investors to lock in gains during the bull market, and protected them during the bear market.

> **TIP:** Rebalancing is another way investors can automate their savings and investment strategy. But if you rebalance your 401(k)s and IRAs annually, do so on the same day each year. Not only does this regiment your investment strategy, it allows you to take an arm's length approach to these decisions. Some investors decide to rebalance only during emotional times in the market. For instance, some plan participants only rebalance when stock prices are falling dramatically. But the whole point of this exercise is to make sure your portfolio is on the right path to meet your long-term goals. By rebalancing on the same day each year, not only will you know when to do it, you won't be influenced to do the wrong thing by short-term fluctuations in the market.

Bottom Line

Next to our homes, our retirement accounts are our biggest assets. In fact, for many of us, 401(k)s and IRAs represent the sum total of our investment portfolios. Yet our retirement accounts aren't nearly as big as they could or should be. Belying the myth of the 401(k) millionaire is a sobering fact: The average 401(k) investor has only around $50,000 saved up, and the average traditional IRA is worth less than $40,000.

In the late 1990s we worried about how best to invest our tax-deferred retirement accounts. There was even a push to get more 401(k)s to offer brokerage windows. As it turns out, the single biggest challenge for retirement investors isn't finding an optimal investment strategy. It's more basic than that: We need to put more money into these accounts.

Figure 9-11. Rebalancing Works in the Long Term Impact of rebalancing a portfolio.

Source: T. Rowe Price Associates

Date	Non-Rebalanced Portfolio				Rebalanced Portfolio			
	Stocks	Bonds	Cash	Balance	Stocks	Bonds	Cash	Balance
12/31/94	60%	30%	10%	$100,000	60%	30%	10%	$100,000
3/31/00	78	17	5	$271,400	58	31	11	$255,300
7/31/02	69	25	7	*$203,800*	56	33	11	*$215,200*

Checklist: Things to Do

- ❏ Max out your 401(k).
- ❏ At the very least, take full advantage of company matches in your 401(k).
- ❏ The next time you get a raise, automatically increase contributions to your 401(k).
- ❏ If you're 50 or older, take advantage of the new catch-up provisions on your retirement accounts.
- ❏ When you switch jobs, roll your existing 401(k) into an IRA.
- ❏ Rebalance your 401(k) and IRAs once a year.

10

FAILING TO DO THE RETIREMENT MATH

Calculating What You'll Need *Before* You Retire

Retirement is the giant elephant in the room that none of us wants to talk about. We know it's there. We see it coming. But many of us are too afraid, indifferent, or in denial to deal with it just yet. That would be a big mistake.

According to a recent survey by the AARP, two-thirds of all Baby Boomers "think about the future often," and about half have given some thought recently to how their finances might affect that future.[1] That's because the vast majority of Boomers understand that in this do-it-yourself era of retirement, they are largely responsible for taking care of themselves. Though Social Security still provides a surprisingly large percentage of many retirees' incomes, personal sources of money—traditional pensions, employer-sponsored 401(k)s, individual retirement accounts, part-time work, proceeds from the sale of a home, and basic savings—pay for the majority of many retirees' bills.

Yet despite this fact only a third of Americans know how much money they'll need in the future to retire.[2] And most 60-somethings—55 percent—don't know how much money they'll need annually in retirement to maintain the lifestyles they've grown accustomed to during their working years. Even worse, among those who think they know, the overwhelming majority underestimate their needs.

The fact is, while we may think about our golden years in the abstract, we don't crunch the numbers. Less than a third of us in 2002 even *tried* to calculate how much we'll need to save for retirement, according to a study by the Employee Benefit Research Institute. That's down substantially from the 51 percent who tried in 2000, before the bear market (see Figure 10-1).[3] And even among those who tried, more than a third still don't know or can't remember how much is needed to fund their lives after work.

"Many people spend more time planning a two-week summer vacation than a 22-year retirement," says Mathew Greenwald, president of Mathew Greenwald & Associates, the polling firm that conducts EBRI's annual Retirement Confidence Survey.[4] He's not joking. While a vast majority of workers—74 percent—routinely spend four or more hours planning holiday trips, only a minority spend that much time in any given year thinking about what they'll do in retirement and how they'll pay for it, surveys show.

Is it any wonder, then, that one of every six workers isn't "at all confident" of having enough money to live comfortably in retirement? One-third fear outliving their savings, a growing concern now that the average 65-year-old man lives to almost 81 and the average 65-year-old woman lives to 84. And more than 40 percent of all workers fear not being able to pay for medical costs, which continue to rise significantly faster than the overall rate of inflation. This is not a minor consideration. According to a study conducted in 2003,

60-somethings who aren't covered by employer-sponsored retiree healthcare benefits may need more than $1 million to pay for their lifetime medical expenses.

This financial insecurity is having real consequences: An increasing number of older workers say they plan to postpone their retirement beyond their original scheduled dates, largely due to financial concerns. The most recent retirement confidence survey by EBRI showed that one-fourth of all workers 45 or older plan to put off retirement in order to shore up their finances. The bear market has only exacerbated the problem. While 29 percent of Boomers in 2001 expressed concerns about their financial readiness for retirement, that number jumped to 52 percent in 2002, according to a separate survey by Allstate.

While it's disappointing that more workers, especially older Boomers who are getting ready to leave the workforce, aren't doing a better job preparing themselves, it's hardly surprising. Consider all the unknown and unpleasant questions involved in estimating how much money you'll need for retirement: How much longer will your company keep you on? How long will you live? How long will your spouse live? Will you suffer any special medical problems? Who will take care of you if you're incapacitated? Will you need long-term care? Then there are more pedestrian concerns: What will your investments return in the future? Will you work part-time in retirement should you require additional income? Will you even be able to find work once retired? What will the future rate of inflation be?

These are all difficult questions. Yet workers who make an effort to calculate their retirement needs tend to feel better about their path to retirement. Indeed, a survey by American Express Retirement Services in 2002 found that workers who did the math ended up more than twice as confident about their retirement readiness than workers who haven't crunched the numbers.

Perhaps that's because once you do the math, you'll come to realize that despite all the obstacles to a comfortable retirement, you have more financial flexibility than you might realize.

For instance, today's 50- and 60-somethings are much healthier and more productive than their parents were at this age. So you might be able—and willing—to work well into your 60s. In fact, surveys indicate that many older Boomers and retirees want to work well into their golden years for both financial and emotional reasons. Plus, with so many two-income households today, many families can improve their chances for a comfortable retirement if one spouse works a few extra years to bring in more income and to extend the family's eligibility for employer-provided benefits. There is ample anecdotal evidence that an increasing number of American families are staggering their retirements in this fashion. And don't forget your home, your one appreciating asset at the start of this decade. At retirement, you might not want to live in such a large house anymore. You might be willing to trade down for a smaller home or condo. Or, you can continue to live in your home but earn additional income off of it through a reverse mortgage.

Another reason to do the math: you might clear up some confusion surrounding your benefits. For instance, recent surveys show that a majority of workers are unaware of the recent increase in the normal Social Security retirement age from 65 to 67, for those born in 1960 or later. In fact, half think they'll be eligible for full Social Security benefits sooner than they actually will. This might explain why a majority of retirees start collecting benefits early. Yet the decision of *when* to start taking Social Security benefits—for instance, should you start at the minimum age of 62 or wait until you're 67 or even older—could mean a 20 to 30 percent difference in your monthly check.

At the very least, workers nearing retirement need to consider how much they plan to *spend* in retirement well before retiring. Here's why:

- *We're falling behind.* While two-thirds of all workers say they've saved money for retirement, 12 percent of those respondents have saved less than $10,000 and another 11 percent have accumulated less than $25,000. In all, about half of all workers have saved less than $50,000 thus far among all their banking and investing accounts, according to EBRI.

Even among Baby Boomers, including those who are only five to 10 years from retiring, four out of 10 have socked away less than $50,000. This would explain why 58 percent of workers say they're "behind schedule" when it comes to retirement planning.[5] The irony is, a growing number of workers who are saving—73 percent—say they can afford to put away an extra $20 per week for retirement. And more than half of those who aren't currently saving admit they can set aside at least $20 a week. As we discussed in *Mistake 1: Shortchanging Yourself,* a small amount of money can grow into a sizable account over time.

- *Retirement often comes sooner than expected.* The average worker today *expects* to retire at age 65. In fact, one-fourth of all workers want to keep on working well past the age of 66. But the fact of the matter is, the average retiree actually leaves the work force at around 62, and nearly a third retire in their 50s. Often, it's not by choice. In 2002, slightly more than half of all retirees said they left the workforce early because of health reasons, and 26 percent were downsized out of a job.[6] So you should prepare sooner rather than later.

- *Meanwhile, seniors are falling into debt.* Nearly half of all seniors carry credit card balances today, something that was unheard of a generation ago, and total household debt among Americans 65 and older has nearly tripled since 1992, to an average of $23,000, according to research conducted by SRI Consulting Business Intelligence.[7] It's no wonder, then, that the 65-and-older set now represents the fastest growing group in the country filing for bankruptcy, according to the Consumer Bankruptcy Project.[8] In fact, the number of bankruptcy filings among senior citizens soared more than 200 percent in the 1990s. This is exacerbating an already troubling situation for many older Americans. Cash and fixed-income investments were generating meager returns at the start of the decade, thanks to record-low interest rates. As a result, more and more seniors are having to dip into their ever-shrinking income to make larger debt payments while in retirement.

- *Fewer and fewer companies offer retiree medical.* While workers
  have spent most of their time fixating on their investment losses
  in recent years, there's an even bigger concern that's often overlooked: How will they pay for health insurance in retirement?
  This is an especially big problem for those workers who are
  forced to retire before they turn 65 and qualify for Medicare.
  Even retirees who are covered by an employer-based plan are
  having to bear a bigger burden of the costs. According to a
  recent study by the consulting firm Watson Wyatt Worldwide,
  80 percent of large companies that offered retiree medical at
  the start of the 1990s reduced those benefits—in some cases,
  considerably—by 1999. And while many large firms pick up 50
  percent or more of a retiree's medical expenses, that figure is
  likely to fall to 10 percent over the next three decades.[9] Meanwhile, a separate study by Hewitt Associates and the Kaiser
  Family Foundation discovered that 13 percent of large employers have terminated retiree medical benefits for *future* retirees
  altogether, while another 22 percent are planning on doing so
  within the next three years.[10]
- *Long-term care insurance decisions should be made soon.* By 2030,
  the population of Americans age 65 or older will likely double
  to 70 million, and the 85-and-older set is growing just as fast.
  Yet many Baby Boomers, a majority of whom are already suf-
  fering from at least one chronic illness, are largely unaware of
  the costs and coverage of long-term care insurance policies. A
  recent AARP study found that only 15 percent could identify
  the costs associated with nursing home care, and more than two
  out of five think Medicare covers assisted living care (which it
  doesn't). And while more than 30 percent of Americans 45 or
  older *think* they have long-term care coverage, industry estimates indicate that only 6 or 7 percent of Americans have actually purchased these policies. There's an important reason why
  50-somethings need to research these issues today, before they
  retire: While the cost of long-term care insurance for a 65-year-
  old was as high as $1850 a year at the start of the decade, accord-

ing to the AARP, your premiums would have been considerably lower if you purchased coverage at an earlier age. That same policy—which provides $100 a day for nursing home care and $50 a day for home care—would cost up to $900 annually if purchased at age 50. (If you wait until you're 75, it could cost nearly $6000 a year.) Though younger Americans are starting to look into long-term care insurance more these days, only about a third of these policies are bought by consumers younger than 65.

Today, about half of all workers say they're not confident about having enough money to pay for long-term care coverage. In fact, only one in seven workers is "very confident" in their abilities to cover these costs. This is precisely why financial planners say it's important for workers nearing retirement to map out their future spending needs. Clearly, health care and long-term care insurance costs must factor into your equation.

Like any other budget, your estimate should reflect necessities such as your housing, transportation, and food costs. And while expenses for health-care and long-term care will likely increase, keep in mind that in retirement, other costs go down. For instance, you're not likely to be funding your retirement savings accounts as you did

Figure 10-1. Few Calculate Retirement Needs

Source: Employee Benefit Research Institute, 2002 Retirement Confidence Survey

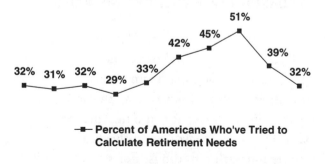

—■— Percent of Americans Who've Tried to Calculate Retirement Needs

1993 1994 1995 1996 1997 1998 1999 2000 2001 2002

as a worker, and your clothing expenses may go down (though surveys indicate that two-thirds of workers nearing retirement say they want to work for pay after they "retire"). Other costs that may go down include taxes, professional dues, and commuting expenses.

Some workers have a hard time estimating their needs because they don't have a clue as to what kind of retirement they want to lead. Some are uncertain about how they want to live, where they want to live, and how much they're willing to spend. For these workers, sitting down with their families to discuss exactly what kind of retirement they want will be key.

Once you have a decent picture of your retirement needs, don't forget to consider inflation. For instance, let's say you figure you need $70,000 a year in today's dollars to fund your lifestyle. A rate of inflation of, say, 3 percent, means you will actually need to come up with about $94,000 a decade from now. In 25 years you'll need about $147,000 to buy $70,000 worth of today's goods and services (see Figure 10-2).

Of course, it serves no purpose to draw up a budget showing only your spending plans. You'll need to determine what type of lifestyle you can afford to fund as well. The good news is, we do know something about the rate at which retirees can "safely" tap their retirement accounts each year to fund their needs—without jeopardizing the longevity of those accounts.

MINI MISTAKE

FAILING TO CONSIDER SAFE WITHDRAWAL RATES

It's a huge fear in the age of self-directed 401(k)s and IRAs: What are the odds that I'll deplete my retirement account prematurely? How much money can I take out each year from my retirement portfolios to fund my spending needs without risking the account?

Three professors at Trinity University in San Antonio—Philip Cooley, Carl Hubbard, and Daniel Walz—recently studied this issue and came up with some interesting findings. For starters, they discovered that even a seemingly conservative annual withdrawal rate

Figure 10-2. Income Needs Based on 3% Inflation, Assuming Need to Replace 100% of Current Income

Today's Dollars	5 Years	10 Years	15 Years	20 Years	25 Years
$40,000	$46,000	$54,000	$62,000	$72,000	$84,000
50,000	58,000	67,000	78,000	90,000	105,000
60,000	70,000	81,000	93,000	108,000	126,000
70,000	81,000	94,000	109,000	126,000	147,000
80,000	93,000	108,000	125,000	145,000	168,000
90,000	104,000	121,000	140,000	163,000	188,000
100,000	116,000	134,000	156,000	181,000	209,000
120,000	139,000	161,000	187,000	217,000	251,000
150,000	174,000	202,000	234,000	271,000	314,000

can bankrupt a retirement account prematurely, depending on stock and bond returns.

For example, many retirees would probably feel comfortable withdrawing, say, 7 percent of their retirement assets each year. That means if you had $100,000 saved up in your 401(k)s and IRAs, you would withdraw no more than $7000 annually. If you had $250,000, you'd withdraw no more than $17,500 a year. While this sounds modest—in fact, living on $7000 sounds downright austere—Cooley, Hubbard, and Walz looked at the performance of stocks and bonds between 1926 and 1995 and found some periods when that 7 percent was too aggressive.

To spell this out: Let's say you retired at the beginning of 1963 with $1 million in retirement savings. And let's assume that half of your nest egg was invested in the S&P 500, while the other half was in high-quality corporate bonds. If you withdrew 7 percent of your assets each year starting in 1963, 30 years later you would still have $784,000 left in your account, based on actual stock and bond market returns.[11] (Remember, even though you're withdrawing money at a 7 percent clip, your stock and bond market gains are also replenishing the account over time.) Indeed, history shows that there is a 90 percent chance that retirees can safely withdraw 7 percent of their money annually (not adjusted for inflation)—and have it last at least 30 years—as long as half of the money is invested in stocks and half in bonds.

However, while the odds are in your favor, it's not guaranteed. Had you started taking withdrawals at the same 7 percent rate just one year earlier at the start of 1962 your $1 million nest egg wouldn't have just fallen to $784,000, as was the case in the previous example. It would have completely run dry in 30 years.

Why the disparity? In 1962 the stock market suffered major losses, which would have significantly reduced your initial $1 million portfolio before it got a chance to grow. And over time, the effects of that initial loss compounded. On the other hand, in 1963 stock prices rose 19 percent immediately, which would have significantly increased your nest egg right from the start.

So what is a "safe" rate of withdrawl? Based on the performance in the stock and bond markets between 1926 and 1995, Cooley, Hubbard, and Walz determined that retirees are almost guaranteed of having their money outlast them if they withdraw no more than 3 percent of their assets each year, adjusted for inflation.

In other words, if you have a $250,000 account, you would take out $7500 in the first year, then $7725 in the second year, and so on, assuming a 3 percent rate of inflation. Between 1926 and 1995, a 3 percent withdrawal rate adjusted for inflation each year enjoyed a 100 percent survival rate over 30 years, as long as at least 25 percent of the money was invested in stocks and the rest was put into high-quality bonds (see Figure 10-3). If you went up to 5 percent, that would yield $12,500 in the first year and $12,875 in the second, adjusting for inflation. But if you invested 25 percent of your money in stocks and 75 percent in bonds, a 5 percent inflation-adjusted withdrawal strategy enjoys only a 27 percent survival rate over 30 years.

Under this latter withdrawal strategy, history says there's a greater than 7 in 10 chance that you'll run out of money before you die.

The problem is, at a 3-percent withdrawal rate you would only have $3000 to live off of, assuming you had $100,000 in your accounts. And even if you had a $1 million nest egg, a 3 percent annual rate of withdrawal would yield just $30,000 a year. So while there's a virtual certainty that your money will last for a lifetime with this strategy, it's virtually certain that you'd be living on a tight budget.

TIP: If a 3 percent inflation-adjusted strategy won't cut it for you, based on your account balances, you might consider an alternative approach. While many retirees make inflation adjustments for their withdrawals—because inflation is a big concern for those living on a fixed income (as discussed in *Mistake 4: Overlooking Risks*)—you might consider withdrawing a higher rate of your assets, say 6 percent, but *not* adjusting for inflation. So instead of taking $7500 out of your $250,000 account in year one, based on a 3 percent withdrawal rate, you can start withdrawing $15,000 in year one. But you have to keep to the flat 6 percent rate for this to be a relatively safe withdrawal strategy. That means taking out $15,000 as well in year two, year three, and so on.

A flat 6 percent rate of withdrawal had a 100 percent survival rate over 15- and 20-year periods between 1926 and 1995, provided that half the money was invested in stocks and half in bonds, according to the Trinity professors' research (see Figure 10-4). And it had a 98 percent survival rate over 25- and 30-year stretches. In comparison, an inflation-adjusted 6 percent withdrawal rate enjoyed only a 51 percent survival rate over 30 years in a 50 percent stock/50 percent bond portfolio.

By relying on a higher withdrawal rate but *not* adjusting for inflation, you're in essence increasing your spending power early in retirement—when, frankly, you're more likely to travel, dine out, and spend more in general—than in the later years of retirement, when we tend to spend less on discretionary items. Retirees who intend to spend more early on and less down the road may want to consider this strategy.

Figure 10-3. Inflation-Adjusted Portfolio Success Rates 1926–1995

Source: Philip Cooley, Carl Hubbard, and Daniel Walz

	Withdrawal Strategies as Percentage of Initial Portfolio Values									
	3%	4%	5%	6%	7%	8%	9%	10%	11%	12%
100% Stocks										
15 years	100%	100%	100%	91%	79%	70%	63%	55%	43%	34%
20 years	100	100	88	75	63	53	43	33	29	24
25 years	100	100	87	70	59	46	35	30	26	20
30 years	100	95	85	68	59	41	34	34	27	15
75% Stocks/25% Bonds										
15 years	100%	100%	100%	95%	82%	68%	64%	46%	36%	27%
20 years	100	100	90	75	61	51	37	27	20	12
25 years	100	100	85	65	50	37	30	22	7	2
30 years	100	98	83	68	49	34	22	7	2	0
50% Stocks/50% Bonds										
15 years	100%	100%	100%	93%	79%	64%	50%	32%	23%	13%
20 years	100	100	90	75	55	33	22	10	0	0
25 years	100	100	80	57	37	20	7	0	0	0
30 years	100	95	76	51	17	5	0	0	0	0

25% Stocks/75% Bonds

	100%	100%	100%	89%	70%	50%	32%	18%	13%	7%
15 years										
20 years	100	100	82	47	31	16	8	4	0	0
25 years	100	93	48	24	15	4	2	0	0	0
30 years	100	71	27	20	5	0	0	0	0	0

100% Bonds

	100%	100%	100%	71%	39%	21%	18%	16%	14%	9%
15 years										
20 years	100	90	47	20	14	12	10	2	0	0
25 years	100	46	17	15	11	2	0	0	0	0
30 years	80	20	17	12	0	0	0	0	0	0

Figure 10-4. Noninflation-Adjusted Portfolio Success Rates 1926–1995

Source: Philip Cooley, Carl Hubbard, and Daniel Walz

	Withdrawal Strategies as % of Initial Portfolio Values									
	3%	4%	5%	6%	7%	8%	9%	10%	11%	12%
100% Stocks										
15 years	100%	100%	98%	98%	93%	91%	88%	77%	63%	55%
20 years	100	98	96	94	92	84	73	61	47	43
25 years	100	98	96	91	87	78	70	50	43	35
30 years	100	98	95	90	85	78	68	54	49	34
75% Stocks/ 25% Bonds										
15 years	100%	100%	100%	100%	96%	95%	91%	79%	63%	46%
20 years	100	100	100	96	94	88	71	51	41	33
25 years	100	100	98	96	91	78	57	46	33	26
30 years	100	100	98	95	88	73	54	46	37	24

50% Stocks/50% Bonds

15 years	100%	100%	100%	100%	100%	98%	91%	71%	50%	36%
20 years	100	100	100	100	96	88	61	41	25	10
25 years	100	100	100	98	96	70	43	22	7	0
30 years	100	100	100	98	90	51	37	15	0	0

25% Stocks/75% Bonds

15 years	100%	100%	100%	100%	100%	100%	91%	50%	21%	14%
20 years	100	100	100	100	100	71	24	12	4	2
25 years	100	100	100	100	78	22	9	0	0	0
30 years	100	100	100	100	32	5	0	0	0	0

100% Bonds

15 years	100%	100%	100%	100%	100%	79%	43%	38%	14%	7%
20 years	100	100	100	96	47	35	16	6	0	0
25 years	100	100	98	52	26	7	2	0	0	0
30 years	100	100	51	27	0	0	0	0	0	0

Once you decide on a withdrawal rate, it's time to work backward. If you calculated that you can withdraw a flat 6 percent of your retirement money every year and feel safe about its longevity, then how much do you need to amass now to deliver that annual income in the future?

Well, 6 percent of $250,000 is $15,000. Six percent of $300,000 is $18,000. Six percent of $400,000 is $24,000. Six percent of $500,000 is $30,000. And 6 percent of $1 million is $60,000. So do the math. Obviously, with average 401(k) balances in the neighborhood of $50,000 and average IRA balances at $40,000, the typical retirement saver has a long way to go.

But before you get overly pessimistic—and give up—remember that your needs during retirement change, as we discussed. Moreover, nearly 7 out of 10 workers say they plan to work after retirement anyway, which would provide another source of income. And again, don't forget the value of your home. Depending on your family situation, you could rent it out for income, you could sell it and move into a smaller house, or you could take out a reverse mortgage to generate an income stream.

Whatever you do, don't underestimate the role Social Security plays in the equation. According to EBRI surveys, only 13 percent of workers assume that Social Security will be their largest source of income in retirement. Among workers 39 and younger, it's even lower. In a 2002 poll, only 7 percent said that Social Security would pay for the lion's share of their bills. But studies indicate that for nearly half of all retirees Social Security represents the single largest contributor to their income stream.

Researchers at Georgia State University's Center for Risk Management & Insurance Research have been compiling data on income replacement needs for retirees. Their research indicates that a single 65-year-old retiree who earned $50,000 a year before retirement need only replace 74 percent of preretirement salary to maintain his or her lifestyle (see Figure 10-5). Part of this is due to the fact that once in retirement, you no longer have to save for retirement. Furthermore, as you enter retirement and as your income drops, so too does your tax burden. And as we discussed, individuals in retirement spend less money on a wide assortment of things.

Figure 10-5. Income Replacement Ratios for Single Worker Age 65

Source: Georgia State University

Preretirement Salary	$40,000	$50,000	$60,000	$70,000	$80,000	$90,000
After-Tax Income	$30,084	$36,359	$42,680	$48,989	$55,247	$61,680
Less preretirement savings	1,056	1,559	2,128	2,740	3,375	4,041
Less spending changes	457	559	661	763	865	960
$ Left for Retirement Spending	$28,571	$34,241	$39,891	$45,486	$51,007	$56,679
Plus Post-Retire Fed Taxes	1,052	2,126	4,072	9,094	11,323	13,653
Plus Post-Retire State Taxes	280	519	935	2,022	2,516	3,133
Total Pretax Income Needed at Retirement	$29,903	$36,886	$44,898	$56,602	$64,846	$73,465
Income Replacement Required	75%	74%	75%	81%	81%	82%
Minus Soc. Sec. Benefit	$14,160	$15,924	$16,836	$17,628	$18,324	$18,492
TOTAL NEEDED FROM SAVINGS AND RETIREMENT PLAN	$15,743	$20,962	$28,062	$38,974	$46,522	$54,973

According to the Georgia State researchers, annual spending in 2001 for the typical single 65-year-old earning $50,000 fell $559 after retirement, since expenses for transportation, clothing, and other needs diminished. Thus, a 65-year-old retiree who earned $50,000 before retiring needed just $36,886 a year to maintain his or her lifestyle at the start of the decade. Since Social Security covered about 43 percent of that figure in 2001, a worker in this situation needs to come up with less than $21,000 a year from savings, retirement plans, and other sources. So cheer up.

Bottom Line

Sometimes, we make saving and investing for retirement more complicated than it needs to be. For starters, we underestimate the role of Social Security. Again, while surveys show that workers think Social Security will only cover a sliver of their living expenses, nearly half of all retirees say government benefits are their biggest source of income. At the same time, we overestimate the role our own personal savings play in our income strategy. While workers believe that their 401(k)s and savings accounts will have to cover the lion's share of their living expenses when they retire, retirees say that personal savings play a smaller role.[12] Meanwhile, we often discount our other assets in this equation, including our homes. Most of us have yet to calculate our retirement needs. If we'd only do the math, we would get it.

Checklist: Things to Do

- ❑ Map out what *kind* of retirement you want to lead.
- ❑ Calculate how much you'll need to spend in retirement.
- ❑ Have a withdrawal strategy. See if you can afford to live on 3 or 4 percent annual withdrawals from your retirement accounts.
- ❑ If you can't live on 3 or 4 percent withdrawals, consider a higher rate of withdrawal, such as 6 percent—but don't adjust it for inflation.

CONCLUSION

Once upon a time, not so long ago, when the bull market was all the rage, when our 401(k)s were A-OK and our stock options were worth the paper they were printed on, managing our personal finances wasn't just simple, it was fun. Well, it's certainly less entertaining today. And nothing about it feels very easy. In fact, the challenge of saving money, investing it, and retiring with it, can be downright maddening.

Having lived through the boom and bust, many of us find ourselves in a financially confusing place.

For instance, we experienced the greatest bull market it's likely we'll ever see in our lifetimes—with the stock market delivering annual gains of more than 16 percent between 1984 and 2000. And this took place during the first time in history when a majority of us were invested in the market, thanks in part to our 401(k) retirement accounts. But being human, with all the baggage that comes with it, many of us found a way to miss out on those remarkable bull market gains.

As savers and investors, we're filled with similar contradictions. Despite years of faithfully putting money into our employer-sponsored retirement accounts, the average 401(k) is worth only about $50,000, and the median account is worse. More of us own homes today than ever before, and they're larger than ever. But many of us own *less* of our homes than we did a generation ago, thanks to the equity we pulled out of our one appreciating asset at the start of the decade. Meanwhile, our total debt has grown to more than 100 percent of our disposable personal income, and American families have more credit card debt (nearly $9000) than ever before. But more of us are doing a better job managing our credit and, despite popular belief (and our average of 14 credit cards), a majority of Americans enjoy good credit scores, which is good news for reducing interest expenses down the road. When it comes to preparing for retirement, we're underfunding our individual retirement accounts—the average IRA is worth less than $40,000. Yet retirement investors have more opportunities than ever to put money away into tax-favored investment plans, thanks to new catch-up provisions and higher annual contribution limits made possible by the federal government.

In general, we're overly pessimistic when it comes to things that we can be good at—like saving money—because we have the math all wrong. Studies show that savers underestimate by as much as half how much a small amount of money can grow over long periods of time.

On the other hand, many of us are overly optimistic about our investing skills. We think our portfolios are beating the market when in fact they're not. Many of us think it's not that hard to beat the market over the long term—but it is. And most of us think our mutual fund managers can beat the market over the long term—but they don't. History has shown that our fund managers generally do a poor job of beating a simple, low-cost, low-hassle index fund.

Bottom Line

We think the things that are hard are easy. Meanwhile, we think the things that are easy are hard. Half the battle in fixing our personal finances, then, is understanding this human contradiction—and finding ways around it. Once you do that, managing your personal finances can be simple, if you let it be. And isn't that the point of it all: to simplify and automate your finances so that you don't fall into the traps that lead to common money mistakes?

Here's a few things we can do:

- *Worry about things you can control.* Try as we might, we can't control the stock market. We can't control interest rates. But we can control how much we save each month—and how much we save in fees to banks, brokers, and mutual funds.
- *Worry about the little things.* Small steps between now and retirement can add up to thousands of dollars. For example, save $125 a year in checking fees by switching to a no-frills "free" checking account, sit back, and watch it grow to $9000 in 25 years. Set aside $25 a week for 40 years, sit back, and watch it grow to nearly $300,000.
- *Manage all your assets.* Our homes and our portfolios are two of our biggest financial assets. A third is our credit. It doesn't cost much to check your credit reports routinely to improve your score, yet the payout could be worth tens of thousands of dollars. So check those reports and improve your score.
- *Manage your risk.* Given the losses we suffered in the stock market, we may feel compelled to take even *more* risks with our money to make back what was lost. But isn't that how we got here in the first place? Keep in mind that stocks aren't the only assets that come with risks. Seemingly safe investments like bonds, company stock, and diversified mutual funds can be dangerous, depending on the circumstances.
- *Take the easy way out.* Don't try to beat the stock market. Take what the market gives you. Don't seek out maximum returns if your short- and long-term goals require much less. Remember that the risk you run by trying to beat the market is underperforming it in the long run and failing to meet your needs.
- *Automate your savings plan.* Inertia is the enemy to savers and investors. But inertia can also be your friend. Set up an automatic savings plan so that money is routinely set aside toward your savings goal. And every time you get a raise, increase the amount you automatically set aside.

- *Automate your investment plan.* An easy way to do this is by playing the averages through an index fund. Another way to automate your portfolio is to dollar-cost average into the market, just like you do with your 401(k). And remember to rebalance your investments once a year to smooth your ride. None of these strategies will deliver the absolute best performance. But one of the biggest mistakes we make with our money is thinking that there's shame in being average.

NOTES

Chapter 1

[1] "Typical American Household Has Net Financial Assets of $1000." Washington, DC: Consumer Federation of America, October 28, 1999.

[2] "The Changing Face of Affluence." *Money*, September 27, 2002: 42.

[3] "Congressional Testimony of Frank Torres on Behalf of Consumers Union Before the Subcommittee on Financial Institutions and Consumer Credit." *Congressional Record*, May 12, 1999.

[4] "The 2002 Retirement Confidence Survey." Washington, DC: Employee Benefit Research Institute, 2002.

[5] "More Than Half of Americans Behind in Saving for Retirement." Washington, DC: Consumer Federation of America, April 26, 2000.

[6] "Study Finds That Many Americans Do Not Expect Their Children to Attend College." Louisville, KY: Aegon Institutional Markets, July 10, 2002.

[7] "CFA Research Reveals Most Americans Have Built Little Wealth." Washington, DC: Consumer Federation of America, February 20, 2001.

[8] "New Report Finds One-Quarter of U.S. Households Are Wealth-Poor." Washington, DC: Consumer Federation of America, May 13, 2002.

[9] "The High Price for America's Low Savings." *National Journal*, October 19, 2002.

[10] "CFA Research Reveals Most Americans Have Built Little Wealth." Op cit.

[11] "Typical American Household Has Net Financial Assets of $1000." Op cit.

[12] "More Than Half of Americans Behind in Saving for Retirement." Op cit.

[13] "The 2002 Retirement Confidence Survey." Op. cit.

[14] "American Seniors Rack Up Debt Like Never Before." *USA Today,* April 25, 2002: A1.

[15] "Small Measures in Unpredictable Times." *Financial Times,* September 11, 2002: 22.

[16] "Rates Notch Up." *Cardweb.com, www.carddata.com.* Posted October 9, 2002.

[17] "Reading Between the Lines: The New Science of Behavioral Finance Can Help Investors Understand Why They Make Mistakes—and How to Prevent the Next One." *Money,* September 1, 1999, 81.

[18] "Fast Food & Cards." *Cardweb.com, www.carddata.com.* Posted November 13, 2002.

[19] Richard Thaler and Shlomo Benartzi. "Save More Tomorrow: Using Behavioral Economics to Increase Employee Savings." Paper. August 2001. *http://www.cbrss.harvard.edu/events/emc/thalerbenartzi.pdf.*

[20] Ibid.

Chapter 2

[1] "Banking on Fees; Rising Charges Have Growing Impact on Bottom Line." *Chicago Tribune,* May 12, 2002: C1.

[2] Ibid.

[3] "Mixed Messages: Consumers' Views on Financial Consolidation." Washington, DC: Council on Financial Competition, 2000.

[4] "Checking Study," Fall 2002. *http://www.bankrate.com.*

[5] Ibid.

[6] "Big Banks, Bigger Fees 2001: PIRG National Bank Fee Survey." Washington, DC: U.S. Public Interest Research Group, November 2001.

[7] Ibid.

[8] "Mixed Messages: Consumers' Views on Financial Consolidation." Op cit.

[9] "Yields Down, Free Checking Accounts Up." Posted September 26, 2002. *Bankrate.com, http://www.bankrate.com/brm/news/chk/-chkstudy/20020926a.asp.*

[10] "Open Letter from Consumers to Senate: You Still Have a Chance to Help the 'Little Guy,' " September 18, 1998. Available at *http://www-consumersunion.org/finance/0918ltrdc998.htm.*

[11] "Checking Study." Fall 2002. *http://www.bankrate.com.*

[12] "Big Banks, Bigger Fees." 2001. Op cit.

[13] "Yields Down, Free Checking Accounts Up." Op cit.

[14] "Mixed Messages: Consumers' Views on Financial Consolidation." Op cit.

[15] Ibid.

[16] "Credit Squeeze." *U.S. News & World Report,* June 17, 2002: 38.

[17] "Credit-Card Firms Collect Record Levels of Late Fees; New Shorter Grace Periods, Tighter Rules Boost Profits; How to Avoid Getting Hit." *Wall Street Journal,* May 21, 2002: D1.

[18] "Late Payers." *Cardweb.com., www.carddata.com.* Posted October 22, 2002.

[19] "Credit-Card Firms Collect Record Levels of Late Fees." Op cit.

[20] "Honest, the Check Is in the E-Mail." *Wall Street Journal,* September 4, 2002: D1.

[21] Ibid.

[22] "The Dark Side of Online Billing; Missed Payments, Glitches Drive Many Back to Checks." *Wall Street Journal,* October 17, 2002: D1.

[23] "Pay Your Bill by Phone." *Wall Street Journal,* May 14, 2002: D1.

[24] "Credit Squeeze." Op cit.

[25] "More $35 Fees." *Cardweb.com., www.carddata.com.* Posted February 14, 2002.

[26] "New Hidden Fees Hit Overseas Travel; Credit-Card Firms Boost Cost of Exchanging Money, Triggering Lawsuits." *Wall Street Journal,* April 23, 2002: D1.

[27] "ATM Surcharges and Fees Climbing Higher." Posted September 27, 2002. *Bankrate.com, http://www.bankrate.com/brm/news/chk/-chkstudy/20020927a.asp.*

[28] Ibid.

[29] Ibid.

[30] "2002 Vanguard/Money Investor Literacy Test." Posted at *http://www.vanguard.com.*

[31] John C. Bogle. "Success in Investment Management: What Can We Learn from Indexing?" Speech. Chicago: Investment Analysts Society of Chicago, October 26, 2000.

[32] Brad Barber, Terrance Odean, and Lu Zheng. "Out of Sight, Out of Mind: The Effects of Expenses on Mutual Fund Flows," July 2002. Posted at *http://faculty.haas.berkeley.edu/odean/papers/mutualfunds.*

[33] *Predicting Mutual Fund Performance 2: After the Bear.* Boston: Financial Research Corp., 2002.

Chapter 3

[1] "How to Improve Your Credit Profile." *U.S. News & World Report,* June 17, 2002: 42.

[2] *www.fairisaac.com*

[3] *www.myfico.com*

[4] "Credit Scoring Secrets Are Soon to Be Revealed." *U.S. News & World Report,* February 5, 2001: 54.

[5] "Trying to Live Down a Bad Credit Rating." *Chicago Tribune,* February 2, 2003: Q1.

[6] "Bad Credit Can Sink Job Hunt." *San Francisco Chronicle,* September 21, 2002: B1.

[7] "Property Insurers Keep Score." *U.S. News & World Report,* June 17, 2002: 41.

[8] "Bad Credit? You Could Lose Your Insurance." *Orlando Sentinel,* December 30, 2001: H1.

[9] "Deadbeat Retreat." *Cardweb.com, www.carddata.com.* Posted June 12, 2002.

[10] "Blending the Ingredients of a Credit Bureau Score." *Credit Union Magazine,* April 1, 2002: 30.

[11] "Credit-Card Firms Collect Record Levels of Late Fees: New Shorter Grace Periods, Tighter Rules Boost Profits; How to Avoid Getting Hit." *Wall Street Journal,* May 21, 2002: D1.

[12] "Mistakes Do Happen: Credit Report Errors Mean Consumers Lose." Washington, DC: U.S. Public Interest Research Group, March 1998: *http://www.pirg.org/reports/consumer/mistakes/index.htm*

[13] "Stolen Names, Stolen Lives." *U.S. News & World Report,* November 12, 2001: 40.

Chapter 4

[1] "Mutual Fund Investors Going with the Flow Trends." *Los Angeles Times*, February 1, 2000: C1.

[2] John Y. Campbell, "Diversification: A Bigger Free Lunch." *Canadian Investment Review*, Winter 2000, 13(4): 14–15.

[3] John Y. Campbell, et al. "Have Individual Stocks Become More Volatile? An Empirical Exploration of Idiosyncratic Risk." *Journal of Finance*, February 2001, 56: 1–41.

[4] "Beaucoup Bucks." *U.S. News & World Report*, February 11, 2002: 53.

[5] "Defined Contribution Plan Survey: Insights Into Participant Investment Knowledge & Behavior." Boston: John Hancock Financial Services, 2002.

[6] "Can This Fund Be Saved? Gold Fever Was This Manager's Downfall." *Los Angeles Times*, June 22, 1999: NC-6.

[7] *How Many Funds Should You Own?* San Francisco: Schwab Center for Investment Research, 2003.

Chapter 5

[1] "Cash Avalanche Suddenly Swamps Tech Stock Funds." *Los Angeles Times*, December 12, 1999: C1.

[2] "Funds' Record Rise Triggers Caution Lights." *Los Angeles Times*, January 4, 2000: A1.

[3] "Increasingly, Value Is in the Beholder's Eye." *Los Angles Times*, October 5, 1999: S1.

[4] "Investors Behaving Badly: An Analysis of Investor Trading Patterns in Mutual Funds & Their Impact on Long-Term Investment Success." Boston: Financial Research Corp., April 2001.

[5] Jay Ritter. "Behavioral Finance." Gainesville, FL: University of Florida, August 31, 2002.

[6] Brad Barber and Terrance Odean, "All That Glitters: The Effect of Attention and News on the Buying Behavior of Individual and Institutional Investors," April 2002.

[7] Roger Ibbotson and Paul Kaplan. "Does Asset Allocation Policy Explain 40, 90 or 100 Percent of Performance?" Association for Investment Management and Research. *Financial Analysts Journal*, January–February 2000.

Chapter 6

[1] "Optimism and Overconfidence in Asset Allocation Decisions."*Morningstar.com*, April 23, 1999, *http://news.morningstar.com/news/ms/Commentary/990423comm-1.html.*

[2] Jack Brennan, with Marta McCave. *Straight Talk on Investing: What You Need to Know.* New York: John Wiley & Sons, 2002.

[3] "Typical American Household Has Net Financial Assets of $1000." Washington, DC: Consumer Federation of America, October 28, 1999.

[4] Simon Gervais and Terrance Odean."Learning to Be Overconfident." *The Review of Financial Studies*, Spring 2001, 14(1): 1–27.

[5] "Did You Beat the Market? Most Investors Who Say They Do Are Just Kidding Themselves." *Money*, January 1, 2000: 55.

[6] Ibid.

[7] "Optimism and Overconfidence in Asset Allocation Decisions." Op cit.

[8] Peter Lynch, with John Rothchild. *One Up on Wall Street: How to Use What You Already Know to Make Money in the Market.* New York: Simon and Schuster/Fireside Books, 1989.

[9] Brad Barber and Terrance Odean. "The Courage of Misguided Convictions: The Trading Behavior of Individual Investors." *Financial Analyst Journal* November–December 1999: 41–55.

[10] "Dalbar Issues 2001 Update to Quantitative Analysis of Investor Behavior Report. More Proof That Market Timing Doesn't Work for the Majority of Investors." Boston: Dalbar Inc., June 21, 2001.

[11] "Investors Behaving Badly: An Analysis of Investor Trading Patterns in Mutual Funds & Their Impact on Long-Term Investment Success," Boston: Financial Research Corp., April 2001.

[12] "Funds with Redemption Fees Rise 82 Percent." *Mutual Fund Market News,* June 18, 2001.

[13] "Growing Number of Mutual Funds Charge Redemption Fees." *Investment News,* May 14, 2001: 3.

Chapter 7

[1] "Who Needs a Money Manager? Index Funds Are Cheap, Easy— and They're Changing the Way Americans Invest." *Business Week,* February 22, 1999: 127.

[2] "Where Have All the Geniuses Gone? The Brilliant Mutual Fund Managers of Yore Are Nearly Extinct." *Fortune,* October 11, 1999: 150.

[3] "Funds in a Funk." *U.S. News & World Report,* April 22, 2002: 40.

[4] "Pulling the Plug." *U.S. News & World Report,* September 17, 2001: 58.

[5] Mark Carhart, et al. *Mutual Fund Survivorship, Review of Financial Studies,* 2002, 15/5.

[6] "Pulling the Plug." Op cit.

[7] Bing Liang. "Hedge Fund Performance: 1990–1999." *Financial Analysts Journal* January 1, 2001: 11–18.

[8] "Pulling the plug." Op cit.

[9] "Ghosts of Dead Funds May Haunt Results." *Wall Street Journal,* April 4, 1997: R1.

[10] Richard Ferri. *All About Index Funds.* New York: McGraw-Hill, 2002.

[11] "Investors Put Index Funds, If Not Their Theory, into Practice." *Los Angeles Times,* September 26, 1999: C1.

[12] Richard Ferri. *All About Index Funds.* Op. cit.

[13] "Bogle Legacy Looms Over Index Sector." *Mutual Fund Market News.* September 10, 2001.

[14] Richard Ferri. *All About Index Funds.* Op. cit.

[15] "Removing Obstacles to Better Investing." *Los Angeles Times,* January 4, 2000: S1.

[16] "Know a Fund's Cost? Look Deeper." *New York Times,* February 9, 2003: Sec. 3, p. 7.

[17] "As Stock Market Returns Shrink, After-Tax Results Gain Importance." *Los Angeles Times,* October 17, 1999: C3.

[18] "What Can Active Managers Learn From Index Funds?" Remarks by John C. Bogle at the Bullseye 2000 Conference in Toronto, Canada, December 4, 2000.

Chapter 8

[1] "Monkey Shines: A Chimp Beats Five Experts at Picking Stocks." *Orange County Register,* September 8, 1993: A1.

[2] Peter Lynch, with John Rothchild. *One Up on Wall Street: How to Use What You Already Know to Make Money in the Market.* New York: Simon and Schuster/Fireside Press, 1989.

[3] Peter Lynch, with John Rothchild, *Beating the Street.* New York; Simon and Schuster/Fireside Press, 1993.

[4] "Most Analysts Remain Plugged In to Enron." *Wall Street Journal,* October 26, 2001: C1.

[5] "Enron in Perfect Hindsight; Plenty of Red Flags Were Waving at the Energy Giant, but from Execs to Auditors to the Media, No One Wanted to Argue with Success." *BusinessWeek Online,* December 19, 2001.

[6] "MFS Gets Caught by the Bear; Fund Group Escaped Collapse of Tech, but Bets on Tyco, Energy and Advertising Hurt." *Wall Street Journal,* March 4, 2002: R1.

[7] Daniel Kahneman and Mark Riepe. "Aspects of Investor Psychology." *Journal of Portfolio Management* 24(4), Summer 1998.

[8] "Secrets of a High Plains Investor: Buffett, the Sage of Omaha, Makes Value Strategy Seem Simple." *International Herald Tribune,* December 20, 1997: 15.

[9] "Despite Down Year, Buffett Optimistic About Berkshire." (Quincy, MA) *Patriot Ledger,* December 18, 1999: 51.

[10] "Buffett Lost His Midas Touch?" *CNNfn: Business Day,* December 28, 1999.

[11] Peter Lynch, with John Rothchild. *One Up on Wall Street.* Op cit.

[12] "You Don't Know Jack." *The Rekenthaler Report,* column at *Morningstar.com,* April 1, 1999.

[13] Peter Lynch, with John Rothchild. *One Up on Wall Street.* Op cit.

[14] Ibid.

[15] "401(k)s Still Heavy in Company Stock." *Chicago Tribune,* November 3, 2002: 1.

[16] "Defined Contribution Plan Survey: Insights Into Participant Investment Knowledge & Behavior." Boston: John Hancock Financial Services, 2002.

[17] "AMR 401(k) Manager Drops Company Stock." *USA Today,* February 4, 2003: B1.

[18] "401(k) Plan Asset Allocation, Account Balances, and Loan Activity in 2000," Washington, DC: Investment Company Institute, November 2001.

[19] "Company Stock in 401(k) Plans Gets Off to Fast Start in 2001." *DC Plan Investing,* February 20, 2001.

[20] *Trends and Experience in 401(k) Plans: 2001.* Lincolnshire, IL: Hewitt Associates, September 2001.

[21] "Fair Shares? Why Company Stock Is a Burden for Many—and Less So for a Few." *Wall Street Journal,* November 27, 2001: A1.

[22] "The 401(k) Stumbles," *U.S. News & World Report.* December 24, 2001: 30.

[23] "Mixed Messages: Consumers' Views on Financial Consolidation." Washington, DC: Corporate Executive Board, 2000.

[24] "The 401(k) Stumbles." Op cit.

Chapter 9

[1] William Arnone. "The 401(k) Time Bomb." *www.bcsolutionsmag.com/Archives/Dec97Jan98/401TIMEB.htm.*

[2] "Losing Altitude: The 401(k) Has Hit Hard Times, As Account Balances Fall, Companies Cut Back, and Workers Grow Disenchanted." *U.S. News & World Report,* April 21, 2003: 58.

[3] *401(k) Future Market Trends.* Chicago: Spectrem Group, 2003.

[4] *45th Annual Survey of Profit Sharing and 401(k) Plans.* Chicago: Profit Sharing/401(k) Council of America, 2002.

[5] *401(k) Plans: Survey Report on Plan Design.* New York: Buck Consultants, 2002.

[6] *45th Annual Survey of Profit Sharing and 401(k) Plans.* Op cit.

[7] "Hewitt Research Shows U.S. Employees Not Interacting with 401(k) Plan for Optimal Benefit." *Hewitt News & Information,* July 8, 2002.

[8] Ibid.

[9] "401(k) Plan Asset Allocation, Account Balances, and Loan Activity in 2001." Issue brief. Washington, DC: Employee Benefit Research Institute, March 2003.

[10] *Participant Report Card for 2002: The Impact of the Bear Market on Retirement Savings Plans.* Valley Forge, PA: The Vanguard Center for Retirement Research, February 2003.

[11] Ibid.

[12] "Recovery Plan." *U.S. News & World Report,* June 3, 2002: 80.

[13] *Trust & Consequences: Closing the Retirement Awareness Gap.* Hartford, CT: Cigna Retirement & Services, March 2003.

[14] Richard Thaler and Shlomo Benartzi. "Save More Tomorrow: Using Behavioral Economics to Increase Employee Savings." Paper, August 2001. *http://www.cbrss.harvard.edu/ events/emc/thalerbenartzi.pdf.*

[15] "Your Savings May Plump Up If Congress Has Its Way." *U.S. News & World Report,* February 19, 2001: 63.

[16] "Borrowing Isn't Usually in Your Best Interest." *Los Angeles Times,* August 29, 1999: C1.

[17] "Layoff Triggers 401(k) Options Benefits: The Decision on What to Do with Retirement Funds May Be One of the Biggest You Face." *Los Angeles Times,* May 15, 2001: C7.

[18] *401(k) Plan Participants: Characteristics, Contributions, and Account Activity.* Washington, DC: Investment Company Institute, Spring 2000.

[19] "Sticking with Equities After a Bear Market." Baltimore: *T. Rowe Price Report,* Fall 2002.

Chapter 10

[1] *Boomers at Midlife: The AARP Life Stage Study.* Washington, DC: AARP, November 2002.

[2] *Quicken Fiscal Literacy Survey 2001.* Mountain View, CA: Quicken, January 2001.

[3] *The 2002 Retirement Confidence Survey.* Washington, DC: Employee Benefit Research Institute, 2002.

[4] *Insights on America's Attitudes Toward Retirement.* Valley Forge, PA: The Vanguard Group. July 9, 2002.

[5] *The 2002 Retirement Confidence Survey.* Op cit.

[6] Ibid.

[7] "Recovery Plan." *U.S. News & World Report,* June 3, 2002: 80.

[8] "American Seniors Rack Up Debt Like Never Before." *USA Today,* April 25, 2002: A1.

[9] *Retiree Health Benefits: Time to Resuscitate?* Washington, DC: Watson Wyatt Worldwide, 2002.

[10] *The Kaiser/Hewitt 2002 Survey on Retiree Health Benefits.* Lincolnshire, IL: Hewitt Associates, 2002.

[11] "Making Your Money Last as Long as You Do." *U.S. News & World Report,* June 4, 2001: 72.

[12] *The 2002 Retirement Confidence Survey.* Op cit.

INDEX

About the Author

Paul J. Lim is a senior editor at *U.S. News & World Report* magazine, where he covers the markets and personal finance. Before joining *U.S. News*, he was a personal finance writer and mutual fund columnist for the *Los Angeles Times* in Los Angeles, as well as a staff writer at *Money* magazine in New York. Earlier in his career, he was twice named by the TJFR Group to its "30 Under 30 List" of the nation's top young financial journalists. A graduate of Princeton University and the University of Pennsylvania, Lim currently resides in Chicago.